The Resurrection of Jesus

# THE RESURRECTION OF JESUS

*History, Experience, Theology*

Gerd Luedemann

FORTRESS PRESS
Minneapolis

THE RESURRECTION OF JESUS:
History, Experience, Theology

First Fortress Press edition 1994. Copyright © 1994 Gerd
Luedemann 1994. Translated by John Bowden from *Die
Auferstehung Jesu: Historie, Erfahrung, Theologie* (Gottingen:
Vandenhoeck & Ruprecht, 1994). Translation copyright © John
Bowden 1994.

Unless otherwise noted, scripture quotations from the New Revised
Standard Version Bible copyright ©1989 by the Division of Christian
Education of the National Council of the Churches of Christ in the
United States of America. Used with permission.

Cover graphic: Icon of the Transfiguration of Christ, c. 1403 by
    Theopan the Greek, from the Tretyakov Gallery, Moscow.
Cover design: Carol Evans-Smith

Library of Congress Cataloging-in-Publication data available
ISBN 0–8006–2722–6

Manufactured in Great Britain                    AF 1-2792
98   97                       2   3   4   5   6   7   8   9   10

# Contents

# Preface

The theses of this book caused quite a stir even before its publication. They were passionately rejected in circles which regard any disputing of the bodily resurrection of Jesus as a betrayal of the gospel, which thought it quite natural to call for legal proceedings to be taken against the author. Others, who present themselves as modern Christians, thought that it was going too far to say that the body of Jesus decayed, and criticized the book for overestimating history and underestimating theology. But despite all the objections and opposition, the book has already started something, and introduced a process of fermentation which will serve to clarify what is meant by 'resurrection'.

The book seeks to teach, to stimulate and to offer a reasonable human approach to 'resurrection'. This is all the more important since the 'resurrection' of Jesus has largely become both an indispensable requisite of theology and an empty phrase. So today many Christians have fallen victim to a schizophrenic split in their consciousnesses. The hallowed precincts of the tradition of the church and theology are often set abruptly over against the natural human feeling for truth. Unless a bridge is built here, the credibility of theology and the church will disappear, and the two, for all their apparent splendour, will become petrified. So this book is specifically not written with a view to its results being useful for the church; its main aim is to investigate the historical truth – honestly and regardless of other factors. Only on the basis of such quasi-empirical work is a theological reflection possible, though the emphasis here is not on such reflection.

The first two chapters describe the lay-out of the present work and the need for it. Readers who are not so interested in theology but primarily in history can begin at Chapter 3. At all events, I would like this book to be read not only by theologians and rising theologians, but above all also by reflective men and women who have some interest in Christianity and want to investigate the Christian case thoroughly at its central point.

Here I also want to mention those people and institutions which have helped me in writing the book. Andreas Technow, a well-tried fellow worker, has helped me to make my thought precise. Christina Abel, Andrea Kilian, Dirk Krah, Ulf Schlimper, Karoline Läger in Göttingen and Birgit Rengel in Nashville have got literature for me or read and made critical comments on several versions of the book. Dr Helga Botermann and Dr Jürgen Wehnert have read the manuscript both critically and in a friendly way. I am grateful to Dr Gebhard Löhr for critical comments on philosophical questions. My secretary Silke Röthke, Christina Abel and Andrea Kilian, Silke Battermann and Alf Özen prepared the typescript for printing. Dean Joseph Hough of Vanderbilt Divinity School granted me the status of a visiting scholar in Nashville from 1992 to 1994. The theological faculties of the universities of Lausanne, Chicago and Copenhagen invited me to give lectures at which some of the theses of this book were tried out. I am grateful to D. Marguerat, H. D. Betz and N. Hyldahl in their representative functions for their hospitality and criticism. Finally, I want to thank the translator, Dr John Bowden, for his great care and my conversation partners in Göttingen over recent years, Manfred Josuttis and Hanscarl Leuner. What I owe my wife Elke and our daughters Amrei, Eyke, Marei and Reiga cannot be put into words.

On the technical side I should remark that for reasons of space there is no bibliography and the complete titles are usually mentioned only initially. Where the abbreviations are not obvious, they come from the list of abbreviations in the *Theologische Realenzyklopädie*.

Göttingen, Spring 1994
Gerd Lüdemann

# 1 Introduction

In the present book I am taking up ideas which have interested me since I began to study theology. As a beginner I found it strange that exegetes had so little historical concern for the central Christian datum of the resurrection of Jesus and at the same time were engaged in a theological exposition of the New Testament which claimed to be scientific. In it, theologians constantly kept using the term 'objective' when what they explicitly meant was subjective faith.[1] The attention to subjectivity was worthwhile, but the refusal to ask historical questions or indifference towards them was disturbing. One might note Rudolf Bultmann's remark: 'How the Easter faith arose in individual disciples has been obscured in the tradition by legend and is not of basic importance.'[2] Reference might also be made to the verdict of Willi Marxsen:

> 'For my faith in Jesus, it is completely unimportant *how* Peter arrived at his faith in Jesus after Good Friday. It is equally unimportant how *the person* found faith who then communicated his faith to *me*, so that *I*, in my turn, could believe . . . The decisive thing is that the faith is always *the same* . . . Our faith is only the Christian faith if it is joined with the faith of the first witnesses and with the faith of Peter.'[3]

This remark formally leads us to ask how anyone who talks about faith like this knows anything about the nature of the faith in the first century which he nevertheless wants to *share*. Is it not also important to measure one's own faith by the faith of the first witnesses or if need be to have it corrected from there? Otherwise it threatens to be arbitrary.

Thus the insistence on the character of faith as decision and the need to venture it gave rise to the danger of losing sight of the historical foundations when talking about faith. Such an attitude led, for example, to an exaggerated polemic against the historical approach of Luke–Acts[4] and a contrast between kerygma and history.[5] The result of this is that everything ends up being subjected to the kerygma, as if this had no connection with Jesus himself, and as if the question of our faith and how it accords with the message of Jesus and the first disciples was not to be discussed in that perspective, i.e. by looking at the relationship between the proclamation of the historical Jesus and the faith of the first witnesses.[6]

The other school which I encountered in my studies attempted ultimately to get round the problem of history by the application of confessional formulae from the early church and entering e.g. into an 'anhypostatic' relationship to them.[7] However, this led to their being finally bracketted off and assigned to the field of christological dogma. A critical remark by Emanuel Hirsch in a lecture published posthumously applies to this approach quite generally: in such an approach 'explicitly or implicitly a presupposition is made: that an authoritative revelation to be ascertained methodologically gives an objective basis to Christian teaching and, rightly used, allows one to ascertain a related group of Christian truths and doctrines'.[8]

In view of the neglect of historical investigation in large parts of German New Testament scholarship and theology generally, it was only consistent that a more recent systematic trend should want to rectify the historical defect. Here it was even bold enough to understand the resurrection of Jesus as a historical event. Thus Wolfhart Pannenberg states on the resurrection of Jesus:

'If the emergence of primitive Christianity, which, apart from other traditions, is also traced back by Paul to appearances of the resurrected Jesus, can be understood in spite of all critical examination of the tradition only if one examines it in the light of the eschatological hope for a resurrection from the dead, then that which is so designated is a historical event, even if we do not know anything more particular about it. Then an event that is expressible only in the language of the eschatological expectation is to be asserted as a historical occurrence.'[9]

The drift of Pannenberg's remarks becomes clear in the following statements:

'There is no justification for affirming Jesus' resurrection as an event that really happened if it is not to be affirmed as a historical event as such. Whether or not a particular event happened two thousand years ago is not made certain by faith but only by historical research, to the extent that certainty can be attained at all about questions of this kind.'[10]

In the face of later criticism that this puts an enormous burden of proof on historical scholarship, Pannenberg has explicitly held firm to these statements. He is concerned 'primarily with a *logical* connection in respect of the claim of the factuality of a past event . . . and the degree to which the claim of such statements can be decided is a different question . . . The claim to historicity of a statement of fact merely implies the expectation that the content of this claim can stand up to historical examination, regardless of different and controversial judgments.'[11] 'Historical' does not mean 'historically demonstrable' but 'what actually took place', for few things can be proved in such a way 'to be beyond all doubt' (ibid.). This statement is amazing in that in the context of the chapter, for Pannenberg himself, 'actually took place' is a much stronger assertion than 'historically demonstrable', and is evidently exclusively a theological conclusion. What if Pannenberg's expectation of a historical examination did not stand the test? In that case, would Christian faith be at an end, as Pannenberg evidently thinks? (We shall come back to this question.)

Regardless of how we may judge Pannenberg's results, it is at all events welcome that at a decisive point of Christian faith he has justified historical enquiry and thus again made it possible for Christianity to come to an understanding with other sciences.[12] Pannenberg is right in noting that 'behind the foggy talk of "Easter faith" many authors shamefully avoid their reader's interest in what they think about the reliability of the Easter tradition, which has become the basis for Christian faith'.[13]

Unfortunately the historical stimuli which follow from Pannenberg's theses on the question of the resurrection of Jesus have been virtually ignored in the subsequent period.[14]

By contrast, to an increasing degree apologists, old-style and new-style, are increasingly making themselves heard. (This represents a retrograde move from the position of Rudolf Bultmann which, while critical, does not seem to me to take enough account of history.) Ultimately these apologists want to remove the resurrection of Jesus from scientific investigation altogether. Thus for example Hans Kessler writes:[15] 'As we know from our experience, there can be real events which have really happened but which cannot be objectified and verified historically' (271). But Kessler immediately goes on to stress that such statements about the resurrection of the crucified Jesus must be capable of proof in order to avoid the suspicion of being subjective and dependent on a world view. He continues:

'If the resurrection of Jesus . . . is to be spoken of meaningfully . . . it must prove possible to give the context which ties the talk of this reality to experiences that can be described and examined. In this sense, the assertion of the "appearances" and the resurrection of Jesus have a high degree of credibility, in particular in the context of historical events which can be demonstrated by historical criticism' (271).

However, these are sheer defensive statements which quite manifestly derive from an 'immunization strategy'. By what criteria is Kessler working? In my view his remarks about the origin of belief in the resurrection of Jesus (136–236) are *a priori* made in such a way that they no longer admit of investigation. Certainly the author often speaks of concretion, but he then refuses to investigate the manner of the appearances (233f.), and regards for example a transference of the insights gained into Paul to the disciples as impermissible, although Paul himself says that the appearances are of the same kind (I Cor.15.1–11)(171).[16]

Like Kessler, Karl Barth had evidently already decided the question of the resurrection of Jesus. He writes: 'There may have been events which happened far more really in time than the kind of things the "historian" can prove. There are good grounds for supposing that the history of the resurrection of Jesus is a pre-eminent instance of such an event.'[17] To this Bultmann replies: 'Barth tells me that the resurrection of Jesus is not a historical fact which can be established by the means at the disposal of historical science. But from this he thinks that it does not follow that it did not *happen* ... My question is, what does Barth understand by "happen" and "history"? What kind of events are those about which it can be said that they "have really taken place as history in time far more certainly than everything that the historian can establish as such"?'[18] According to Hans-Georg Geyer the real difference between Barth and Bultmann is 'that in a historical perspective Bultmann speaks of the events of Easter only as the rise of faith in the saving efficacy of the cross, whereas Barth understands and expounds the resurrection of Jesus Christ as the providing the basis for faith distinct from the act of faith'.[19] But even this precise grasp of the difference between Barth and Bultmann cannot alter the fact that Barth removes the grounding of faith from historical investigation (just as Bultmann does not ask behind the kerygma).

In his understanding of the resurrection, Eugen Drewermann, who in his work so far has sharply criticized the historical-critical method,[20] goes very much by the analytical psychology of C. G. Jung, and also by Paul Tillich. He writes: 'The mystery of the resurrection cannot be "established" externally; one can only believe it and it can only be communicated in images and symbols . . . One can perceive the reality of Easter morning only with the eyes of the heart, for everything that makes us live comes from the invisible sphere of eternity . . .'[21]

Later we shall ask whether such an interpretative approach helps to overcome the aporias of historical-critical research. Much will depend on how the question of the historicity of the resurrection of Jesus is to be decided. If Bultmann should be right in disputing its historicity, in fact a symbolic understanding might perhaps be a possible way of continuing to be a Christian even today. Or does one then have to grant that such a faith is too far removed from that of the first witnesses and honestly bid farewell to Christianity?[22] Or should not a contemporary faith be orientated much more than before on Jesus himself? All these questions are waiting for an answer.

After lengthy reflection on the problem of Easter faith and the resurrection of Jesus, in what follows I want to attempt a clear and understandable introduction to this topic and the problem it poses. Of course this enterprise is not an *answer* in the narrower sense, but an attempt at thinking which can perhaps help others to arrive at an intermediate result which is beyond an unhistorical certainty of salvation and a 'know-all' attitude about history. It is evident here, as Maurice Goguel remarked, that most of those who have occupied themselves with the resurrection of Jesus have unconsciously had a preconceived notion or prejudice which often cannot be backed up historically. So in what follows it will also be important time and again to become aware of one's own presuppositions and to ask critically behind them.[23]

The main emphasis in this book is not on methodological questions and the history of research.[24] In the interest of brevity I shall be referring only to a selection from the flood of secondary literature, but will deliberately often be quoting the basic works, old and new. I shall be discussing things as they emerge from a study of the sources and attempting to stimulate readers to arrive at their own verdicts on the basis of an analysis of the sources. To that extent this book does not take the line of Karl Martin Fischer, which is ultimately church apologetics: in his book on the resurrection he wants to help Christians 'who are seeking a unity of thought and faith in responsibility for our world. It seeks to offer a possible way of thinking for those who are troubled or questioning, but not to condemn those who are loyal to the faith.'[25] My contribution does not move within the same framework as Fischer's book, which is otherwise so sympathetic, because it is an attempt at a new departure, a new approach. For how in the end does Fischer know what being a Christian still really means? In a mainstream church and in today's world – also given the 'incredible diversity of Christian symbolism, doctrine, belief, and moral practice'[26] – that itself has become questionable.

Rather, the present book is to be understood in the way in which Gerhard Marcel Martin understands his work on the Gospel of Thomas. He writes: 'I think that it is good, for once, for people who feel such a close bond with the Christian tradition that they are almost imprisoned in it [and no longer know the real meaning of what has been handed down, GL] for once to be shown their own tradition as if it were an alien one.'[27] I would add that there are many within the church and theology who no longer know what Christian experience as experience of 'resurrection' was and is, and therefore urgently need an undistorted look at what is basically Christian. That means a look at the resurrection, if it is right to assume that this has a bond with what is elementally Christian.[28]

On the question discussed above Eugen Drewermann writes:

'At any rate it seems absurd out of duty to have to concern oneself for years as a student (or a teacher!) of theology with reports of appearances of God, experiences of a call, heavenly visions and prophetic discourse without having or getting the slightest inkling of what could be meant by such religious experiences in real life!'[29]

Here the application of psychological methods[30] is quite natural. Maurice Goguel already pointed out that if one worked here in an exclusively historical and literary way, one would simply skirt round the problem and not penetrate to the mystery of early Christianity. Nevertheless, the purely historical-literary method is usually mis-used in these questions. It is not enough to study the reports and the facts; one must also work out the feelings, the emotions, the ideas which would have gone with the faith of the first Christians in the relevant narratives about the resurrection.[31]

These requirements of Goguel's, which in part relate to conscious-ness psychology,[32] need to be supplemented. For in historical study of the resurrection of Jesus or the belief of individual early Christians that they 'saw' Jesus after his death it is important in addition to use the methods of depth psychology.[33] This is no lapse into psychologism, but a consistent development of the historical-critical method.[34] 'The analytical psychology of religion is simply a matter of taking for granted the consistent extension and deepening of the historical concerns of the doctrine of faith. It continues the historical investigation in the life of the individual and pursues it to the sources of the unconscious.'[35]

It is unnecessary at this point to give an account of the principles of the historical-critical method and of psychoanalytical theories, since the decisions are made on the individual texts, and any considerations from depth psychology that are advanced must be capable of demonstration from the texts.[36] (Where that happens, in each instance they will be presented in direct association with the exegesis and without any great theoretical apparatus.)

> Like Albert Schweitzer, I regard 'the investigation of historical truth as such . . . as an ideal for which scientific theology has to strive. I still hold fast to the opinion that the permanent spiritual importance that the religious thought of the past has for ours makes itself most strongly felt when we come into touch with that form of piety as it really existed, and not as we make the best of it for ourselves. A Christianity which does not dare to use historical truth for the service of what is spiritual is not sound within, even if it appears to be strong. Reverence for truth, something that must be a factor in our faith if it is not to degenerate into superstition, includes in itself respect for historical truth.'[37]

However, in my meetings with many theologians in university and church my experience has been similar to that of Karl Jaspers when he writes:

> 'For me, one of the pains of a life concerned for the truth is that discussion with theologians stops at decisive points: they fall silent, utter an incomprehensible sentence, talk about something else, make some unconditional assertion, speak in a good and friendly way without really having noticed what one has just said – and in the end probably have no real interest in it. For on the one hand they feel confident, terrifyingly confident, in their truth, and on the other it does not seem worthwhile for them to be bothered with us people who seem so stubborn. But to talk together calls for attention and a real answer; it prohibits silence or avoiding questions; above all it requires any statement of faith, which

after all is made in human language, which is directed at objects and is a disclosure in the world, to be put in question and examined again, not only externally but also internally. Anyone who is in final possession of the truth can no longer talk properly with others – he breaks off real communication in favour of the content of his belief.'[38]

One simply cannot stop at a point at which – to exaggerate somewhat – theology possesses without seeking and philosophy seeks without finding. For 'in the end being human and being Christian go together, so that Christian faith loses nothing by dedication to the human awareness of truth, and the human awareness of truth loses nothing by dedication to Christian faith'.[39] However, in some quarters one can see that even in academic theology there is no longer a *search* for the truth, and in the church the serious crisis of present-day Christianity is not *recognized*.[40] But I cannot believe that, since that would be the end of our religion.

# 2  The Need for Further Work on the Resurrection of Jesus

For Hans Grass, there is need for work on the resurrection of Jesus above all 'because this event has come to us in the form of historicizing reports, and therefore the reliability and credibility of this side of the act of revelation which is turned towards history *must* be examined'.[41] The question 'of the basis and justification for this testimony remains decisive. Without this basis any theology of the resurrection, even the theology of the New Testament, is groundless speculation' (14). At another point Grass emphatically affirms 'historical questioning of the Easter accounts and the Easter events which nowadays is often too quickly pushed on to one side or even dismissed altogether. This last is true of many statements about the problem of the resurrection in kerygmatic theology'(4).[42] As the situation has not changed since this fundamental book by Grass was first published in 1956, the concern of this Marburg theologian continues to be justified,[43] even if the end of the historical method is formally being proclaimed on all sides – for different reasons and under another name.[44]

Another reason for renewed concern with the resurrection of Jesus is that historically it was of decisive significance for the origin and development of the Christian religion. Without the 'halo' of the risen Lord, the preaching and proclamation of Jesus of Nazareth handed down in the New Testament would not have had the force that it has exercised in church history to the present day, since the Gospels have always been read as words of the risen Christ. David Friedrich Strauss remarked that it is humbling for human pride that all the words and teachings of Jesus, however true and good, one-sided and terse they may have been, 'would have been tossed and scattered like individual leaves by the wind were these leaves not held together by the deluded belief in his resurrection as by a tough and firm bond, and consequently preserved'.[45] To that Rade's pupil Samuel Eck replied: 'However, this "deluded belief" achieved precisely that. And the fact that it did calls for much more energetic reflection than we usually engage in . . .'[46] He goes on to say that faith in the resurrection of Jesus 'gave imperishable value to all that memory of him could retain. But the same faith which spreads in such a protective way over this precious treasure of the past, the earthly history of Jesus, creates a new heaven and a new future, a heaven and a future of the kind that no piety and no wisdom had previously known, in which Jesus's personal life forms the magnet towards which hope is drawn.'[47]

Finally, renewed work on the resurrection of Jesus is necessary in view of its present significance in church and theology.[48] Every day pastors comfort mourners with the message of the resurrection of the dead; the church derives its right to exist from the authority bestowed on it by the risen Christ; and the risen Christ still serves academic theology as a guarantee of theological epistemology,[49] as may be demonstrated with quotations from three distinguished theologians:

> 'The question of the resurrection of Jesus Christ poses a key question, perhaps even *the* key question, of Christian faith. Even though the average Christian is hardly aware of the fact, almost all other questions of faith and theology are decided by this question.'[50]

> 'Christianity stands or falls with the reality of the raising of Jesus from the dead by God.'[51]

> 'Christianity, inasmuch as it is a confession of Jesus of Nazareth as the living and powerfully effective Christ, begins at Easter. Without Easter there is no Gospel . . . no faith, no proclamation, no church, no worship, no mission.'[52]

Now the purpose of a historical work on the resurrection of Jesus in the sense described above is not new, and the arguments against such an undertaking are also generally known. I shall take up the most important of them, which in part overlap, and go on to discuss them:

1. We have no eye-witness accounts of the resurrection of Jesus.
2. The resurrection traditions cannot be disentangled, and the historical sources are inadequate.
3. The resurrection of Jesus is a miracle which completely evades our grasp – what can historical work achieve here?

Ingo Broer depicts the situation in which Roman Catholic theology finds itself as a result of historical criticism:[53]

> 'If one yields to it at least in part in the case of the miracles and possibly also the virgin birth, no pardon can be granted to historical criticism in the case of the resurrection . . . Only in the case of the resurrection is such an approach, which has found its way into the widest circles, said not to apply. At least in the view of many theologians the resurrection should, must and can provide what used to be provided by the Gospels as a whole, especially by a combination of miracle, resurrection and virgin birth, namely a basis for faith. The more difficult the historical understanding of the miracles and the virgin birth became, the more people concentrated on the resurrection, and here again particularly on the appearances, thinking that there they would find the point of points.'[54]

4. Moreover it is said to be impossible to talk meaningfully about the resurrection of Jesus outside the experience of faith and testimony, 'even if Jesus' personal, bodily resurrection precedes any experience of faith and any testimony to it in logical and ontological (not necessarily chronological) priority'.[55]

5. Event and interpretation are always interlocked, so that it is impossible to have access to the event of the resurrection without the interpretation. Therefore many resurrection texts resist historical investigation, e.g. the Emmaus story (Luke 24.13–35).

Detailed criticism of the objections:

On 1: At any rate we have Paul's own testimony and the accounts in Acts, which, if they agreed with Paul, would provide a good supplement to Paul's own reports. And that would also shed light on the other witnesses to the resurrection, since Paul puts his own 'encounter' with the risen Christ in parallel to that of the other witnesses (I Cor.15.8). Moreover, even if the above objection is correct, is not the *question* of the manner of the resurrection legitimate as long as Christian theology makes a claim to be scientific and feels an obligation to the Enlightenment? Of course whether any *results* can be achieved here, and if so what, is another question. For the moment I am concerned only to stress the obligation to ask about the manner of the 'resurrection'.[56]

On 2: The church historian Hans von Campenhausen has rightly commented that this way out is too easy. A reference to the tangled nature of the sources only helps what thinks of itself as especially radical faith 'to avoid its own tribulations as a result of history and historical reason'.[57] In other words, to say that what really happened at Easter is inexplicable seems formally to turn into an indispensable requisite for the doing of theology!

On 3: On the one hand the miraculous or revelatory character of Jesus indeed cannot be the object of scientific *historical* work; it can only be the object of philosophical and theological reflections. David Hume already demonstrated that a miracle is defined in such a way that 'no testimony is sufficient to establish it'.[58] But on the other hand, as long as theology is formally 'paired' with historical thought, as it is *on the one hand* because of the character of its central sources and what they say and *on the other* because of our modern awareness of truth,[60] then if it is to remain credible and not lead to a split in the consciousness it must be interested in the question of the manner of the 'resurrection' of Jesus as a question of the context of the resurrection *testimony* and expect an answer to this 'question of miracle' to be of some use for *theological* knowledge,[61] even if right down to most recent times these historical questions have time and again been blocked off.[62] Indeed, a reconstruction of the manner of the 'resurrection' of Jesus or an explanation of how the resurrection of Jesus came to be asserted are unavoidable for an understanding of how the resurrection was proclaimed at the time and how this proclamation can be continued or reformulated today.

Even Willi Marxsen dodges the question that arises in the present and writes: 'The miracle happens today. *For the miracle is the birth of faith.* But since it is a miracle, it eludes my description.' The resurrection is a miracle: 'For "Jesus is risen" simply means: today the crucified Jesus is calling us to believe.'[63]

The more recent systematic work of Bernhard Bron[64] comprehensively works through the discussion of the understanding of miracle against the horizon of the modern concept of nature and history. But its limitations immediately emerge when the question of historicity is not discussed in connection with any of Jesus' miracles – despite the title of Chapter VI, 'The Cross and Resurrection of Jesus Christ as the Horizon for the Understanding of Miracle' (240–2), which promises so much. Anything and nothing can be proved with his thesis on p.243 (the theological concept of miracle will find its criterion and norm from the category of creation from nothing).[65] Of historical research Bron writes:

'It has constantly to free itself from all ideological premises and remain aware of the limits to what it can say, and on the other hand in the very attempt to demonstrate divine action in singular miraculous events it will lose sight of miracle as God's miracle and an event which transcends all possible categories of immanent knowledge. Only where this twofold limit, the impossibility of denying miracle and the impossibility of recognizing miracle in the framework of imment criteria of research, is not broken through, can miracle stand as an event which is completely without derivation and analogy, exclusively and absolutely bound to the revelation of God in Jesus Christ and capable of being recognized against his horizon' (114).

'However, impossible though it may be for historical criticism to demonstrate a miracle, it certainly does not pass the verdict of "un-historicity" on most miracles. Nor is the opposite judgment possible, of affirming miracle in principle as objective facts. Only where this tension is maintained can one do justice to the testimony of the New Testament' (234).

In my view, true historical research cannot accept these curtailments, well-meaning though they may be, unless arguments are adduced for them from historical theory (i.e. arguments which are accessible to autonomous historical reason at least as a description of its own limits). Furthermore, what Bron says reveals a widespread attitude which gives the impression that theology knows better than a historical discipline which is allegedly not self-critical and which demotes history to being an auxiliary science, the arguments of which are taken over where they fit the theological position. Moreover here again we have another instance of the problematic attempt essentially to ground faith and theology in a gap in historical knowledge.

Hoffmann himself evidently takes Bron's line: 'Thus the Easter question points comprehensively to the question of God and can only be solved from that perspective in a systematic theological way.'[66] One may ask in return: is not the Easter question *also* the object of historical research? After all, the early Christians under-stood it as the statement of a historical fact in their discussion with Jewish (Matt.28.15) and pagan (Celsus,[67] Porphyry[68]) contemporaries.

On 4: In this way one avoids the world while accepting its privileges (the author teaches in a state faculty) and everything ends up in '*I believe in order to understand*', a statement which cannot be left to stand in the context of modern scholarship, or at least needs explanation and justification.[69] This objection is based on an 'immunization strategy'.[70] In other respects I would refer to what I said on 3. above and to the remarks of Karl Jaspers on pp.7f. As long as absurdity is not to be made the criterion of the truth of theological statements, academic theologians (*and* church preachers) must be concerned that their remarks are comprehensible. In other words, theological science has the task of ascertaining and interpreting Christian testimonies of faith from history and today, defining their status and content both categorically and conceptually. Theology and proclamation which do *not* share in this understanding – even in respect of what they say about the resurrection – could be understandable only as a private religion or sectarianism.

On 5: The interlocking of event and interpretation applies to all texts with which the historian deals, and thus is in no way a peculiarity of religious or Christian source-texts. This normal fact leads one to see and respect any given source as an expression of human life. Hermeneutically, the objection stated is as important as it is banal. So it must not and cannot put anyone off investigating the New Testament texts to see to what extent, given their nature, they can be used as historical material. It is indeed a shame that as a result of the artificial division into Christian and non-Christian sources, hardly any ancient historian (or even classical philologist), outsiders apart, has adopted any position on the resurrection of Jesus.[71] (Might that possibly be misguided respect, out of an unwillingness to hurt anyone?) Perhaps one can compare the work to be done by historical research at this point with psychoanalysis, where similarly the reports of the patient have to be read against the grain, i.e. against his or her explicit interpretations in the framework of a 'hermeneutics of suspicion'. No analyst is forbidden to use such a method simply because it is in tension with what there is in the statements or texts. Experience teaches that the tradition opens up anew precisely when one approaches it with all available scientific means (in other words, means which are justified and differentiated). At the same time a remark of Ferdinand Christian Baur applies: 'Either scholarship discloses really weak sides of faith or it attacks faith without a reason. If the former is the case, what is introduced is merely the recognition of the truth . . . ; if the latter, then the attack of knowledge on faith can . . . first of all only raise doubt about what was previously believed; now doubt in itself is not regrettable and reprehensible, but for the thinking person the necessary means of arriving at a knowledge of the truth.'[72]

So the investigation which follows will look in a purely historical and empirical way at the historical context of the testimonies to the resurrection, in short at the manner of the 'resurrection' of Jesus – in agreement with Hans von Campenhausen, who writes:

'Now it seems that the many kinds of literary-critical, traditio-historical, motive-critical and form-critical investigations have excessively concealed the simple historical question, i.e. the question of the historical nucleus of what is historically attested by the tradition. Interest in the Easter stories threatens to conceal the Easter history. But the philological work which of course has and must keep the first word in an assessment of the sources may not lead to a Philistine marginalization of the real historical question of what happened, in which the real course and internal connections in the event appear secondary. Legitimate critical objections to a naive psychologism and historicism have made us cautious about exploiting and interpreting the old texts directly; but they do not yet dispense us from the task of putting the old unavoidable question of the historian anew on the basis of a better method, and one that is used more cautiously, and even giving an answer, i.e. making out how far and with what degree of probability we can still ascertain the actual events and their course.'[73]

The aim of this book as a whole is to present a hypothesis on the 'resurrection' of Jesus which causes the least offence and solves the most difficulties – taking into account the requirement of David Friedrich Strauss 'to express myself without ambiguity and reserve, leaving all caution aside',[74] for it is still the case that large parts of so-called critical theology have developed the capacity 'to say nothing with many words' (ibid.). Emanuel Hirsch's Foreword to his 1940 book on the resurrection could have been written, in the Strauss tradition, in 1993:

'Nowadays theologians, by spinning out general theological concepts, have often obscured the real state of our historical knowledge of the Easter event and how far the vast majority of all Protestant scholars have already moved from the New Testament Easter legend. But our non-theologians have no idea what we theologians know and think about the legendary character of the Easter stories. What we need to do here is to require unqualified clarity. The theologian owes it to himself and his community to give an account here to himself and to others of what he really regards as historical and also what he rgards as unhistorical.'[75]

At this point Emanuel Hirsch meets David Friedrich Strauss's demand, which nowadays is often regarded as 'superseded', where it is still noted at all by New Testament scholars.[76]

See also Karl Barth's evaluation of David Friedrich Strauss, in his *Protestant Theology in the Nineteenth Century. Its Background and History* (1947), 1972, 541–68. Barth depicts Strauss as a fickle opportunist (549), a mediocre bourgeois. By denying Strauss any credibility and academic consistency, in the end he spared himself the need of discussing the content of his work: 'Proper theology begins just at the point where the difficulties disclosed by Strauss and Feuerbach are seen and then laughed at . . . But where that is not the case, Strauss could not and must not be pensioned off' (568)

'Is it not a fact that the goal of historical research can at best only be a historical Christ and that this implies a Christ who as a revealer of God can only be a relative Christ? Is it not a fact that such a Christ can only be a helper of those in need, who as such requires all sorts of associates, and figures to supplement him, who at best could only be related to a real, eternal revelation to mankind as a most high and perhaps ultimate symbol is related to the thing itself, who could on no account be the Word that became flesh, executing God's judgment upon us and challenging us ourselves to make a decision? This is what D. F. Strauss asked theology, just as Feuerbach asked it whether the Godhead man sought and thought he had found in his consciousness was anything but man's shadow as it was projected upon the plane of the idea of the infinite. Strauss was no great theologian . . . we are still bound to conclude that his theology ultimately only consisted in the fact that he saw through a bad solution of the problem of theology, gave up any further attempt to improve upon it, abandoned the theme of theology and departed from the field of action' (566).

By way of criticism: does Barth think that he can get beyond the symbol to the 'matter himself'? But his 'proper theology' laughs when asked such a question.

It is almost superfluous to say that the accounts which follow move within the realm of the probable and that the argument is hypothetical; this *a priori* sets limits to this investigation. The predicates 'purely hypothetical', a 'series of hypotheses', and so on which are conceivable as a possible refutation rest on a misunderstanding of historical work. Like any form of interpretation, historical reconstruction cannot proceed without hypotheses and assessments of probability. Indeed it is the real task of historical work to work out the most appropriate hypotheses and clearly weigh probabilities in the process. The value of a reconstruction is decided by whether it is based on the best hypotheses, i.e. those which answer the most (and most important) open questions or solve existing problems and provoke the least (or only weak) counter arguments.[77] Indeed according to Immanuel Kant probability *is* truth, the knowledge of which may be defective but is not for that reason deceptive.

However, an investigation of this description with its aims and possible answers is significant for the theological question as long as theology maintains its reference to history and the critical research that it has entered into since the Enlightenment. One of the decisive insights of modern times is that historicity is a basic category of human make-up which cannot be passed over. Even theologians who are sceptical about a historical approach to theology cannot do other than themselves make historical statements, or statements with necessarily historical implications. Since David Friedrich Strauss, a theology which evades *radical* historical-critical questions 'has been marked for ever with the brand of being unscientific',[78] although of course there have been plenty of attempts to stop the thrust of historical results with apologetic ploys.[79] Dogmatic theologians can no longer move so-called saving facts around dialectically as objective realities, as they did at the time of the Reformation.[80] All statements, including those with a claim to objectivity or revelation, are made by human subjects. This dispensing with a naive concept of objectivity by no means represents the end of the criterion of truth and universality by branching off into subjectivism. For objectivity is rightly to be understood as the intersubjective validity of a notion. And the term subjectivity does not mean empirically individual subjects as such, but denotes a human basic structure in an essential sense.

The thesis that historical knowledge is deceptive (Kierkegaard)[81] and therefore that the question of the historicity of the resurrection is unimportant or cannot be decided must therefore be regarded as a mistake or as appeasement, in both cases with the thought that it is possible to avoid the difficulties of the task of reformulation which grow out of the insights mentioned.

If one assumed that the resurrection of Jesus were not a historical fact (so Jesus did not rise, and remained in the tomb – in contradiction to the classical confessions of the church and probably also to Paul[82]), but was grounded in the vision of Peter and Paul, a new explanation would have to be given of whether in that case Easter can still be regarded as an experience from outside (*extra nos*) or whether it does not prove, rather, to be a wish of the human spirit, as critics of Christianity, ancient (Celsus) and modern,[83] have claimed.[84] Hans von Campenhausen spoke in this connection of the painful 'expedient of following the early Christians in the confession of the Risen Christ but following the Jews in what this confession called forth',[85] but evidently not only saw no difficulties in a bodily resurrection but even took it for granted theologically, since 'here in fact we are said to be dealing with an event which is unique in any sense' (ibid.).

Now following Maurice Goguel, attention should be drawn to the next point. If it could have been proved that the body of Jesus remained in the tomb, the religious consequences of belief in the resurrection at that time would probably not have been destroyed and Christianity would not have been finished off.[86] Had it been possible to present the body of Jesus rotting in the tomb, faith would have found a way out, for example on the basis of the notion of the resurrection in Jubilees 23.31 ('And their bones will rest in the earth, and their spirit will have much joy'), which proves to be disinterested in the physical body.[87] If on the contrary it could be proved that on the morning of the third day the tomb was found empty, that would compel no one to accept the interpretation of this by the first Christians, that Jesus had also risen.[88] (For example, the women could have gone to the wrong tomb [cf. Kirsopp Lake, *The Historical Evidence for the Resurrection of Jesus Christ*, ²1912, 251–3] or Joseph of Arimathea could have moved the body previously.) According to Maurice Goguel and Hans Lietzmann, the reason for this is as follows: 'All events in history take place in the phenomenal world and we can grasp them only in the manifestations of natural causality. But any attempt to understand the deepest essence and the meaning of history in general or in individual instances leads into religions which lie beyond this limit, into the metaphysics of the philosopher or the theologian. And only at this depth do the sources flow from which any consideration of history draws life and gains value.'[89]

Now Lietzmann takes it for granted that criticism of the early Christian Easter accounts is made solely on the basis of natural experience of earthly regularities and leads to a great variety of visionary hypotheses. He continues: 'But the verdict on the true nature of the event described as the resurrection of Jesus, an event of immeasurable significance for the history of the world, does not come within the province of historical inquiry into matters of fact; it belongs to the place where the human soul touches the eternal.'[90]

What 'event' is Lietzmann talking about here? About the historical Jesus? About the visions? I find the easy juxtaposition of historical investigation of facts and metaphysics in Lietzmann too harmonious. And similarly, the remarks of Goguel quoted above apply only to the early Christians and not to us, for whom the question of history has become our fate.[91] Only a ruthlessly honest 'quest for the truth'[92] of the resurrection of Jesus can help us further here.

The plan of the work:

Chapter 3 gives a survey of the early Christian sources for the resurrection of Jesus. Here there is not only a comparison of the content of the individual texts, but they are also classified by characteristics of *form*, in order to arrive at a starting point for the history of the resurrection traditions. That is all the more important for the present work, since it is on the one hand about the resurrection of Jesus and on the other about the origin of the resurrection traditions. In other words, should certain texts about the resurrection from the earliest period prove e.g. to be of defective historical value in this section, there would be no need to subject them to a detailed historical investigation.

Chapter 4 investigates all the relevant texts about the resurrection in three stages (redaction, tradition, historical content). Now it is almost 'universally recognized . . . that the accounts of the appearances in the Gospels are secondary kerygmatic narrative expressions of resurrection faith made by relatively late communities. Thus historical investigation is directed towards the earlier forms of confession.'[93] So the analysis begins with the old kerygmatic formulations and only after that turns to the texts of the Gospels, without establishing a result *a priori*. The aim of Chapter 4 is the exegesis of all the New Testament texts on the resurrection and the recovery of the traditions underlying them, in order at the same time to prepare for a historical reconstruction of the events between cross and resurrection or between the cross and the visions of the risen Christ. This creates the presuppositions for Chapter 5, which will depict the history and the nature of the earliest Christian belief in the resurrection. In Chapter 6 there follows the question of the relationship of the earliest Christian resurrection faith to us, i.e. whether in view of the evidence found we can still call ourselves Christians.

The book has a subtitle: 'History, Experience, Theology'. The term 'history' marks the task of investigating the ascertainable and to some degree assured facts surrounding the resurrection of Jesus, i.e. the circumstances of his burial, the resurrection itself, his appearance and the time and place of the appearance.

The term 'experience' relates to the subjective side of the disciples, to their experiences, which are to be distinguished from theology. In my view this division already presupposes a partial result, since it is assumed (and in my view this cannot really be disputed) that at the beginning we do *not* have the statement 'God has raised Jesus from the dead', but a particular experience of this which later found expression in a theological statement like the one mentioned.[94]

Given what I have said, the triad 'history, experience, theology' exclusively related to the resurrection of Jesus or his appearance. But the texts to be investigated are relatively late; their authors were not eye-witnesses to the life of Jesus but hand down and interpret the texts about the resurrection in a way related to experience. The reason for this may also lie in a particular experience which led them to hand down these texts and these texts in particular. However, in the texts mentioned the first member of the triad, history, drops out, since the narrators concerned are not primary witnesses.

# 3 The Resurrection Texts in Early Christianity – Survey and Classification

Joachim Jeremias described the Easter accounts[95] so precisely in his day that his report will be cited to set the atmosphere for this chapter. He writes:

'The most striking literary problem that we face when we concern ourselves with the Easter stories is the great structural differences between the passion narrative and the Easter stories. In the passion narrative, all the gospels, apart from some differences in detail, have a basic framework of common traditions: entry – last supper – Gethsemane – arrest – hearing before the Sanhedrin – Peter's denial – the Barabbas story – condemnation by Pilate – crucifixion – burial – empty tomb. The Easter stories are quite different. At best we can speak of a common framework in the sequence: empty tomb – appearances. Otherwise the picture is quite a varied one.'[96]

He continues:

'This is true, first, of the *people involved*. The Risen one appears now to an individual, now to a couple of disciples, now to a small group, now to an enormous crowd. The witnesses are mostly men, but also women; they are members of the inmost group of disciples, other followers like Joseph and Matthias (cf. Acts 1.22f.), but also sceptics like the oldest of the family group, Jacob (cf. I Cor.15.7); and at least in one case we have a fanatical opponent', namely Paul (I Cor.15.8) (301).

Jeremias then refers to the various *locations*: in a house, in the open air, before the gates of Jerusalem, in a Judaean village, by the shore of Lake Genessaret, in the hill-country of Galilee, once even outside Palestine, before Damascus.

He goes on to ask what the explanation of this structural difference between the passion narrative and the Easter stories is, and thinks that it is grounded in the events themselves:

'Whereas the passion was an observable happening that took place in Jerusalem over the course of a few days, the Christophanies were a variety of events of different kinds which extended over a long period, probably over a number of years; the tradition limited the period of the Christophanies to forty days only at a relatively late stage (Acts 1.3)' (301). 'The mere fact of the expansion of the Christian community as far as Damascus makes it probable that there is a not inconsiderable interval between the crucifixion of Jesus and the appearance to Paul' (301 n.6).

Following on from this summary Jeremias then extracts three secondary motives which attached themselves to the Easter stories. First, people shaped the reports of the christophanies by words of the risen Jesus and by conversations with him;[97] secondly, the apologetic with which the community reacted to the doubt and ridicule of outsiders which influenced the accounts of Easter (cf. the legend of the watchers by the tomb [Matt.27.62–66; 28.11–15] and the emphasis on the physical nature of the Risen Christ [Luke 24.39; John 20.20; Luke 24.41–43]); and thirdly, the development within the church shaped the Easter stories; cf. the church formulation (Matt.28.19), the church calendar (John 20.26; Acts 2.1ff.) and above all the missionary obligation of the church (Matt.28.16–20; Luke 24.44–49;: Acts 1.4–8).

By contrast, according to Jeremias:

'the characteristic feature of the earliest stratum of tradition is that it still preserves a recollection of the overpowering, puzzling and mysterious nature of the events: eyes opened at the breaking of the bread, beams of heavenly light, a figure on the shore at break of day, the unexpected appearance in a closed room, the outbreak of praise expressed in speaking with tongues, the sudden disappearance – all these are ways in which the earliest tradition is formulated. The same mysterious chiaroscuro surrounds the earliest accounts of the reactions of the witnesses: now they fail to recognize the risen One, now the heavenly brightness blinds them, now they believe that they have seen a ghost. Fear and trembling, anxiety, uncertainty and doubt struggle with joy and worship' (cf. John 21.12; Matt.28.17; Luke 24.41 [303]).

Here already, with due recognition of the precise description of the Easter texts by Jeremias it can be remarked that his verdicts on the earliest stratum of tradition (probably meant historically) may be too optimistic. For the 'opened eyes at the breaking of the bread' (Luke 24.30), Jesus' 'sudden disappearance' (Luke 24.31), the 'figure on the shore at break of day' (John 21.4) – all these features come from a later time (for justification see the detailed exegesis). In this connection it is worth listening to the position of Lyder Brun:

> 'In general, quite often historical judgments find their way into a traditio-historical approach rather too early, when the important thing may be first to work closely through the existing traditions from a traditio-historical perspective, for the moment putting the question of the historical results in the background.'[98]

The same point might be made on more recent works, like e.g. that of François Bovon, who concludes from the pluralistic character of earliest Christianity that evidently contemporaneous (?) appearances took place.[99]

Nevertheless, Jeremias's summary introduction retains its value, even if not all the historical verdicts in it are equally apt. At this point one might refer to Goguel's thesis that it follows from the varied character of the resurrection texts as compared with the passion narrative[100] that these are not historical accounts but narratives of faith (with no historical character?).[101] This proposal shows that a quite different evaluation of the resurrection texts in comparison with the passion tradition is possible. But in reply it should be emphasized that even narratives of faith contain historical elements, and the present book is also concerned with reconstructing these.

Depending on their form, the statements about the resurrection can be divided into six groups. They occur:

I     as a participial phrase, 'God who has raised Jesus from the dead';
II    as catechetical statements about the resurrection of Jesus and about his appearance ('he [Jesus] appeared to XY'), which are already being developed into sequences;
III   in extended appearance stories and
IV   (perhaps) in stories about the tomb
V    in resurrection stories which were dated back into the life of Jesus and
VI   in various others.

On I: The participial phrase, 'God who has raised Jesus from the dead'

The earliest example of this type appears in I Thess.1.10;[102] cf. further II Cor.4.14; Gal.1.1; Rom.4.24b; 8.11a (Eph.1.20; Col.2.12; I Peter 1.21). These formulations are formal throughout, and are therefore older than the particular writings in which they occur; thus in part they go back even beyond the earliest letter of Paul (I Thess.). So – depending on the dating of that letter – they come from at least the forties or even thirties of the first century, and it is sometimes thought that these are the earliest statements of all about the resurrection in the New Testament.[103]

> Jürgen Becker has considerably advanced the discussion of these state-ments, but at the same time moved it in a direction which needs to be examined. He writes: 'In this connection the resurrection of Jesus meant . . .: the God experienced in Jesus' resurrection says yes to Jesus' picture of God and allows the disciples to understand themselves as those who are to hand on this God' (224). According to the earliest confession it took 'such a new act of the experience of God for the early original community to restore the validity of Jesus' image of God' (ibid.). *Historically*, Becker thinks in terms of 'visionary experiences . . . which were interpreted by the belief that the crucified Jesus has been raised by God' (240). Jesus' picture of God is regarded 'as the real cause of his death, deeply inherent in all the details' (206). 'As surely as Jesus was a Jew, so surely the official Judaism of the time silenced him, and immediately early Christianity had considerable problems with his attitude in connection with Judaism. This suggests that we should look out for an opposition between Jesus and the Judaism of his time generally' (206 n.4).
>     Criticism: 1. Becker's remarks systematize far too much: for example, he contrasts a person (Jesus) with an abstract (Judaism). 2. The content of the formula can hardly be limited to the affirmation of Jesus' picture of God 'as in all its variations it proclaims the divine action in one person, not the authentication of his spiritual legacy'.[104] 3. The participial phrase 'God who raised Jesus from the dead' is possibly already a secondary variation of the formula of faith in Rom.10.9b,[105] in which case it cannot be used in a unilinear way to affirm Jesus' picture of God.[106] 4. Becker speaks of an experience of *God* without making it clear what he means historically by the aspect of *experience*. 5. The visionary experiences of the first Christians with which Becker also reckons were primarily 'experiences of *Christ*' and consisted in seeing Jesus (see above in the text).

At this point – anticipating the detailed exegesis – reference must already be made to the close parallel between these formulae and other pre-Pauline formula-like passages: II Cor.1.9, 'God who raises the dead'; Rom.4.17: 'God who gives life to the dead and calls into existence things that do not exist'. The two passages have a parallel in the second of the Jewish Eighteen Benedictions. It differs only slightly in the various recensions and goes back to the first century BCE:[107]

'You are blessed for ever, Lord. You bring the dead to life, you are rich in help. You hold all things living in love, give life to the dead with great mercy. You support the falling, heal the sick and free the captives. You show your faithfulness to those who sleep in the dust. Who is like you, the almighty Lord? Who is like you, a king who kills and brings to life and makes salvation flourish? You are faithful to bring the dead to life again. You are blessed, Lord, who brings the dead to life.'[108]

On II: the catechetical statements

These can be divided into: (a) statements about the resurrection of Jesus and (b) statements about his appearance:

(a) I Thess.4.14; I Cor.15.3–4; Rom.4.25 and Rom.14.9 are related to the type described under I and presuppose it. But in them sometimes Jesus is the active subject, and often the statement about his resurrection is combined with one about his death. So here they are to be classified with the catechetical statements.

(b) I Cor.15.5–8; Luke 24.34; Mark 16.9–20

1. I Cor.15.5–8 says the following about the appearances of the risen Christ:

He appeared (*ophthe*) to Cephas, then to the Twelve (v.5), he appeared to more than 500 brothers at once (v.6), then he appeared to James, then to all the apostles (v.7) he appeared to Paul (v.8).

The statements about christophanies listed here (vv.5–7) are doubtless very old, since they all go back to the time *before* the appearance of Christ to Paul. However, there needs to be an explanation of how many of the appearances mentioned Paul had already communicated to the Corinthians in the preaching with which he founded the community. If one reads I Cor.15.1–11 straight through, it is not clear which verses are merely reporting what has been related in the foundation preaching and what information Paul is adding *ad hoc*. (For these questions see below, 35f. There it is argued that what was reported in the original preaching extends to the end of v.5.) At this point the presupposition may merely be introduced that the statement about the appearance to Cephas was already communicated to the Corinthians during the first mission to the community. In that case Paul is speaking of the appearance to Cephas in Corinth only a short time after the foundation of the Thessalonian community. That would mean that since the christophany to Cephas was handed down to Paul (by his own confession already as tradition, I Cor.15.1f.) before he came to Europe, it is chronologically at least as old as the information under I (above, 24f.), which indeed goes back even before the time of the composition of I Thessalonians. So here one may conjecture that both groups I and II (in the latter at least the appearance to Cephas) belong closely together not only chronologically but also genetically. It should also be noted that in I Thess. both a pre-Pauline participial phrase (I Thess.1.10 = group I) and a resurrection formula (I Thess.4.14 = group IIa) are used. Furthermore, a tradition roughly corresponding to I Cor.15.3–5 may also be presupposed as the ingredient of Paul's first preaching in Thessalonica, since Paul probably used a somewhat similar tradition in every community founded by him.[109] *So we may formulate as a working hypothesis that the conclusion was drawn from the appearance to Cephas* (= group IIb) *that God has raised Jesus from the dead* (= group I). (The reverse order is historically impossible.)

2. In Luke 24.34 we have a formula corresponding to I Cor.15.5, 'The Lord has risen indeed and has appeared to Simon',[110] in which the mention of the resurrection of Jesus in the first place already derives from theological reflection.

3. Mark 16.9–20, the secondary long ending to Mark, recalls I Cor.15.3–8 in its list of the sequences of appearances (v.9 'first to Mary Magdalene'; v.12 'then to two of them . . .'; v.14 'lastly . . . to the eleven'). The passage was certainly not composed as a conclusion to the Gospel of Mark but was already in existence previously,[111] probably as a kind of 'Easter catechism in community instruction',[112] which strictly speaking does not presuppose a narrative about the empty tomb at all. (This is also suggested by the fact that the bodily resurrection of Jesus is not a theme.) This is a kind of Gospel harmony of Easter reports;[113] knowledge of the Gospels of Mark and Matthew cannot be demonstrated, but that of Luke, John and Acts can.[114]

In what follows the parallel passages are put in brackets behind the relevant verse of the Mark ending: vv.9f. (Luke 8.2; John 20.1,11–18); v.11 (Luke 24.11); vv.12f. (Luke 24.13–35); v.14 (Luke 24.36–43; Acts 1.3); vv.15f. (Luke 24.47); vv.17f. (Acts 16.16–18; 2.1–11; 28.3–6;

3.1–10; 9.31–35; 14.8–10; 28.8f.);[115] v.19 (Acts 1.9; Luke 24.51); v.20 (Acts generally).

The text has various striking features. It presupposes the first appearance to Mary Magdalene and thus probably suppresses the protophany to Cephas inferred above. But at the same time the significance of the first appearance to Mary Magdalene is weakened by the fact that she appears at the head of a chain of witnesses,[116] and all the emphasis is put on the appearance to the eleven, to whom moreover the detailed insructions are given by Jesus (vv.15–18).

It has already often been observed that the theme of unbelief runs through the section (vv.11,13 and 14) and that the section is a call for (true) faith (vv.16,17). Arnold Meyer has interpreted it as follows:

'The summary thus sets out to say: Guard against a lack of faith in the resurrection. All salvation is based on belief in the power of God in the resurrection which overcomes the world and death; he alone in alliance with the mysterious power of baptism brings about the liberation of the world from demons and from the corruption that is there before this whole world. Unbelief has already been harshly rebuked by Jesus and will also be regarded by God as the decisive crime against his majesty. You can already see that God and faith really have such power, from the signs which kept happening in the early church and continue to happen now. So this is a defence of belief in the resurrection by reference to the miracle of the church!'[117]

On III: The extended appearance stories

We may follow C. H. Dodd in dividing the detailed appearance stories into two groups.[118]

1. The first group is to be found in Matt.28.9–10; 28.16–20 and John 20.19–21. It consists of five elements:
  (a) Exposition: the followers of Christ are robbed of their Lord;
  (b) Appearance of the Lord (Matt.28.9,17; John 20.19);
  (c) Greeting (Matt.28.9; John 20.19);
  (d) Recognition (Matt.28.9,17; John 20.20);
  (e) Commission (Matt.28.10,19; John 20.21f.).

Dodd reckons that this group 'embodies the "formed" tradition which became stereotyped through a relatively long tradition in the community' (314).

2. The second group of narratives comprises Luke 24.13–35 and John 21.1–14 (302–5). It differs from the first group of resurrection stories in the fact that the Risen One – although he can be seen and heard – is not immediately recognized as the risen Jesus. Thus these narratives betray a higher stage of reflection, and their historical value in relation to what really happened diminishes accordingly.[119]

Mark 16.14–15 (the appearance to the eleven), Luke 24.36–49 (the appearance to the Eleven and those who were there), John 20.26–29 (doubting Thomas) and John 20.11–17 (Mary Magdalene at the tomb) are mixed types of resurrection stories. On this pericope Dodd remarks:

'I have to confess that for a long time I have not been able to avoid the feeling (and it can be more than a feeling) that in an undefinable way there is something first-hand about this pericope. At any rate it stands by itself. There is nothing comparable in the Gospels. Is there anything comparable in the whole of ancient literature?' (311).

On IV: The stories about the tomb

The story about the tomb in Mark 16.1–8 has a special role. Thus it does not contain a real report of an appearance of the Risen Christ himself, but rather the *proclamation* of the resurrection of Jesus by a disciple (v.6). To this degree it is perhaps a resurrection story, but one already in the form of a reflection (with a kerygmatic purpose).

Another possibility would be the hypothesis that the appearance of an angel suppressed a christophany in Mark 16.5, to safeguard the first appearance to Cephas. In that case the tomb story would go back to an earlier tradition and would be of even greater interest for our work than it already is. Furthermore, the question would arise whether the first appearance to Cephas might not have competed with a first appearance to the women. Yet another situation would arise if Mark 16.1–9 should be based on an earlier epiphany story.[120]

To the question of the right way to understand Mark 16.1–8 must be added the question of the order of the other New Testament stories about the tomb which put the accent in very different places (epecially Matthew and John). Certainly we may generally presuppose that Mark is the basis for Matthew and Luke and John 20 is later in terms of literary form or tradition. But 'we may not in any event take it that the innovations from Matthew and Luke are simply conditioned by a literary revision of Mark and the peculiarities of

John by a literary reshaping of the Synoptic texts. Behind the traditio-historical movement attested by the texts is an oral-written tradition . . .'[121]

### On V: The resurrection stories dated back into the life of Jesus

The stories from the life of Jesus contained in the Gospels which can perhaps be called resurrection stories dated back into the life of Jesus form a further complex. Certainly it is always difficult at this point to arrive at statements which are anything like certain, but in general the possibility of dating Easter stories back into the life of Jesus should not be disputed. Even the words of the earthly Jesus were only worth telling for the community in that at the same time they were read and understood as words of one who was (now) exalted. Scholars have understood the following pericopes as original Easter narratives: Mark 6.45–52 (Jesus walking on the lake) and the Matthaean addition Matt.14.28–31 (Peter first goes to meet Jesus walking on the lake and then loses his nerve);[122] Mark 9.2–8 (the transfiguration of Jesus); Luke 5.1–11; Matt.16.17–19.[123] But by way of qualification it should already be remarked here that only the last two pericopes will be considered in the subsequent analysis.

### On VI: Various others

Finally, reference should be made to the so-called apocryphal Gospels, the content of which is Jesus' resurrection or his appearance. The Gospel of the Hebrews decribes the epiphany of Jesus to James (for the text see below, 108f.). The Gospel of Peter describes the event of the resurrection of Jesus and, following that, probably the appearance to Peter. Nikolaus Walter[124] and B. A. Johnson[125] derive the narrative of the Gospel of Peter from an 'eschatological epiphany narrative' (on which Matthew also drew). But here we must ask whether this is a secondary traditio-historical development on the basis of the canonical Gospels. At any rate the writing claims to be an eye-witness report of the Lord's disciple ('Now I, Simon Peter, and my brother Andrew took our nets and went to the lake' [124.60]), which suggests a secondary character. One might compare the similar stress on the eye-witness of the twelve apostles in the Gospel of the Ebionites.[126] But that does not necessarily demonstrate that the *whole* writing is later, only the stylistic form mentioned. Only a detailed comparison can bring clarity here. (For pragmatic reasons I shall be discussing the Gospel of Peter in connection with the analysis of Matt.28, without presupposing a general verdict on its age.)

Furthermore, reference might be made to the dialogue of the Risen One with his disciples in the Gnostic writings, in which Jesus gives instructions to his disciples.[127] Here too what has just been said about the first-person style (a claim to being an eye-witness) applies. The dialogue form is secondary, but that does not say anything about the age of the content.

The following intermediate results and consequences arise from the previous section on the classification of the texts on the resurrection:

1. A large number of the existing narratives do not come from eye-witnesses but passed through the hand of the community and/or a theological personality. Only in the relatively numerous passages in Paul, our primary source, do we have an eye-witness report – not of course of the event of the resurrection itself but of the appearances of the Risen Lord. As Paul explicitly puts the appearance of Jesus to him in parallel to that to the other witnesses (I Cor.15.8), it is above all from *here* that we are to expect access to the manner of the appearance of the risen Christ to the rest of the eyewitnesses.

Here David Friedrich Strauss already rightly observed: 'When Paul there places the christophany which occurred to himself in the same series with the appearances of Jesus in the days after his resurrection: this authorizes us . . . to conclude that, for aught the Apostle knew, those earlier appearances were of the same nature with the one experienced by himself.'[128] So the analysis of the Pauline texts occupies a key position. Here it goes without saying in a work which adopts a primarily historical procedure that these testimonies or Paul's 'Easter' need also to be related, in a further step, to the pre-Christian period of his life.

Anyone who does not share the presupposition made here will not be able to make anything of what follows. Of course it is also clear to me that in I Cor.15 *ophthe* is a collective term for a variety of appearances. For example, it is used for appearances both to individuals and to groups, and is shaped by the language of the Septuagint (for details, see 48f. below). Therefore one could assume theoretically that different things were meant here, so that the presupposition mentioned in the text would be improbable. What tells against this is that Paul knew the people in Jerusalem and Cephas personally (Gal.1) and must have known what he was talking about. In other words, the above presupposition is right.[129] Since the historical objections to the presupposition introduced here can be rejected, it should be asked: what *resistance* is at work in any possible criticism of that presupposition?

2. According to the texts, the second personal eyewitness alongside Paul is Peter. But we do not have a first-person report. Nevertheless, the tradition of an appearance to Peter[130] remains extremely valuable, all the more so since other *pre*-Easter traditions about Peter are to be peeled off (cf. the denial of Jesus by Peter [Mark 14.54, 66–72]) and we can relate these *ex hypothesi* historically to the appearance to Peter. Therefore the Peter tradition similarly has an important role, and here as in the case of Paul we must examine the relationship between the appearance to Peter and his 'pre-Easter' period.

3. At this point we can already differentiate between the historical value of the individual narratives. Because of its age, Paul's report in I Cor.15.3ff. and the details in the Gospels and Acts which accord with it are of paramount significance. Within the Gospel narratives we are to suppose that those reports which stress the bodily nature of the risen Christ are relatively late,[131] though we cannot exclude the possibility that elements in them may be earlier. For the emphasis on the reality of the resurrection body of Jesus shows signs of later apologetic concern with the reality of the resurrection in the face of the docetic challenge to it, according to which Jesus only seemed to have risen.

4. The stories about the tomb pose a separate problem (cf. already 28f.). Closely connected with this we need an answer to the question whether the tradition of the appearance to the women or to Mary Magdalene is historically valuable. If, for example, the 'young man' (Mark 16.5) has suppressed the Risen Christ, at any rate the appearance to the women would be pre-Markan. So we need to work thoroughly through Mark 16.1–8 and John 20. We must further ask whether the tradition of an appearance to women could not have been preserved in non-canonical texts. And finally a first appearance to women would not necessarily be irreconcilable with Paul's report in I Cor.15, since the apostle could deliberately have omitted a first appearance to women, especially as according to Jewish law women were not legitimate witnesses (see below, 158).

5. As for the place of the resurrection appearances, as is well known, there is a choice of two localities: Galilee and Jerusalem (and its surroundings). But as the appearances in Galilee can hardly be

explained on the assumption of the priority of the appearances in Jerusalem (in any case, that would be like the Reformation first gaining a footing in Rome and then later in Wittenberg), we may now consider whether the first appearances took place in Galilee and those in Jerusalem occurred only at a later point in time.[132] In that case, however, the first appearance to Mary Magdalene which has often been emphasized recently would have to be disputed, since this is probably conceivable only in Jerusalem (also because of its presumed proximity to the tomb tradition). The flight of the disciples after the death of Jesus or before his crucifixion (Mark 14.50) would fit the priority of the Galilee tradition, since Galilee would be a plausible destination, as it was their home and the place of Jesus' activity. However, we should be extremely cautious in resorting to a theory of the flight of all the disciples. At any rate Peter may not have fled immediately, if the circumstances of his denial of Jesus have been described with any degree of accuracy at all in Mark's account. Probably the internal situation in the group of disciples before and after the crucifixion of their master was in any case so diffuse that we should presuppose unknown intermediary stages. For example, von Campenhausen supposes that the word of the angel in Mark 16.7, which, while legendary, is ultimately historical, made Jesus and the disciples go to Galilee, where the first appearances then took place (but it should already be asked at this point whether and how Mark 16.7 is an 'authentic' angelic saying).[133] It follows that the question of the place of the first appearance needs to be raised again after the exegesis of all the texts.

6. The time of the resurrection or the appearance of the risen Christ also has to be governed by an answer to the Galilee/Jerusalem controversy. At least it can already be said here that an appearance on the third day is incompatible with the priority of the Galilee tradition. The disciples could hardly have travelled from Jerusalem to Galilee between Friday and Sunday. Moreover, the sabbath lay in between, and they would hardly have travelled on that day. But at the same time we should note that in the earliest kerygma I Cor.15.4, the resurrection of Jesus and *not* the appearance is dated to the third day. To this degree the question of the priority of Galilee or Jerusalem is again open.

# 4 Individual Analyses

## 4.1 I Corinthians 15.1–11

### 4.1.1 *Redaction*

The position of I Cor.15 at the end of the letter can be explained on traditio-historical grounds: the instruction about the end-time always comes at the end (cf.I Thess.4.13–5.11; Mark 13; Didache 16; Barnabas 21.1).[134] I Corinthians 15 is a well-rounded unit on the resurrection of the dead. However, that does not become clear immediately but only as a result of vv.12–34 ('the fact of the resurrection') and vv.35–38 ('the manner of the resurrection').

In vv.1–11 Paul takes up the confession of faith which he communicated on the visit which led to the foundation of the community: this spoke of the death and resurrection and Christ's appearance to Cephas and the Twelve (I Cor.15.3b–5), the appearances of Christ that had been made known to him. This probably had the purpose, *first*, of providing a 'historical' guarantee of his resurrection[135] (cf. v.6b, one can indeed investigate it; moreover 'at one time' ([v.6a] on the redactional level is probably meant to 'intensify . . . the objectivity, because 500 witnesses at one time could not easily all have been deluded'[136]). *Secondly*, Paul was evidently concerned to continue up to himself the tradition which he had given the Corinthians on his first visit, which already included Jesus' appearance to Cephas (for the reason see below). Now in that case it was necessary for him to add appearances of the same kind which chronologically preceded his own.[137] That makes it clear that according to v.8 Paul received the same vision as all the other people listed in this sequence. In this way the statements in vv.5 and 7 lose the task that they perhaps had at the stage of the tradition. They are now used by Paul to bear witness to the fact of the appearances of Christ to himself (compare v.6b, which is certainly redactional),

whereas originally and for the main part they probably stressed the
first vision and thus the legitimacy of Cephas and James.

Why did Paul want to continue the appearances of Christ up to
himself? Why does he stress the identity of his vision with that to all
the people mentioned earlier? We cannot avoid the assumption that
this was to defend his apostolic authority. Verses 8–10 clearly have
an apologetic character. How else are we to understand the reference
to his own work (v.10b)? How else are we to understand the
surprising length of his comments about himself, the designation of
himself in v. 8 as 'one untimely born' (in relation to those mentioned
previously)? It emerges quite plainly from I Cor.9.1b–18 that this
apostolic authority was doubted by some people in Corinth.[138] At
the least there was criticism of it in the Corinthian community which
he had founded. In I Cor.15.8–10 he wanted in advance to provide
himself with credentials for the teaching which follows, all the more
so since he understands himself (as in I Thess.4.14) as an authorized
expounder of the Christian confession of faith which he summarizes
yet again in v.12a ('if[139] Christ is preached as being raised from the
dead'), and from which, unlike some[140] Corinthians, he concludes a
future resurrection (of Christians).[141] The one is inconceivable
without the other. Therefore, 'If the dead are not raised, then Christ
has not been raised' (v.16).

In what follows, among other things Paul gives a brief sketch of the
last things to be expected (I Cor.15.20–28). Here we evidently have
an overall understanding of the resurrection of Jesus which can see it
only in the framework of Jewish apocalyptic and not in the
Hellenistic pattern of epiphanies, according to which the exalted
Lord is present in the spirit without the horizontal coming into view.
Accordingly the apostle can also answer the question of the
corporeality of the resurrection ('with what kind of body will the
dead be raised' [I Cor.15.35]) only from his Jewish apocalyptic
background (the distinction between the fleshly and the spiritual
body in vv.35–49), which was alien to Hellenistic thought. So Jewish
and Hellenistic thought clash in the controversy in Corinth.[142]

According to Karl Heinrich Rengstorf, in what Paul says about the
resurrection body (vv.35ff.) he wanted to develop the Palestinian
Easter testimony that he had given in I Cor.15.3–5,[143] so that in the
end the testimony of the earliest community is present in his account.
This thesis is possible, but cannot be proved, since in vv.35ff. it is
primarily *Paul* who is speaking or writing.[144] It cannot be demonstrated that these statements depend on a tradition of the earliest

community, although it is clear that both Paul and the earliest community stand in a Jewish apocalyptic tradition which is stamped throughout by the idea of the bodily nature of the resurrection.[145]

## 4.1.2 *Traditions*

First of all we should clarify how far the formula which Paul had communicated to his community in Corinth at the time of its founding actually extended.

There are basically two reasons for suggesting[146] that the tradition communicated to the Corinthians on Paul's initial visit extends to '*then to the Twelve*'(v.5, end). (a) Another sentence construction begins after 'then to the Twelve'. (b) As the words 'most of whom are still alive, though some have fallen asleep' (v.6b) certainly do not belong to the tradition handed on at the first visit, it would seem probable that Paul was no longer recalling something already known but was giving his own account, using other traditions.

Now it is clear that the tradition in vv.3–5 handed down at the foundation visit is itself not all of a piece. Thus for example the statement about Jesus' resurrection or being raised and the statement about Jesus' death 'for our sins' originally did not stand side by side[147] and were first put together at the level of pre-Pauline tradition (cf. the similar combination of statements about the death and resurrection in Rom.4.25; 14.9; II Cor.5.15; I Thess.4.14). The 'that' (*hoti recitativum*, cf. I Cor.8.4) which appears four times and perhaps goes back to Paul himself also gives a clear external indication that different formulae are being put side by side.[148]

In addition, it can be noted that vv.3–5 provide a twofold proof, (a) from scripture and (b) from a confirmatory fact. Thus 'he was buried' is connected with the dying and not the resurrection of Jesus.[149] So vv.3–5 consist of two lines and are to be read as follows:

(a) Christ died (*apethanen*) for our sins according to the scriptures[150] and he was buried (*etaphe*);

(b) he was raised (*egegerthai*)[151] on the third day according to the scriptures and he appeared (*ophthe*) to Cephas, then to the Twelve.

There are various views about the origin of the tradition in I Cor.15.3b–5. Some scholars derive it from the Greek-speaking communities around Antioch and Damascus;[152] others, including Joachim Jeremias,[153] from the earliest community in Jerusalem, in which case a translation from the Aramaic must be presupposed. On the whole the alternative 'Jerusalem or Antioch' seems to be exaggerated. 'For even if the tradition came to Paul by way of the community in Antioch, it would only have reproduced what it too had received – from Jerusalem.'[154] Moreover, an argument in terms of content supports Jerusalem as the origin of the tradition: the closing remark in I Cor.15.11 that Paul's 'kerygma was identical with that of the first apostles'.[155]

We now come to the question of the tradition of the first appearance of Jesus to Cephas (v.5) and its relation to the christophany to James (v.7).

The clause in v.5, 'he appeared to Cephas, then[156] to the Twelve' can be detached as an independent piece of tradition.[157] In favour of this is first the parallel to Luke 24.34 ('Jesus has risen indeed and has appeared to Simon') and Mark 16.7 ('the disciples and Peter'), and secondly the parallel formula in v.7 which follows.

The christophany to James (and all the apostles) in I Cor.15.7 contains two statements: first, that James has been granted an appearance, and secondly, that James has a special position in the circle of apostles.

A more precise traditio-historical definition of v.7 follows from the observation that vv.7 and 5 are constructed in the same way. Here, apart from Cephas/James and the Twelve/all the apostles, the same words are used; cf. 'he appeared to Cephas, then to the Twelve' with 'he appeared to James, then to all the apostles'.

The parallelism between v.5 and v.7 could be explained in two ways: (a) Paul himself has shaped the language of v.7 on the basis of v.5, having before him a tradition about an appearance to James and all the apostles; (b) in each case Paul is giving an independent tradition. In that case either one formula was modelled on the basis of another at a secondary stage prior to Paul, or both formulae have a common origin. In any case it remains clear that both in v.5 and in v.7 there is a tradition[158] which on each occasion may be described as a 'formula'.[159]


*The historical context of I Cor.15.5–7*

The traditions handed down in I Cor.15.5,7 contain the brief report that a specific group of Christians (the Twelve and Peter or the apostles and James) experienced an appearance of the Risen Christ. The possible function of such a 'formula' becomes clear if we look at

Paul's writings. In his battle against adversaries Paul refers at several points to his vision of the Risen Christ (I Cor.9.1; cf.Gal.1.15f.; Phil.3.8) in order to legitimate his authority. The traditions in I Cor.15.5,7 probably have a similar function and are therefore best described as 'legitimation formulae' (Wilckens).

However, it should not be claimed that the legitimation formulae do not allow us to make any inferences about the process of legitimation, as Rudolf Pesch still argued in 1973, claiming that the phrase 'he appeared' was only a literary form of expression of the authority of the one legitimated.[160] That is improbable, because *ophthe* is a verb of seeing and Paul must have expected the Corinthians to understand this term historically.

The rivalry between the two formulae in vv.5 and 7 can be explained if we connect them with the development of the earliest Jerusalem community in the first two decades. According to this, Peter had the first appearance. For the formula legitimating Peter and the Twelve is earlier than than that of I Cor.15.7. It comes from the time when the circle of the Twelve existed and was linked to a pre-Pauline stage of tradition with the christological confession of faith.

The text I Cor.15.7 arose when followers of James (or James himself) claimed Peter's role as witness for James. To this end they adapted the account of the appearance of Jesus to James to the formula of I Cor.15.5; here James's historical vision was certainly already received at a time when Peter was leader of the community.[161]

## Summary of the analysis of the tradition

I Corinthians 15.3–8 contains the following individual traditions[162] about the death and resurrection of Jesus:

(a) I Cor.15.3b: a formula (perhaps catechetical) about the death of Christ 'for our sins'[163] with a general reference to the scriptures;

(b) I Cor.15.4a: a reference to the burial of Jesus;[164]

(c) I Cor.15.4b: a statement (perhaps catechetical) about the resurrection on the third day with reference to the scriptures.

(d) Finally, four individual statements about witnesses:

(1) I Cor.15.5: he appeared to Cephas, then/and to the Twelve.

(2) I Cor.15.6a: he appeared to more than 500 brethren at one time.

(3) I Cor.15.7: he appeared to James, then/and to all the apostles.

(4) I Cor.15.8–10: he appeared to Paul.

We can assume that all the elements in the tradition are to be dated to the first two years after the crucifixion of Jesus. At any rate this thesis is probable for I Cor.15.3b–5.[165] It is also likely for I Cor.15.6a,7 since the conversion of Paul lies at the chronological end of the appearances cited and is probably to be thought of as not later than three years after the death of Jesus.[166]

Now I remarked on p.35 above that Paul did not hand on to the Corinthians other appearances of Christ (as e.g. that to more than 500 brethren or that to James and all the apostles) on the visit on which he founded the community, but merely the credal formula mentioned above, together with the appearance to Cephas and the Twelve. I gave this as the reason why the apostle lists these appearances in I Corinthians (as a historical guarantee of the resurrection of Jesus and to back up his own apostolic authority). From that it follows for I Corinthians, *first*, that Paul cited all the appearances known to him, and *secondly*, also that the information was extremely reliable and complete.[167]

At this point the question arises why Paul did not report the other appearances in his preaching when the church was founded. The answer is that they were not (yet) the basis of salvation in the same way as the creed of the death and resurrection of Jesus, whereas the appearance(s) to Cephas and the Twelve were particularly significant in founding the church in the very earliest period, and therefore were part of the gospel. It cannot be concluded from this that the other appearances only took place historically after the founding of the Corinthian community. Such an assumption already comes to grief on the fact for example that the appearance to more than 500 brethren was told for no other reason than that it had really happened (in the same way as the appearance to James).[168] It is hard to say what the relationship is here between fact and the linguistic development of the tradition. Because of the extraordinary nature of each of these events we may reckon that appearances of Jesus were talked about *immediately* after they happened.[169] How is it conceivable that an event could have taken place and only have been talked about, shall we say, ten years later?

Conclusion: *the formation of the appearance traditions mentioned in I Cor.15.3–8 falls into the time between 30 and 33 CE, because the appearance to Paul is the last of the appearances and cannot be dated after 33 CE.*

### 4.1.3 Historical

#### 4.1.3.1  I Cor.15.3 (Jesus' death)

The fact of Jesus' death as the consequence of crucifixion is indisputable.[170]

#### 4.1.3.2  I Cor.15.4a
#### (The burial of Jesus: Mark 15.42–47 parr.; John 19.31–37)

The burial of Jesus is reported in the early Christian writings in two ways:
(a)  Joseph of Arimathea buried Jesus (Mark 15.42–7 parr.);
(b)  Jews buried Jesus (John 19.31–37).

On (a) = Mark 15.42–47

> Bultmann regards this text as 'a historical account, which creates no impression of being a legend apart from the women who appear again as witnesses in v.47, and vv.44,45, which Matthew and Luke in all probability did not have in their Mark, creates no impression of being a legend. It can hardly be shown that the section was devised with the Easter story in mind. The first indication of that cannot be seen before the note in v.46 that a stone was rolled in front of the tomb, though that could also be simply a descriptive touch. The age of the tradition here preserved cannot of course be established.'[171]

Bultmann's thesis needs to be examined. So first we shall discuss the position of the pericope in the context of the passion story and then return once again to the divide between redaction and tradition.

*The position of Mark 15.42–47 in the context of the passion narrative*

The present pericope links the narrative of the crucifixion (15.20–41) with that of the empty tomb (16.1–8). The note of time 'in the evening' (v.42) takes up the 'third hour' (15.25) when Jesus was crucified and the 'sixth to the ninth hour' (15.33) during which time darkness fell. In other words, Jesus died at three o'clock in the afternoon ( = ninth hour), and by the time he was put in the tomb it was already evening. There are two references to the crucifixion scene in v.44: the amazement of Pilate at Jesus' rapid death makes sense above all in the context of the Markan passion narrative, since according to that, against the rules, the time of Jesus' suffering was unusually short.[172] (*That* was why Pilate was surprised.) The scene is connected by the question of the centurion on duty (v.44) with what has gone before (cf. v.39 the centurion under the cross). There are further links with the context in the fact that 15.46b and 16.3 correspond almost word for word and the women both stand under the cross and observe the burial from afar, and go to the empty tomb (15.40, 47; 16.1).

## Redaction and tradition in Mark 15.42–47

[42] The note of time, 'and when evening had come', is redactional, as are Mark 4.35; 6.47; 14.17. There is probably a basis in tradition for the naming of the day of rest. Mark explains it for his readers as the day before the sabbath (cf. the similar explanation of Jewish customs in Mark 7.3f.).

[43] The characterization of Joseph as a 'respected member of the council (*euschemon bouleutes*)' occurs only here in Mark. However, we cannot without further ado infer that the whole phrase comes from tradition. The remarkable note could also be understood as redaction: in this way Joseph is identified as a member of the Sanhedrin which condemned Jesus to death (Mark 14.55; 15.1).[173] However, for Mark the note seems to have positive connotations: the fact that Joseph was 'also himself looking for the kingdom of God' shows that others than he were doing the same thing. This includes not only the disciples (Mark 4.11) but also the scribe whom Jesus claims to be not 'far from the kingdom of God' (Mark 12.34).[174] In other words, while Mark does not depict Joseph as a Christian, he does single him out from the opponents of Jesus in the Sanhedrin by the characterization mentioned, and given the completely positive significance that 'kingdom of God' has in Mark (see 1.15), he dissociates him from the opposition of the Sanhedrin to Jesus.[175] Certainly Mark would have preferred to report a burial of Jesus by his followers (cf. Mark 6.29, the burial of John the Baptist by his disciples). However, as he had no tradition and on the other hand a report was going the rounds about the burial of Jesus by a counsellor Joseph of Arimathea, he made the above-mentioned improvements to Joseph's character. In that case, there is something to be said for the assumption that Joseph's membership of the supreme council was an element of tradition, but that his character-

ization as 'eminent' is redactional. The information that 'he took courage and went to Pilate' is passed over by the parallels. Does it not make Joseph, who risks a good deal, more sympathetic to the readers? Certainly it also contributes towards toning down his membership of a supreme council which was hostile to Jesus.

[44–45] These verses are certainly redactional and bracket the scene with the context. They are official authentication of the death of Jesus and have the subsidiary apologetic aim of stressing its reality.[176]

[46] The statement that Jesus was buried by Joseph comes from the tradition. The information about the rock tomb with a stone rolled in front of it is redactional preparation for Mark 16.3. As this specific detail of the tomb of Jesus is *presupposed* in 16.1–8 (otherwise the story would make no sense), whereas in the existing pericope at any rate it is an expansion, it possibly comes from the former passage.[177] It is striking that Joseph *buys* linen. That implies that it is new. If we said that the burial of Jesus by Joseph goes back to tradition, the *new* linen may derive from the redaction, which shows an interest in protecting the burial of Jesus from any disrespectful element.[178] Here the shrouding in (used) linen may come from the tradition. It is customary in all forms of burial in Judaism (cf. the Jewish horror of nakedness with Acts 5.6). On the other hand, there are indications of some differences from the circumstances of a normal burial. Thus we must note that Jesus was certainly not buried in his family tomb in Nazareth, which would have been an essential feature of an honourable burial. Furthermore Mark had reported the burial of Jesus *before* his death in ch.14 and understood it as an anointing for death. But there is no anointing of the *body* of Jesus, which is known as part of the burial ritual from MSabbath 23.5.[179] Is there not a suspicion here that Mark wanted to reinterpret the tradition of a dishonourable burial?

[47] Cf. 111f. below.

*Conclusion*: The investigation of the redaction and tradition of Mark 15.24–27 to some degree confirms Bultmann's judgment above, but it needs to be made more specific, as follows. The tradition reports a burial of Jesus by a member of the supreme council, Joseph of Arimathea. However, we cannot discover any more historical information about the nature of the burial. Still, there are reasons to suspect that Mark was confronted with the tradition of a burial which was in some way dishonourable and reinterpreted it. We shall have to see whether there is also any sign of similar knowledge of this tradition of a dishonourable burial of Jesus in the parallels and the other sources for the burial of Jesus.

### The revision of Mark 15.42–27 by the parallels

The parallels Matthew and Luke and also John have Christianized the figure of Joseph or drawn it in an even more positive way than Mark before them. Matthew differed from his Markan model by making Joseph of Arimathea a rich man and a disciple of Jesus (Matt.27.57); Luke describes him – redactionally – as a good and just man (Luke 23.50), who did not take part in the hearing (by the supreme council) against Jesus (Luke 23.51), and according to Gospel of Peter 6.23 Joseph 'saw all the good that he (sc. Jesus) had done'.

In John, too, Joseph of Arimathea is described as a disciple of Jesus (John 19.38), but he keeps this discipleship hidden for fear of the Jews (cf.John 12.42; 9.22). The story contains the further detail that Nicodemus, 'who had at first (viz. John 3.2) come to Jesus by night' (John 19.39a), came to help Joseph prepare the body of Jesus for burial (19.39f.).[180]

The *tendency* in the early Christian narrative tradition of the burial of Jesus by Joseph of Arimathea may have been made sufficiently clear. The counsellor has become a disciple of Jesus – one could almost say that the enemy has become a friend – and finally yet a further friend of Jesus, Nicodemus, takes part in the burial.[181]

But the burial, too, is painted in increasingly positive colours. Whereas Mark merely says that it was in a rock tomb, the parallels not only presume this but also know that it was Joseph's own tomb (Matt.27.60; Gospel of Peter 6.24[182]), and John 20.15 and Gospel of Peter 6.24 even locate it in the garden, which is a distinction (cf. II Kings 21.18,26). Finally, Matt.27.60; Luke 23.53 and John 19.41 describe the tomb as new: this is a mark of honour for Jesus and also excludes the possibility that Jesus was put, for example, in a criminals' grave.[183]

At this point it may already be said that only the Markan account or the tradition worked on in it is a source for the question to be raised below about any historical value in the tradition.[184] At the same time it should be noted that if the post-Markan tendency is to Christianize Joseph, the thesis I presented above, that probably already the Markan report takes this line in its portrayal of Joseph as someone who expects the kingdom of God, is reinforced. So we have to ask: if the story of the burial increasingly becomes a mark of honour for Jesus, did not it perhaps displace a dishonourable burial? In other words, is there not already in the Markan version a developed tradition which seeks to work over the terrible fact of Jesus' death to indicate that Jesus was at least given an orderly burial by a prominent counsellor?

On (b) = John 19.31–37
The text John 19.31(–37)[185] mentioned above is a further source for the burial of Jesus. The Jews ask Pilate for the legs of Jesus (and the other two crucified with him) to be broken and for them to be taken down from the cross. This is done to the two who were crucified with Jesus but not to Jesus, as he is already dead. To get to the heart of the tradition it is first of all necessary to peel off the shell. The text is shaped by a redaction which translates Ps.34.21 (Ex.12.46) and Zech.12.10 (cf. the explicit phrase: '. . .that the scripture should be fulfilled . . .' [v.36]) into action. But that does not prove that the whole narrative is a redactional formation, as Theodor Keim already sought to demonstrate.[186] What remains as the core of the tradition is the request of the Jews to Pilate for Jesus' body to be taken down from the cross (v.31); what tells here against a purely redactional construction and for the existence of a tradition is that their wish is not acceded to in this narrative. Verse 38 begins all over again with Joseph's request, and he himself (not the Romans) takes the body from the cross (*arhe* refers back to *arhthosin* [v.31]). The part of the narrative which originally concluded vv.31ff., about the 'burial' of Jesus, has evidently been broken off and replaced later by the (other) account of a burial of Jesus by Joseph and Nicodemus (John 19.38–42).[187]

The reconstructed nucleus of tradition behind John 19.31–37 has a parallel in Acts 13.29 (Jews 'took him [Jesus] down from the tree and laid him in the tomb'). Certainly it is often asserted that this verse is exclusively governed by Lukan language and theology.[188] But that is questionable. In the mission speeches in Acts Luke indeed lays the blame for the death of Jesus on the Jews (Acts 2.23; 3.13–15; 4.27; 5.30; 7.52; 10.39; 13.28). However, at this point Jews see to taking the body away and to the burial, and that cannot be linked with the motif of attaching blame. So this is an independent tradition which corresponds to the one behind John 19.31–37.[189]

Be this as it may, in all probability we are to conclude that the tradition of a burial of Jesus occurs in two different narratives:

(a) Joseph of Arimathea asks Pilate for the corpse of Jesus and buries it; (b) Jews ask Pilate for the corpse of Jesus and bury it. Tradition (b) is clearly earlier,[190] because (a) with the tendencies demonstrated above is probably already a Christian interpretation.[191]

## Historical

That brings us to the historical question: how was Jesus of Nazareth really buried?

Roman legal practice normally provided for someone who died on the cross to rot there or to be consumed by vultures, jackals or other animals – as a warning to the living.[192] This possibility is excluded for Jesus, as the traditions relating to him agree in reporting that his body was taken down from the cross (I Cor.15.4 also presupposes this). So the 'burial of Jesus' may be one of those cases in which the Roman authorities released the body.[193] Presumably Jews took Jesus from the cross because a crucified dead person might not hang on the cross overnight (Deut.21.23), and because it was about to be a festival (Passover). Moreover the release of Jesus' body and its removal from the cross might also have suited Pilate, because this would *a priori* avoid unrest among the large number of visitors for the festival.

We can only conjecture the precise place of the burial of Jesus. The assumption that Jesus was buried in a cemetery for those who had been executed,[194] the location of which moreover it is impossible to discover by archaeology,[195] is almost impossible, as Jesus was not executed by the Jewish authorities. The hypothesis of a burial of Jesus in the family tomb of Joseph of Arimathea comes to grief on the tendency of the early Christian accounts, which betray a knowledge of a dishonourable burial of Jesus or fear one. The anointed bones of a crucified Jew named Jejochanan from the first century CE, buried (reburied!) in an ossuary in a rock tomb in the north-east of present-day Jerusalem (Giv'at ha-Mivtar),[196] are often cited as an analogy to the burial of Jesus reported in Mark 15.42–47.[197] However, that is not much help, since in that case we have an ossuary,[198] while the case of Jesus involved the burial of a corpse (with flesh on). As neither the disciples nor Jesus' next of kin bothered[199] about Jesus' body,[200] it is hardly conceivable that they could have been informed about the resting place of the corpse, so as later to be able to bury at least the bones.[201] Thus we must doubt whether the instruction about mourning customs in the brief Talmud tractate Semachot II 12[202] illuminates 'both the burial of Jesus and the return of the disciples and relatives of Jesus to Jerusalem (Acts 1.14)',[203] and the sources say nothing at all about a reburial.

The two strands of tradition reconstructed above perhaps agree in knowing Joseph of Arimathea. In that case he would have been the one who was charged with seeing to the burial of Jesus. It is improbable that he was a disciple or a friend of Jesus. The opposite conclusion, that he was one of Jesus' enemies, is equally improbable, since – historically speaking – there are serious doubts about a condemnation of Jesus by the supreme council.[204] We can no longer say where Joseph (or Jews unknown to us) put the body. '*Nobody knew what had happened to Jesus' body.*'[205] Evidently not even the earliest community knew. For given the significance of the tombs of saints at the time of Jesus[206] it can be presupposed that had Jesus' tomb been known, the early Christians would have venerated it and traditions about it would have been preserved.[207] However, we do see what Christian legend in Mark has made of this ignominious end of its Lord.[208] (The summary note about the burial contained in the kerygma in I Cor.15.4 leaves the details of the 'burial' open, just as the note of Jesus' death there [I Cor.15.3] does not specify the nature of his death.)

### Paul and the empty tomb

Does Paul also know the tradition of the empty tomb? It is often concluded from the fact that Paul makes no mention of the empty tomb that this was unknown to the apostle, all the more so since he could well have used it for his argument in I Cor.15, had the Corinthians taken offence at the Jewish notion of resurrection, including corporeality (see above, 34). Against this it is often objected that Paul or the tradition presupposes the empty tomb. The reason: if Jesus had risen and had been buried beforehand, the tomb *must* have been empty. Thus, to take one example from many, Paul Althaus writes:

'The notion that the tomb was empty has been a necessary part of Easter faith from the beginning. So people must also immediately have been certain of the empty tomb . . .'[209]

However, this reflection, which is at first sight illuminating, comes up against the observation that Paul explicitly rejects the 'resurrection' of flesh and blood (cf. I Cor.15.50: 'Flesh and blood will not inherit the kingdom of God'). Similarly, one might add, the image of the grain of wheat that must die (I Cor.15.36f.) is also orientated on – to put it in concrete terms – the corruption of the old body.[210] For that reason alone it is questionable whether the apostle was interested in the empty tomb. In this connection one might consider the remarks of Willi Marxsen:

'What is laid in the tomb is according to Paul precisely not the body (or "I") which is going to be; it is the passing, perishable and corruptible body (cf.v.42). Hence the spiritual body (the risen "I") is not something like an ethereal body . . . With the term "spiritual body" the identity of the earthly "I" is maintained; but the spiritual body eludes *any* imagination. Paul can only express what he means through images and analogies.'[211]

But the thought here is perhaps too modern. Johannes Weiss conjectured with good reason that Paul would have imagined the resurrection of Christ as being like that of Christians: 'The dead will be raised incorruptible' (I Cor.15.52), i.e. 'Christ will have left the tomb with an already transfigured body.'[212]

Now occasionally in mischievous apologetic it is pointed out that, if asked, Paul would have imagined the tomb of Jesus to be empty. But that evades the problem. For initially the main question is whether Paul knows any witnesses to the fact that the tomb was really found empty by others. This can be ruled out, especially since – as I pointed out above – the statement about the burial of Jesus (I Cor.15.4) is connected with the death and not the resurrection.

*Conclusion*: We have a dilemma here. For on the one hand Paul knows no witnesses to the empty tomb,[213] but on the other hand he imagines the resurrection of Jesus in bodily form, which seems to require the emergence of the body of Jesus from the empty tomb. That is probably also the case even if Jesus left the tomb with a transfigured body, since despite I Cor.15.50 the fate of the physical body of Jesus cannot have been unimportant to Paul,[214] unless fleshly and transfigured corporeality stand side by side in his work and there is hardly any precise reflection on the relationship between the two. For example, in I Thess.4.13–17 both (in relation to Christians) are parallel as they are in Syrian Baruch 49–51. Something similar may be inferred for the Pauline view of the exalted Jesus.[215] So one consequence would have been to connect the notion of the empty tomb with that of the bodily resurrection (in transformed and/or physical form). However, it must be emphasized that Paul did not explicitly draw this conclusion.

### 4.1.3.3  I Cor.15.4b (Jesus' resurrection on the third day)

The question of the third day as the point of time of the resurrection of Jesus[216] cannot really be decided finally until all the texts have been analysed. So the following reflections are only provisional. As I demonstrated on 31f. above, the Galilee tradition, if it is original, could be an important objection to this indication of time. For if the first appearance took place in Galilee, it cannot have been on the third day in Jerusalem. The assumption that the appearances took place simultaneously in Galilee and Jerusalem, including the first appearance to Mary Magdalene in Jerusalem on the third day, would be one possible way of avoiding this conclusion. Another understanding results from the following observation. If we read I Cor.15.4 precisely, what took place on the third day was not the appearance to Cephas but the resurrection of Jesus, whereas the christophany remains undated (in contrast to Luke 24.21). In my view this prompts the reflection that the origin of the date on the third day is not to be sought in historical recollections (e.g. Mark 14.58?) but in scribal reflection.

The main point of reference of the phrase 'according to the scriptures' (I Cor.15.4) is Hos.6.2. In the LXX translation the passage reads as follows: 'will make us whole after two days, on the third day we will rise and live before him'. This passage from Hosea was evidently used in Judaism to infer the date of the eschatological resurrection of the dead.[217] In that case the resurrection of Jesus would have been understood as the fulfilment of an Old Testament prophecy. The fact that Hos.6.2 is never cited in the New Testament[218] and that it appears only relatively late in rabbinic exegesis[219] seems to tell against a derivation of the third day from it. However, the point in time of the testimony need not coincide with the origin of the relevant exegesis. Rather, conversely, I Cor.15.4 is a possible instance of a Jewish eschatological interpretation of Hos.6.2.[220]

### 4.1.3.4  I Cor.15.5 (The appearance [*ophthe*] of Jesus)

Before considering the event expressed by *ophthe* it is worth first of all making a linguistic investigation of the verb. The importance of this step is clear from the fact that *ophthe* is used with reference to all the persons mentioned in I Cor.15.3f.

Grammatically, *ophthe* (= third person aorist passive of *horao* = see) in the phrase *ophthe Kepha* can be translated in three ways:[221]

1. Passive: he was seen by Cephas.
2. Deponential; he allowed himself to be seen by Cephas, he showed himself to him.
3. Theological passive: he was made visible to Cephas by God: God showed him to Cephas.

Possibility 1 can be ruled out, since according to Greek linguistic usage in that case we would expect a 'by' (*hypo* = genitive).[222]

In favour of possibility 3, scholars are fond of pointing out that 'he was raised' (v.4) is a theological passive and that this suggests the same thing for *ophthe*. It is also pointed out that the theological passive contains elements of both possibilities 1 and 2: in being made visible to Cephas by God, Christ was seen by Cephas (possibility 1) and showed himself to Cephas (possibility 2).

But this proposal is improbable. The predicate *ophthe* = dative requires an active subject, which here is most probably the Christ who shows himself (deponential understanding).[223]

The expression *ophthe* = dative has a prehistory in the Old Testament.

The niphal formation of *r'h*, which corresponds to the New Testament formulation, is used about 45 times in the Old Testament. It reports an appearance of Yahweh or his angel to Abraham (Gen.12.7; 17.1; 18.1), Isaac (Gen.26.2,24), Jacob (Gen.31.13; Gen.35.19), Moses (Ex.3.2). The LXX usually renders the phrase with *ophthe* + dative or + proposition (*pros/en*).[224]

In view of the evidence that in the LXX *ophthe* + dative is the preferred use for an appearance, scholars have spoken formally of a 'theophany formula' which appears in the creed I Cor.15 and drawn far-reaching conclusions from it. In that case it would be almost impossible, given its usage as a formula, to arrive at the event lying behind it (cf. already above, 30). No wonder then that some exegetes could speak of a legitimation formula without any real background relating to experience.

However, it should be pointed out that in the LXX *ophthe* can also have other subjects than God: II Kings 14.11 (Joash and Amaziah), I

Macc.4.6 (Judas), I Macc.4.19 (Judas's enemies), I Macc.9.27 (a prophet), II Macc.3.25 (a horse). Here one may speak of a well-worn or unspecific use of *ophthe*.[225]

Now it should be noted that Paul draws together very different phenomena (individual encounters, mass manifestations) under the one bracket of the *ophthe*. There are also further differences between the appearances: for Cephas the experience denoted by the *ophthe* is not combined with a previous process of communication or even with the consolidation of a community (as with the other members of the chain of witnesses), but is first of all an immediate event, a primary experience. The latter also applies to Paul (see below). But a difference between Peter and Paul lies in the fact that Peter saw Jesus *again*, whereas Paul had not previously seen Jesus. In other words, the christophany of Peter (and the Twelve) is '*also at least* based on their converse with Jesus, but that of the later ones is based on the proclamation of Jesus as the risen Christ by the earlier ones'.[226] And the christophany to Paul must be further distinguished from those to the 'later figures', because it affects the persecutor of the community. (To this degree it is a primary experience.)

Since on the other hand Paul uses 'he appeared' with reference to himself (v.8) and thus puts his encounter with Jesus in parallel with the appearances of Jesus to the other witnesses, and moreover in other places uses different verbs to express the same thing, one may legitimately attempt to clarify the phenomenon mentioned in I Cor.15 by these passages. So for methodological reasons we shall first of all discuss the appearance of Jesus to Paul and only after that the tradition of the appearance of Jesus to Peter.

### 4.1.3.5 I Cor.15.8 (The vision of Christ or Paul's Easter)

#### 4.1.3.5.1 *The primary Pauline texts: I Cor.9.1; Gal.1.15f.; Phil.3.8; II Cor.4.6*

This next section is a critical discussion of the modernizing understanding of Willi Marxsen,[227] even if his views are not set out in detail. First of all, here are some of his programmatic statements:

> 'It is wrong to call . . . the Damascus road experience "Paul's Easter" – unless one understands by Easter the experience of finding faith in Jesus . . .' (107).

'We cannot discover what really happened on the Damascus road . . .
Whatever it was that Paul experienced, he says here: *God* did something
to me' (106).
' . . . a subjective vision hypothesis breaks down because it cannot be
brought into accord with the texts. They (the texts) are absolutely
unequivocal. They at least intend to speak of an objective vision – if one
presents them with the alternative' (116).


By way of criticism: at this point it is certainly not a matter of what
the texts 'want' to say to the Corinthians; it is rather a matter of what
*really* happened before them. Here it must be permissible to examine
what the texts about Easter say and to investigate behind them. For
as in any work with sources, it is to be expected that the
reconstruction of the historical situation to which the statements
point or on which they are based can contribute something to an
appropriate understanding of these statements.

In what follows I shall go in sequence through the passages in the
letters of Paul in which the apostle speaks about the 'Damascus
event'. (Here it is presupposed that some characteristics of the
Damascus event can be got out of these retrospects of Paul, after
more than twenty years and despite some problems in the communities related to his day.)[228]


## I Corinthians 9.1

Here Paul says that he has seen Jesus (cf. John 20.18, 25). He uses the
first person perfect of the verb *horao*, i.e. a form of the active
(*heoraka*). Thus he is expressing the same substantive content as in I
Cor.15.8 as his own active sensual perception, without resorting to
possible appearance or legitimation formulae. So Paul is claiming a
visual side to the appearance mentioned in I Cor.15.8. The thesis that
Paul is using *ophthe* + dative in the sense of a literary legitimation
formula is untenable in this exclusive form given what the apostle
himself says, and is to be supplemented with the visual aspect which
Paul takes for granted. I Corinthians 9.1 is then the active perception
of Jesus for which the appearance stated in I Cor.15.8 is the
presupposition. In my view it is certain that here the apostle is
thinking of a vision of Jesus in his transformed spiritual resurrection
corporeality. Otherwise it would be hard to understand why Paul
can refer to *ophthe* (I Cor.15.4ff.) for the certainty of the bodily
resurrection. The statements about the future resurrection body of

Christians (I Cor.15.35–49) might also be claimed for the resurrection body of Christ, all the more so as Paul accepts the principle: as
Christ, so Christians (cf. I Cor.15.49; Phil.3.21).[229]

Now it is occasionally even disputed that Paul is giving any
appropriate description of the Damascus event at all in I Cor.9. In the
view of Hans-Willi Winden[230] the 'polished rhetoric of this verse . . .
bears witness to the *self-legitimation of the apostle* as the sole aim of
his argument' (104). 'I have seen the Lord' (I Cor.9.1) does not in his
view reflect 'any revelation event . . . and might have been formulated by Paul first of all on the basis of his knowledge of his
traditional *ophthe* statements from I Cor.15.5–7' (ibid.). To this it
should be pointed out that the remarks on *ophthe* above have
confirmed the *visual* aspect of the event connected with it. So in I
Cor.9.1 Paul is quite appropriately expressing the subjective aspect
of the event.

## *Gal.1.15f.*

At another point the apostle describes the same event by saying that
God revealed his Son in/to him (Gal.1.15f.). As the verse stands in the
framework of an account of his pre-Christian and early Christian
period, he might be referring to a *particular* event.[231] Here v.12
combined with v.16 makes it clear that the content of the event was a
revelation the subject (objective genitive) or author (subjective
genitive) of which was Christ. *en emoi* can be translated either 'to
me' or 'in me'; perhaps these two possibilities are not opposites. At
all events the theme of revelation fits the seeing in I Cor.9.1 and its
presupposition, the appearance in I Cor.15.8.

However, Hans Kessler takes another view. He thinks that
Gal.1.12,15f. 'does not *necessarily* include the visionary element, the
seeing. The crucified Jesus is revealed to Paul as the risen and exalted
Christ, and in this revelation Paul receives the gospel (which in any
case has to be explained and to be preached in words).'[232]

Is there any thought at all without imagery, whether that of a
written word, a colour, a written number – above all in religion?
Why does Paul resort to concepts from the sphere of visions if
'seeing' did not adequately render his experience of revelation? That
it may have been provided for him by his religious horizon is not a
refutation but reinforces the hypothesis that revelation at that time
was experienced in precisely this way – also as seeing.

In connection with Gal.1.15f., where Paul uses the verb 'reveal' instead of the formula 'he appeared + dative', Paul Hoffmann asks whether talk of a revelation – in contrast to I Cor.15 – must not be regarded as the genuinely Pauline rendering of his Easter experience. He then concludes:

> 'The fact that Paul refers so emphatically to the revelation of the Son of God that has been given him in the face of opponents who are playing off the Jerusalem apostles against him shows that precisely this was the decisive criterion (cf. Gal.1.12) . . . So the genuine designation of the Easter experience of the first witnesses may still have been preserved in the term . . . In the light of Gal.1.15f. and its prehistory, the use of LXX terminology in I Cor.15.5 is to be understood as making an originally apocalyptic statement more precise.'[233]

Willi Marxsen arrives at a similar conclusion:

> 'One may therefore at least suspect that Paul earlier described his experience in provisional and general terms as a revelation. The further defining of this revelation as seeing only came about through assimilation to what was (probably) common linguistic usage. The possibility of an assimilation of this kind cannot be excluded, for we know that Paul certainly practised it in I Cor.15.8.'[234]

*Criticism*: 1. Both authors presuppose that Galatians was written before I Corinthians. But the reverse order is just as good a historical possibility.[235] 2. The sharp division between revelation and seeing that underlies the approaches of Hoffmann and Marxsen is unnecessary. From the realm of early Christian writing one might refer to Rev.1.1–2,[26] where revelation and seeing stand side by side: 'The *revelation* of Jesus Christ, which God gave him to show to his servants what must soon take place; and he made it known by sending his angel to his servant John, who bore witness to the *word* of God and to the testimony of Jesus Christ, even to all that he *saw*.'

Certainly the character of revelation is emphasized in Gal.1. But it remains incomprehensible how it can be used to dispute visionary elements in the 'Damascus event'.[237] The terms 'revelation' and 'appearance' or 'see' are not mutually exclusive. 'Revelation' denotes an experience in terms of its *religious* character as being immediate to God; 'appearance' describes its *spatial* quality. By the change in terminology Paul is emphasizing different aspects of the same thing.

## Philippians 3.8

In Phil.3.8 Paul returns to the 'Damascus event'; here he is speaking of the knowledge (*gnosis*) of Christ which has led him to see his life hitherto as 'refuse'. The section (vv.2–11) is strongly stamped with polemic. Here Paul is led by Judaistic opponents,[238] as already in Gal.1.13f., to stress his blameless life in Judaism (vv.4–6), and distinguishes from it the righteousness from faith that was revealed to him by the knowledge of Christ (v.9). In this section we again have a theological interpretation of the Damascus event and only a sparse description of what *really* happened in it. So those various scholars who think that there is no visionary element in Phil.3 are missing the historical point.[239] The question to be put in the historical framework is whether the visionary element of the experience of revelation attested in other passages is *excluded here*. There can be no question of that: I Cor.9.1, Paul's statement that he has seen Jesus, provides the key for our historical understanding of the polemical statements of Phil.3.4ff.

## II Corinthians 4.6

Finally, II Cor.4.6 is a possible reflection of the Damascus event. Here Paul writes: 'For it is the God who said, "Let light shine out of darkness", who has shone in our hearts to give the light of the knowledge of the glory of God in the face of Christ.' If the passage refers to the conversion,[240] that would make it probable that at this conversion Paul saw Christ in the form of light, and this would fit his remarks about the heavenly man (I Cor.15.49).[241] But not only this: Paul would be putting his vision of Christ in parallel with the dawning of light on the morning of creation to express what had happened to him before Damascus.[242]

*Conclusion*: Specifically, 'Jesus **appeared to** Paul' means that Paul saw the risen Jesus in his glory, which need not tell against an inner vision of the outward vision. This vision was felt to be an extraordinarily event and a revelation. In other words, in it the visionary received insights into an other-worldly sphere which had an esoteric character and therefore represented secret knowledge. The whole event had the character of light and happened, like the vision of John (Rev.1.10), in the spirit, i.e. in rapture/ecstasy.[243] In it, seeing and hearing were probably not mutually exclusive. – Thus far our provisional description of the Damascus event, which the characteristics of a vision fit.[244]

In connection with the other traditions in I Cor.15.3ff., this means that the persons mentioned there also saw the risen Jesus. David Friedrich Strauss, Christian Hermann Weisse and Carl Holsten among earlier scholars and Hans Grass and Ingo Broer among more recent scholars have seen this correctly and explained *ophthe* within the framework of a vision hypothesis.

### Excursus: A retrospective survey of the vision hypothesis in the nineteenth century

In the present controversy over the vision hypothesis in the context of the 'Easter events' it is too easily overlooked that important arguments for and against it were already exchanged in the nineteenth century. Moreover, a reading of the most recent work on Easter by Hans Kessler[245] gives one an impression which cannot be contradicted emphatically enough. This is what the author says about the vision hypothesis.

'The view which can be found since D. F. Strauss, and which is becoming popular in more recent times, that these are visions that can be explained in purely psychological terms, in other words as mere products of the imagination or sub-conscious of the disciples, must also be excluded. This view claims that the emotional and reflective way in which the disciples came to terms with the crucifixion of Jesus (he and his cause cannot be dead!) produced deep in them the picture of a Jesus who was again with them or who gave them the certainty that he was alive; this certainty caused them to have psychogenic visions in which moreover they saw (as hallucinations) what they longed for and dreamed of. This view has no basis . . . in the New Testament sources. There is no trace either in the early statements about the appearances or in the stories of the appearances in the Gospels of a visionary seeing, of elements of an enthusiastic kind along the lines of a purely psychological concept of vision. There are no indications whatsoever that early Christianity derived Easter faith from inner psychological events. And in any case a purely psychological explanation fails to do justice to the seriousness, the religious claim of the texts' (221).

*Criticism*: This statement is misguided. First of all we have to ask whether a psychological approach helps us to understand the religious earnestness, which cannot well be disputed. Moreover it is quite unimportant for a scholarly account of the 'Easter events' whether early Christianity derived the Easter faith from inner events within the soul. (In any case, that would not be to be expected, since visionaries *always* see things differently.) Rather, it is a matter of communicating an approach to the 'Easter event' which is comprehensible to us today.

Kessler continues: 'The Easter "vision" is evidently quite incomparable; the texts bear witness that the appearances were something exceptional' (227). He continues:

> 'Beyond the limits drawn by the historical state of the text we need to draw attention to a systematic problem: it is fundamentally questionable whether a process of revelation, be it a prophetic process or the Easter process, can be illuminated by an idea which attempts to trace its course. In fact if one seeks to get right "behind" it to explain it, one reduces it to certain factors which can be defined in advance and thus fails to do justice to the substance of its fundamental and central claim, namely its character as the revelation of something underivably new, which cannot be developed from experiences accessible to us. For all our desire to know, this compels us to fundamental modesty' (234).

Does that not end up in an abandonment of the idea of understanding? Where and by what criteria are the limits to historical work to be drawn? For Kessler, consistent historical research and faith seem mutually exclusive: the one destroys the other or makes it impossible. *Because* faith makes a claim which historical reason cannot *confirm*, is historical research *therefore* to be compelled to an attitude of 'fundamental modesty'? To ask such a question demonstrates the totally apologetic character of Kessler's book.[246]

In this respect, I think more fruitful than a further detailed reference to Kessler's view, which in my view ultimately ends up in a sublime fundamentalism or biblicism,[247] a recollection of the debate about the circumstances of the vision at Paul's call which was prompted by Ferdinand Christian Baur in the postscript to his 1845 book on Paul and developed by his remarks on the conversion of Paul in his book *Christianity and the Christian Church in the First Three Centuries*, the second edition of which appeared in 1860, shortly before his death. Here Baur writes on Paul:

> So if we can only see his conversion, the sudden transformation of him from the most vigorous opponent of Christianity to its most decisive herald, as a miracle, it seems to us all the greater, since in this change of

consciousness he also broke through the limits of Judaism and sublated
Jewish particularism in the universal idea of Christianity. And yet this
miracle, great as it is, can only be understood as an intellectual process,
and precisely for that reason cannot be thought of without an element
which mediates the one to the other. Now if no analysis, whether
psychological or dialectical, can investigate the inner mystery of the act in
which God revealed his Son in him, surely we can still rightly ask whether
what mediated that transition into something else cannot be posited in the
powerful impression which the great fact of the death made all at once
upon his soul?'[249]

M. A. Landerer, a colleague in Baur's own faculty, said in a
memorial address on him: as in his last book Baur called the
conversion of Paul an inexplicable miracle, his previous view of
earliest Christianity and its history, which had been critical of
miracle, had to be corrected.[250]

Carl Holsten,[251] a member of Baur's Tübingen school, reacted to
this statement as follows:

'Hardly had death closed Baur's mouth, so that he could give no
explanation, than conservative theology leapt on that remark and sated
. . . its hunger for miracle with the certainty that the old master of
historical criticism, at the end of his life's work, which had been devoted
to removing miracle from the gospel history, at this point recognizes the
reality of miracle in the gospel story and that if at one point, then in
principle at all points, he has again restored miracle to its rights. But
critical theology was puzzled. For not subjectively for himself, but
objectively in itself Baur seemed to have recognized an enigma in the
conversion of Paul that could only be resolved by the assumption of a
miracle. That in principle put in question the basic presupposition of
historical-critical theology, the certainty of the thinking spirit and the
conviction of the religious disposition of the present, that, just as only one
God moves the one world, so only one law of the one God rules nature
and spirit everywhere, including the religious development of
humankind.'[252]

So Holsten, in the wake of Baur, saw the basic presupposition of
historical-critical theology and the consciousness of the modern
spirit put in question. He felt compelled to demonstrate scientifically
that just as the present develops in a regular way through immanent
divine forces without miracle, so also the past (= the new element in
the person of Jesus and the apostolic preaching of a Peter and a Paul)

must have shaped itself without miracle through immanent divine forces.

Let us listen to Holsten again: according to what Paul himself says (I Cor.15.8), the conversion of Paul goes back to a vision of Jesus:

'For Paul's consciousness, this vision was a matter of seeing an objectively real heavenly figure which had appeared to him from its transcendent invisibility ... For Paul, this vision was the embodiment of an alien transcendent power in his spiritual life. But under the domination of the law of the immanent development of the human spirit through this-worldly causalities, historical criticism *must* seek to understand the vision as an immanent, psychological act of its own spirit' (65).

How does Holsten proceed in his work? First of all he states that the vision of Jesus (= conversion of Paul) corresponds to those visions and revelations which the apostle reports in II Cor.12.1ff.

'So that first vision was only the beginning of a series of similar events of a visionary spiritual life in which Paul not only saw the forms of heavenly figures and but also heard their words – facts of a kind which occur everywhere in other historically attested visions in the same way' (69).

Here Paul saw Jesus in the form of the heavenly man which according to I Cor.15.50,54 is incorruptible. And God 'determined this heavenly human being to be Messiah and the one who performed the work of the Messiah' (75).

Holsten then concerned himself – in keeping with his starting point – with the condition and possibility of visions. He writes that there could only be a vision

'where the elements of the vision were already present in the spirit of the visionary. The visionary imagination is a reproductive activity; what is seen is only what has already lived as a notion or an image of the free imagination in the consciousness of the visionary. What the vision adds to these elements which are already present in the spirit is only the sensory side of the objectivity, though the formation of the image in the visionary is only achieved in the way in which the ideal image living in the artist is achieved through objectification ... the first condition is that there is a world of the transcendent in the consciousness of the visionary and that this is filled with forms which can be seen by the imagination, but at the same time in such a way that the vision does not call forth the reflection, that this transcendent world of visible forms is recognized as real truth in the consciousness of the visionary' (81f.).

In other words:

> 'Criticism must be able to demonstrate that the vision of the Messiah in
> the form in which Paul saw it did not contradict his general world-view,
> that in its substantial content it had already previously been in his
> consciousness and conscious imagination, that it corresponded to the
> particular situation in which we must think Paul to have been at the time
> of the vision, and as a result that it was a significant image for him' (84).

Holsten believes that he can demonstrate all these conditions on the
basis of Paul's individuality, which Baur had already discussed in an
appendix to his 1845 book on Paul. According to Holsten, Paul was an
epileptic and had an extremely excitable and restless character (877): '. . .
these traits give us the picture of a sanguine, choleric temperament on the
basis of which everything of any significance that entered the periphery of
his life immediately kindled itself at the centre of his feelings as individual
and personal excitement' (87f.).

In addition to the *natural* determination of the individual there is
the *spiritual* determination, which Holsten describes as follows: Paul
had an

> 'unusually thoughtful, logical nature. For in every activity of his spirit,
> thought is at work to trace back any appearance to its inner nature, to
> grasp its principle, to take it up into the uncontradictory unity and
> context of his whole thought-world . . . a special manifestation of this
> power of thought in Paul was the rational element of his spirit.
> Everywhere we come upon a need of his thinking spirit to reflect from the
> actual to the spiritual basis of what is there, to recognize in the particular
> the efficacy of universal categories, to understand in the fortuitousness of
> the individual with its rational basis also its necessity . . . A second
> particular phenomenon of the logical nature of Paul's spirit was the
> inexorable consistency of his thought . . . And with this penetrative
> sharpness was combined, finally, the victorious dialectic of Paul's
> thought' (88f.).

What specific picture, then, are we to have of Paul's conversion?
With the persecution of the community his theoretical interest had
moved towards its faith in the crucified one. Here the notion of the
death of the Messiah on the cross had occurred to him as a religious
idea. According to Holsten, Paul's conversion is 'the development of
his Jewish consciousness into a Christian consciousness through the
victory over Judaism in him, the victory over that Jewish consciousness which was present in him in a more marked and more lively

form than in any other contemporary from Judaism and Jewish Christianity.'[253] For the Jewish ideal of the Messiah which can be characterized as a national ideal was replaced by a new view of the work of the Messiah which had stifled all nationalistic features.

Holsten ends his defence of Baur with the following sentences:

> 'That brings us to the end of our task of demonstrating the vision of Christ which the zealous Jewish Pharisee Paul had and with this vision the genesis of the gospel of the anti-Jewish apostle Paul as the immanent act of a human spirit. A satisfactory resolution of this task is neither for one man nor for one time. But this much seems certain, that historical criticism can now already assert with a clearer consciousness and clearer rights that in this point in the development of the human spirit, too, no rift will run through its world-view' (114).

Thus far Holsten's work on the conversion of Paul and the vision of Christ as the origin of his theology. It differs from that of Kessler in that its procedure is historical and does not presuppose what is *a priori* inexplicable. Rather, Holsten's starting point is that the conversion of Paul *must* in principle be accessible to historical criticism, even if at present not all the details are yet known. Only through the mediation of an understandable approach to the event of Paul's conversion is it possible to discuss its meaning and its significance.[254]

In conclusion, it should be stated emphatically that the introduction of the objective vision hypothesis[255] (as opposed to Baur's and Holsten's subjective vision hypothesis) is no further help here either. It stands 'entirely in the sphere of supranaturalism and its objectifying notion of God and is thus exposed to the severest objections'.[256] It is piquant to see that Pastor Weingart of Osnabrück, who was dismissed from office in 1899, put forward the objective vision hypothesis,[257] whereas the hypothesis of subjective visions was common property for the History of Religions school,[258] including its marginal figures and its ancestors (Adolf Harnack, Heinrich Julius Holtzmann, Carl Weizsäcker, Richard Adelbert Lipsius, Otto Pfleiderer).[259]

I shall now go on to analyse the accounts of the conversion of Paul in Acts, in order to test whether these can be connected to the primary evidence of the letters. If the result proved positive, we would have a broader basis for defining the Damascus vision more closely.

## 4.1.3.5.2 *The conversion of Paul in the Acts of the Apostles*
(*Acts 9; 22; 26*)

*Redaction*

It is best to introduce the redactional analysis by a synoptic comparison with the parallel accounts Acts 22 and 26. As all three accounts relate to the Damascus event and are genetically inter-connected, it is a reasonable assumption (which will be further vindicated below) that a close comparison may further the re-daction-critical question and also prepare for a reconstruction of the tradition. Acts 9 may serve as a guiding thread.

### A synoptic comparison of the three accounts of the conversion of Paul[260]

Acts reports the conversion of Paul at three points: Acts 9 is a report in the third person singular, while Acts 22 and 26 are in the first person singular. In 22.3–16 Paul is delivering a speech in the temple to his own fellow countrymen, while in 26.4f.,9–18 he is speaking to Agrippa, Festus and Berenice. (In both speeches he is defending himself.) We begin with 8.3, because that section is the prehistory to the conversion and is taken up in all three accounts:

8.3 corresponds to 22.4 and 26.9–11. All three passages say that Saul has Christians put in prison. 26.10b (which is perhaps a concrete form of 22.4) intensifies this by saying that Paul was involved in death sentences ('If they were to be executed, I gave my consent'). 26.11b intensifies the matter yet further by extending Paul's acts of persecution to the cities outside Jerusalem.

9.1–2 corresponds to 22.5b and 26.11b–12. In both 9 and 22 there is mention of letters which Saul asks for from (9.2) or has been given by (22.5b) the high priest or the Sanhedrin. 26.12 asserts that Paul travelled to Damascus with the authority and permission of the high priest (cf. already v.10b). Whereas 9.1f. (with reference to 8.3) and 22.4 start from (8.3 or 22.6) massive activity by Saul as a persecutor (in Jerusalem, 8.1a), in 26.10–12 this activity is already thought to have been extended before the Damascus vision through Jerusalem (26.10; cf. 8.1a) to the cities outside (25.11; cf.8.1b). In accord with this universalizing of Saul's persecution, the detail of Saul's approach to the high priest with the request for letters to Damascus (9.1f), which gives the impression of being a special plan, is not reported. Instead of this, 26.12 mentions the already existing authority for persecution (which is possibly imagined as not being limited to Damascus). Therefore 26 presupposes 9 and 22 and intensifies the statements made there (see also the other intensifications in chs.22 and 26 [q.v.]).

9.3–9 has a parallel in 22.6–11 and 26.12–16a:

9.3 corresponds down to its vocabulary with 22.6. However, the verse contains no note of time, whereas 22.6 speaks of 'around midday' and 26.13 similarly of 'in the middle of the day'. In all three accounts the appearance to Saul is described as light (26.13 again intensifies this by saying that the light is brighter than the rays of the sun [hence the mention of midday]): on each occasion it comes from heaven. 9.3 and 22.6 make the appearance take place 'suddenly'; in 9.3 and 22.6 the light shines (only) around Saul; according to 26.13 it shines round Saul and his companions.

According to 9.4 and 22.7 Saul falls to the ground; in 26.1 Saul and those with him; in contrast to the parallels the light shines around Saul's companions as well. All three narratives again agree that Saul hears a voice which says to him, 'Saul, Saul, why are you persecuting me?' However, 26.14 has two significant additions: 1. the voice speaks in Hebrew; 2. the question to Saul as to why he is persecuting the speaker is supplemented by the comment: 'It is hard for you to kick against the pricks.' The two additions are redactional. The *first* addition (speaking in Hebrew) explains to the reader the Hebrew form of the name, Saul, which is to be found in all three versions. However, the fact that in the *second* addition the persecuted Jesus quotes a Greek proverb does not fit the Hebrew language. Here in fact the writer Luke is speaking: on the one hand he wants to demonstrate the complete dependence of Saul on Jesus and on the other to show off his own wide reading.

9.5 corresponds almost completely with the parallels 22.8; 26.15: when Saul asks who is speaking, he is told, 'I am Jesus (the Nazorean) whom you are persecuting'.

9.6 is closely parallel to 22.10: Saul is to rise, go to Damascus, and there he will be told what to do. 26.16a contains only the order to rise, and no command that Saul is to go to Damascus. It is only logical that ch.26 also has no information about Ananias. Rather, 26.16b immediately describes the real command to Saul to preach, which the parallel versions give only later (see below on 9.15 and 22.15). Therefore in what follows, only the first two versions of the Damascus event will be compared.

9.7: The statement that Paul's companions heard the voice but saw no one conflicts with 22.9, where the opposite is said: Saul's companions saw the light but did not hear the voice[261] which spoke to Paul. The question left open (!) in 9.7 as to whether his companions had seen a light is thus answered in the affirmative.

9.8 corresponds to 22.11: Saul cannot see anything, and his companions lead him by the hand to Damascus.

9.9 has no parallel in 22. The observation that Saul could not see anything and did not eat or drink anything for three days is perhaps a redactional addition. At all events 'three' is a symbolic number (for Luke). The fasting significantly precedes the healing and the gift of the Holy Spirit (cf. v.17).

9.10–17, the Ananias episode, has only a partial parallel in 22.12–13. Acts 9.10–17 depicts a vision of Christ by Ananias. In it he is told that Saul is in Damascus, living with Judas in the Straight Street and praying (v.11). In a vision Saul has seen Ananias coming (v.12). Verses 13f. contain an objection by Ananias which is grounded in Saul's previous actions against the Christians. The prehistory of Ananias's encounter with Saul which has just been described has no parallel in ch.22. In 22.12 Ananias is introduced as a 'pious man after the law, in good standing with all the Jews there'. Immediately after this the text depicts the healing of Saul by Ananias (v.13), which in ch.9 is only narrated later, in v.17. The introduction of Ananias in 22.12 without further explanation of the prehistory of his intervention is abrupt and can only happen because readers have already learned something about him in ch.9. At the same time that means that the report in ch.22 refers back to ch.9. (Chapter 26 continues the abbreviation of the account of the conversion of Saul begun in ch.22 and completely passes over the Ananias episode.)

9.15–16 has a parallel in 22.14–15 and 26.16b. But different accents are clear: 9.15 describes Saul as a 'chosen instrument' who will bear the name of the Lord before the peoples, kings and sons of Israel. Verse 16 gives the reason for this statement: 'I will show him how much he is to suffer for my name.' Without wanting to anticipate the subsequent redactional analysis, one can already say that here Saul is depicted (at least primarily) as a martyr. The situation in ch.22 and especially 26 is different from this: 22.14 has a different subject from 19.15: (Not Christ, but) God has chosen Saul in advance to know his will, to see the holy one and to hear a voice from his mouth. The verb 'choose beforehand' similarly appears in 26.16b (but here it is related to the same subject as 9.15, Christ). The second part of v.14 ('to know his will and to see the righteous one and to hear the voice from his mouth') has no direct parallel in 9.15 or 26.16. But there is a parallel with 26.16 in connection with seeing Jesus.

22.15 has a close parallel in 26.16b. Cf. the 'for you shall be a witness for him (sc. Christ) to all men of what you have seen and heard' (22.15) with 'I appeared to you for this purpose, to appoint you to serve and bear witness to what you have seen and what will be shown you' (26.16b). So according to both versions Saul is a witness. The special task of the witness seems to be developed following 26.16b, i.e. in vv.1–18, which has no parallel in ch.22. Cf. vv.17–18: 'And I will deliver you from the people and from the Gentiles to whom I send you to open their eyes, that they may turn from darkness to light and from the power of Satan to God, that they may receive forgiveness of sins and a place among those who are sanctified through faith in me.' This expresses the call of Saul to be the missionary to the Gentiles, a theme which was probably not contained in ch.9 and only indirectly in 22.1–16 (however, it appears in the immediate context, vv.17–21).

9.17–19 depicts the healing of Saul by Ananias, which in ch.22 was already reported in v.13.

*The result of the synoptic comparison*

All three accounts belong genetically together. At the redactional level the second account in 22.12 presupposes the first, just as the third version (26.9ff.) can be understood as an abbreviation of the two previous ones. In the third version the contrast between Paul's pre-Christian and Christian periods (cf. the elaboration of Paul's activities as a persecutor) is intensified and the conversion of Acts 9 is seen as a call to the Gentile mission.

As Acts 22 and 26 do not contain any additional elements from the tradition, in what follows we can limit ourselves to Acts 9 and first of all carry out a redactional analysis of Acts 9.1–19a.

[1–2] The two verses represent an exposition. The author connects the episodes previously reported (redactional episodes), of Saul's involvement in Stephen's martyrdom (7.58; 8.1a) and his subsequent activity as a successful persecutor (8.3), with a story about the conversion of the persecutor before Damascus. He makes this happen on the way from Jerusalem to Damascus and motivates the journey by a commission of the high priest to arrest Christians in Damascus and have them brought to Jerusalem. This skilfully makes a contrast between the zealous persecutor of Christians and the convert.

[3–9] The introduction (v.3a, 'as he journeyed . . .') derives from Luke, who introduces an episode in a similar way in Acts 10.9; Luke 18.35; 19.29. Verses 4b–6 may be termed an appearance conversation which has analogies within the three accounts of Saul's conversion, in 22.7–10/ 26.14–16 as well as in vv.4–6 (cf. 9.10f.), and also in the Old Testament: Gen.31.11–3; 46.2f.; Ex.3.2–10. The Old Testament form is tripartite: 1. Address or call; 2. Answer with question; 3. Introduction with charge. If it has been *imitated* by Luke, vv.4b–6 would have to be regarded as redactional. But the same form also occurs in JosAs 14 and TestJob 3, where we would not expect an imitation of LXX but the use of an independent narrative scheme.

However, the question whether vv.4b–6 in their present form are redactional or part of the tradition is not decided by the derivation of this scheme. The tripartite form of vv.4b–6 also occurs outside the present text in a redactional context (9.10f.; 10.3–5) and arouses the suspicion that it originates from Luke. This assumption is confirmed by two further factors: 1. vv.4b–6 can be dispensed with for the action. 2. Luke has a predilection for shaping scenes with dialogue. (For the question whether individual elements of vv.4b–6 are part of the tradition, see below.) Moreover in v.4 the duplication 'Saul, Saul' is striking; it has a parallel in the duplication of the address in Luke 8.24 (Mark differs); 10.41; 22.31.

Verses 10–19a:

[10a] The introduction of Ananias reflects Lukan language (cf. Luke 10.38; 16.20; Acts 5.1; 8.9; 10.1 etc.).

[10b] A vision as the communication of divine decisions is an important literary device for Luke (cf. e.g. Acts 10f.; 16.9f.; 18.9f.),[262] the function of which will shortly become clear:

[10c–16] Here particular note should be taken of the context of the section. As in the precious narrative about Philip and the Ethiopian eunuch (8.26–40) and the story of Cornelius (Acts 10), the actions of two people are interwoven through visions. In the Cornelius story this comes about through duplicate visions, as in the previous story (however, Saul's vision is not developed in narrative, in contrast to that of Ananias). By contrast, the eunuch in 8.26–40 has not received any corresponding vision. That may make it clear that the progress of the action is depicted as being increasingly governed by divine visions, so Luke's three stories are combined to provide a cumulative effect.

[17–19a] These verses extend the charge of healing Saul given to Ananias in v.12: Saul is additionally filled with the Holy Spirit and baptized. Verse 19a rounds off the story.

*Traditions*

[3–9] After the removal of the redaction, the following elements of tradition can be extracted:
1. Saul, the persecutor of Christians, is near Damascus;
2. A heavenly light shines out and Saul falls down;
3. His companions, who have heard the voice speaking to Saul, take him (blinded?) to Damascus.

Reconstructed in this way, the tradition can be described as a legend of the punishment of one who despises God (cf. on II Maccabees below). But it should be noted that vv.4b–6, which in this form are certainly redactional, may possibly have a foundation in tradition (cf. v.7, which certainly at the level of tradition refers back to the voice [v.4] that has spoken to Paul). Moreover it remains uncertain whether Luke has deleted elements of the tradition. The definition of form will vary, depending on what one assumes as a basis. In what follows I shall speak of a *christophany* in order to maintain two things: 1. vv.3–9 are not about visions *generally* in analogy to those in Acts 9.10–19a and 10–11. 2. The subject of the event and content of the vision before Damascus is the persecuted Jesus. Such a definition of form thus allows the story to be classified as the story of a conversion or call. Historical considerations will help here.

At this point we also need to discuss whether the blindness of Saul was an element of the tradition. Hans Grass regards the statement in Acts 9.8 as historically not impossible, making general references to instances of ecstatic blindness. But he then decides, referring to the narrative type of the text,[263] to regard the information about this as unhistorical.[264] Against this it may be argued that the account of an event which really happened is often given in typical forms. A typical form does not exclude historicity; on the contrary, recurring historical patterns in particular provoke historical types of narrative (cf. below on Gal.1.23) which may then go on to influence people in their behaviour. The decisive question here is whether the witnesses themselves give yet further indications that a sickness or a blindness was associated with the Damascus event.

We can also consider whether the basis of the tradition in Acts 9.3–9 comes from Damascus. Further, we might see one of the starting points for the tradition in Gal.1.23 ('he who once persecuted us now proclaims the faith that he tried to destroy'). Moreover, Paul's share in the formation of the tradition about his 'turning point' is not to be underestimated; he will doubtless have told of it himself.

[10–19a] The basis of the tradition of this section is even harder to define than that of the previous section. Probably the only element of tradition is the disciple Ananias in Damascus, who healed Paul there and perhaps also baptized him (9.18). Luke will hardly have added this name to the tradition (cf. the negative connotations of the bearer of the same name in Acts 5.1ff.; 23.2). It is unclear whether the house of Judas on Straight Street is genetically part of the tradition. The elements of tradition mentioned above were either the basis of a story along with the basis of vv.3–9 or Luke himself was the first to put them together.

## Historical

[3–9] The tradition behind vv.3–19a reports with historical accuracy, in agreement with the letters, that a particular event made a persecutor a proclaimer, the enemy of Christ a disciple of Christ (cf. Gal.1). Furthermore, the information that the conversion or calling took place in or near Damascus is also accurate. In Gal.1.17 Paul himself also says that he went to Arabia in connection with the conversion and then returned to Damascus. So he must have been near or in this city soon after his conversion.

The tradition further agrees with Paul's own testimony in reporting a christophany. In I Cor.9.1f. Paul speaks in Easter language (cf. John 20.18,25) of seeing the Lord, as he does in I Cor.15.8 of Jesus showing himself (cf. Luke 24.34 and I Cor.15.3–7). Both passages reflect one and the same event: I Cor.9.1 formulates the active perception of Jesus and I Cor.15.8 its presupposition.

Now a striking point of difference between Acts 9.3–9 and what is worked out under 4.1.3.5.1 on Paul's 'vision' is that Acts here does not expressly speak of seeing the 'Lord', but of hearing his words (vv.4b–6) – in so far as this goes back to tradition at all – and of the appearance of light from heaven and Paul's falling down. At all events, vv.3–9 say nothing about Saul seeing the Lord, even if the character of light in that appearance is maintained in both instances.[265]

By comparison, we might refer to Acts 9.17c, where Ananias, looking back on vv.3–9, describes the appearance of light before Damascus as a showing of Jesus to Saul (*Iesous ho ophtheis soi*, cf. 26.19), and to 9.7 (the companions of Saul did not see anyone); here it is probably presupposed that Saul did see someone, i.e. Jesus.

Therefore there is probably no conflict over the mode of Jesus' appearance between the tradition behind 9.3–9 and the letters of Paul – both in fact attest that Paul has seen Jesus. Johannes Lindblom rightly calls the Damascus event 'a vivid vision with a strong auditive element'.[266]

But differences seem to emerge in another respect. Paul himself emphasizes that the christophany before Damascus marked his calling to be a missionary (cf. esp. Gal.1.15f.), but this is not contained in Acts 9.[267] However, this can be explained simply from the narrative intention of the tradition (or first that of Luke), which (or who) at this point puts the emphasis wholly on the overcoming of the persecutor of Christ by Jesus. On the other hand the call of Paul the persecutor to be a missionary introduces a conclusive shift which is described in Acts 9. Therefore it is quite *possible* that what Luke has narrated in Acts 9 and 26 in two stories with different focal points in fact took place historically within a short space of time (indeed Acts 22 comes in between). In that case Acts 9 and 26 simply contain different aspects of one and the same event.

That is even almost the norm with ecstatic visions. Visionaries have often had difficulties in recounting precisely what they have experienced, so that the interpretation of the experience, which at a later stage in the telling – although in some instances chronologically later – fuses into one with the experience, plays an important role. Reference might be made to the opening visions of the prophet Ezekiel (Ezek.1 and 10) as examples of different forms of one and the same vision.[268]

It should be clear that in a vision the boundaries between fact (= appearance) and interpretation are fluid. The phenomenon of the vision in particular indicates the difficulties of an all too naive use of the distinction between fact and interpretation, objectivity and subjectivity, *extra nos* and *en emoi* (Gal.1.16). One might also compare the difficulty of defining philosophically the relationship between language and thought, perception, experience, interpretation and expression in language. Tillich's method of correlation[269] and Schleiermacher's reflections on the structure of the religious consciousness[270] might also be recalled here. But however much we need to note the points mentioned, they should not lead us to neglect completely the question of what actually happened. The fact of the vision and its historical(!) interpretation by Paul cannot be sharply separated. Each needs unconditionally to be distinguished from the other.

For the question of Paul's blindness cf. the discussions on II Cor.12 (below, 77ff.). (Already at this point in anticipation of what is said there about the apostle's sickness, we cannot rule out the historical possibility that he was blinded in connection with the Damascus event.)

[10–19a] It is hardly possible to make any well-founded historical judgment on the person of Ananias and his involvement in the conversion/call of Saul. However, it is illegitimate to cite Gal.1.12, that Paul does not have his revelation from a human person, against any involvement of Ananias in whatever form. For this information hardly excludes the involvement of Ananias, as it would not put in question the particular character of the conversion/call (cf. I Cor.11.23ff.). Similarly Paul can attribute the report of the last supper (I Cor.11.23–25) directly to the Lord (v.23, 'I received from the Lord'), although beyond doubt the tradition was given to him by the community.

### A retrospective survey of the analysis of the tradition in 9.1–19a, taking into account the historical reconstruction

I said above that it was possible to make final comments as to whether the tradition narrates a conversion or a call only after historical considerations. Now the most important result of the historical reconstruction was that the tradition essentially corresponds with Paul's own testimony. It reports a christophany and depicts its circumstances (aspect of conversion). Certainly no call to become a missionary can be found in Acts 9, but we can *ex hypothesi* attribute its absence to the redactor Luke because of the other parallels between the tradition and Paul, since in Luke's plan for Acts Paul's mission is not yet a theme in Acts 9; however, the appropriate mention does occur in anticipation in v.15. Accordingly, in Acts 9 he probably deliberately interpreted the *tradition* of a calling of Paul (cf. Acts 22 and 26) as a conversion and put it in a series of three conversion stories (8.26–40; 9.1–19a; 10.1–11.18). In my view the tradition of the Damascus event at Luke's disposal is the account of a call which essentially corresponds to Paul's own testimonies. For narrative reasons Luke has repeated it three times and in Acts 9 has moved away from historical truth by interpreting the calling as a conversion.

Conclusion: The accounts in Acts enrich our historical knowledge of Paul's vision of Christ. The tradition worked over by Luke may go back to an account by the apostle himself.[271] It contains details which could already be noted in the letters of Paul. But by way of qualification it should be said that we can no longer determine whether the aspect of call in the Damascus event was a part of the event itself. It seems probable to me that Paul's understanding of the conversion as a call first arose out of an interpretation which may have been made within a short period (before his first visit to

Jerusalem about two years after the Damascus event). We need to
maintain that before Damascus Paul 'saw' Jesus. Whether or not we
want to call this a 'conversion' does not matter much, as the content
is clear. What tells against the expression 'conversion' is that Paul
was and remained a Jew and that he did not, like for example the
later pagan converts in Thessalonica, turn away from idols to the one
God (I Thess.1.9). What favours the term 'conversion' is the
reflection that Paul did a one hundred and eighty degree turn from
persecutor to proclaimer and that a revolution of values formally
took place within his person, from the law to Christ (see below 79–
84 on the pre-Christian Paul).

To sum up, it thus seems certain that the Damascus event was a
vision[272] (cf.n.244) of a kind that occurs in the Old Testament,[273] in
intertestamental Judaism,[274] in numerous parallels from the Hellenistic and Roman environment of the New Testament,[275] and in the
New Testament itself.[276] That raises the question whether Paul also
experienced anything similar at a later date. Is Eduard Meyer even
right in saying that the apostle continually[277] experienced visions
and revelations analogous to those in II Cor.12?[278] Against Meyer's
thesis, Wilhelm Michaelis argues that one may not 'see *any*
characteristic of his piety in this experience (viz. of II Cor.12). It is
hard to say what further events are summed up under the plural II
Cor.12.1'.[279] Dieter Lührmann makes similar negative comments
on Ernst Benz (as in n.277) and writes: 'The attempt . . . to work out
"the visionary basis" for particular theological statements in Paul is
quite wrong.'[280]

However, it seems to me that behind all such objections lies an
inability to perceive Paul's piety or his religious life as it was.[281] The
reasons for this lie in a resistance to the fact that Paul's piety could
have been different from one's own. Whether here one's own lack of
religious experience needs to be overcome I do not know, but that
would be a completely vain undertaking. Only the truth – in
historical things too – will make us free.

Furthermore, one cannot get rid of the suspicion that the failure
of historical criticism to take note of the significance of visions for
Paul is the result of a negative prejudice. In fact the 'history of
prejudice, indeed the incapacity of historical-critical exegesis to
understand phenomena like visions and auditions, has still to be
written'.[282] Has modern Protestant theology and exegesis even an
'anti-visionary complex'?[283] But enough of suppositions and
questions. We now turn to a specific text, II Cor.12, to see whether

visions were also significant for Paul in his Christian period, and if so, to attempt to define the relationship of this passage to the Damascus vision.

### 4.1.3.5.3 *II Cor.12.1–10*

*Exegesis and historical reconstruction*

The substance of the charge which led Paul to write II Cor.10.12–12.18 was apparently that his endowment with the spirit of God was defective: cf. II Cor.10.1 (probably a quotation: Paul is 'weak (*tapeinos*) when face to face with you, but bold to you when I am away'. The assumption that this is a quotation is confirmed by the anti-Pauline polemic in II Cor.10.10 ('For they say, "His letters are weighty and strong, but his bodily presence is weak, and his speech of no account."'). The last-mentioned charge recurs in II Cor.11.6: Paul is 'unskilled in speaking'.[284]

The same theme is taken up again in II Cor.13:

'"This is the third time I am coming to you. Any charge must be sustained by the evidence of two or three witnesses. [2]I warned those who sinned before and all the others, and I warn them now while absent, as I did when present on my second visit, that if I come again I will not spare them – [3]since you desire proof that Christ is speaking in me. He is not weak in dealing with you, but is powerful in you.'

The last sentence shows that those addressed are pneumatics, i.e. Christ is powerful in them. They are calling for proof that the same thing also applies to Paul. Until it is given they have to criticize him for not being sufficiently pneumatic.

When Paul writes in II Cor.12.1b, 'but I will go on to visions (*optasias*)[285] and revelations (*apokalypseis*) of the Lord', he is taking up a new topic in the current discussion. By means of II Cor.12.2–9 he is seeking to prove that he too can boast of visions and revelations of the Lord. Evidently these have been denied him in Corinth. It was probably part of the charge of weakness (II Cor.10.10) that Paul could not point to any visions or revelations. The section, then, stands in the context of an argument, so we must be very careful in trying to derive any historical information from it.

*A priori* we need to guard against too precise an identification of Paul's adversaries and at the same time to attempt to understand the text on its own terms. It is also important to guard against developing questionable historical theses in the interests of hermeneutics, without reflecting on this interest and on historical plausibility.[286]

### Construction and redaction

[1a] 'I must boast' quotes II Cor.11.30a word for word, where there is a reference to the need for boasting of weakness. There after an oath (v.31 [cf. Gal.1.20]) Paul tells of his flight from Damascus (vv.32–33). This is evidently meant to illustrate his weakness. So in II Cor.12 the apostle is giving an account of an event which is similarly meant to show his weakness (vv.5b,9).

[1b] 'Visions' and 'revelations' are almost synonymous. *Ex hypothesi* vision can be understood as seeing and revelation as hearing (cf. Dan.10.1[Th]). But 'revelation' does not just happen through words. Cf. I Cor.14.6,26, where it seems to denote an inner illumination. In the present passage, as the context shows, Paul is probably thinking only of the revelation fourteen years before, which was associated with vision(s) and rapture(s).[287] Visions and revelations 'of the Lord' are either an objective genitive[288] or a *genitivus auctoris*,[289] although the two are not necessarily exclusive;[290] because of what follows, the assumption of an objective genitive seems to me more probable.

[2–4] Paul writes in the third person,[291] although he is talking about himself. In 12.7–10 he speaks of the temptation to be elated because of this special experience. So he was promptly given a 'thorn in the flesh' to remind him of this life on earth.

Some parallels to this way of talking about oneself in the third person: Muhammad about himself: 'God gave a person the choice between this world and the other world, and he chose the other' (see Windisch, *II Corinthians*, 370 n.2). Cf. also the New Testament Son of Man sayings and I Enoch 71.5: 'Then the Spirit took up Enoch into the heaven of heavens, and I saw there ...'[292] ApocEzr 1.1,10,13 (third-person account) – interrupted by 1.2–9 (first-person account). Cf. also the examples of speaking in the third person about the first or second person quoted from rabbinic Judaism in Bill.III, 531.

By using this style the apostle gives his statements an objective character and at the same time maintains a modesty of style which becomes particularly clear in vv.5f.[293]

The note 'fourteen years' emphasizes the real character of the events described in what follows. The dating of the call visions of the Old Testament prophets (Isa.6.1; Jer.1.1ff.; 26.1; Ezek.1.1; 3.16; 8.1; Amos 1.1; Hos.1.1; Zech.1.1; 7.1, cf. IV Ezra 3.1; SyrBar 1.1) probably has a similar function.

> E.g. Zmijewski (as n.286) differs: the notes of time 'serve there (viz. in the Old Testament prophets) to *legitimate* the prophetic *mission*! But this does not apply to II Cor.12.2ff., because here we do not have a vision connected with a mission and charge but rather a private event which does not directly affect Paul's apostolate and his legitimation' (341).

That is inaccurate, to say the least. In the prophets, too, the notes of time themselves do not serve legitimation: that function is served by the narrative of the call which they introduce. Furthermore, in the case of the prophets, too, the call (vision) is primarily a private event, i.e. one related to the prophet's own person, even if it immediately assumes a 'public' character. The only difference between the notes of time in the Old Testament prophets and those in Paul lies in the fact that Paul does not use them in connection with his call but in an argument with opponents. But the issue in both instances is what actually happened.[294]

Verses 2 and 3f. have a parallel structure:

| | |
|---|---|
| know a man in Christ who fourteen years ago | I know this man |
| whether in the body I do not know | whether in the body |
| or outside the body, | or outside the body, |
| I do not know | I do not know |
| God knows – | God knows – |
| that this man was caught up into the third heaven. | that this man was caught up into Paradise. |

Either vv.3f. are a variation of v.2[295] – third heaven would be identical with paradise – or vv.3f. contain a second heavenly journey,[296] into the paradise which lies beyond the third heaven.[297] Because of the careful parallel stylization, preference is probably to be given to the former possibility, especially since in Judaism paradise could be located in the third heaven (otherwise it is in the seventh heaven).[298] (Were these two different events, only one note of time would be hardly comprehensible, i.e. it applies to both v.2 and v.3.) So in vv.2–4 Paul is depicting a *heavenly journey* which has many parallels in the world of early Christianity.[299] The repetition of the narrative stresses the extraordinary event and the mention of the year the historicity of the account.[300] However, it would also be possible to regard the event described by Paul as a rapture: *harpazein* (= grasp) in v.2 is the terminology of a rapture.[301] Still, it is not always possible to make a clean distinction between ascension and rapture.

In a variety of publications Gershom Scholem[302] associates II Cor. 12 with Jewish chariot mysticism.[303] He refers to the Talmud tractate Hagigah 14b, which says: 'Four went into "paradise", Ben Azzai, Ben Zoma, Aher and Rabbi Akiba. Rabbi Akiba said to them: "When you get to the place do not say 'Water, water'. For it is written: he who speaks lies shall not stand before my face"'(56). Scholem also thinks 'that the "Paradise" to which the Mishnah teachers ascend is none other than that "paradise in the third heaven" to which Paul ascended in the ecstasy which followed shortly after his conversion, according to his account in II Cor.12.1' (395 n.45).[304]

The journey to heaven or rapture described by Paul anticipates for a moment the 'going home' to the Lord which he hopes for so ardently in Phil.1.21 (cf. II Cor.5.1f., 6–8).[305] Here he did not know whether he was 'in the body or outside the body'. The statement which is added immediately, 'God alone knows', interprets this event as caused by God – in grace (see also II Cor.5.13). Although Paul does not describe the circumstances more closely, we may assume that the heavenly journey/rapture was associated with ecstasy. The way in which he speaks of himself in the third person fits this. 'The one enraptured in ecstasy distinguishes himself from normal people and speaks of himself as though he were someone else.'[306] Visionaries 'often have the awareness . . . of experiencing their ecstasy in the form of a bodily rapture; in many other instances it is not clear to them whether their rapture is only in the spirit or also in the body.'[307] Since for Paul the result of this ecstatic experience is a temporary communion with the heavenly Christ – anticipating the eschatological communion – and on the other hand for him the Lord is the Spirit (II Cor.3.17; Rom.8.9f.),[308] it can be said that in *II Cor.12 Paul is describing ecstasy as a pneumatic experience.*[309]

'He heard things which cannot be told' (v.4) can mean either words which cannot be told or words which may not be told. Because of the continuation, 'which man may not utter . . .', the second possibility is to be preferred.

In Jewish and Greek accounts of ascensions, what the persons concerned saw and heard is often reported in greater or lesser detail. By contrast, Paul merely states that he 'heard things that cannot be told, which man may not utter' (v.4). He does not say whether he saw anything or, if he did, what it was. However, he hints at this with the word 'paradise'. He felt the place where the 'journey' ended to be paradise and 'knew', i.e. probably also saw, what there was in paradise. 'Above all in addition to angels and the righteous he will have seen "the Lord" himself in this place on his throne, Acts 7.56; Rev.1.9ff.'[310] However, once again it should be emphasized that there is no explicit mention of any seeing in the present text.[311] Still, it should probably be presupposed.

The following instances show that seeing and hearing belong inseparably together in such heavenly journeys and revelations: IV Ezra 10.55f.: 'Go in and *see* the splendour and the glory of the building . . . Then you will *hear* as much as your ears can grasp and hear'; Rev.1.2: John 'bore witness to the *word* of God, and to the testimony of Jesus Christ, even to all that he *saw*'. That seeing and hearing go together is also suggested in this context by the great wealth of imagery which the visionary language contains.[312]

These comments are made in criticism of Becker, *Paulus* (see n.266), who states: 'The result of the rapture is stated in the brief extra final clause 12.4b: his eyes saw no heavenly topography. Only his ears perceived something, but his tongue is incapable of expressing the sound' (248f.). 'So the "lack of results" from Paul's journey to heaven is . . . for Paul precisely the result, the reason why he now speaks of it. It is good enough to show that there is no revelation with a content of its own beside the gospel' (249). But by way of criticism it must be pointed out that on the contrary, for Paul 'the gospel' is embedded in religious experiences to which II Cor.12 bears witness.

[5] As far as the vision given by God is concerned, Paul wants to boast of this man. As far as it concerns himself, he will boast of his own weakness. This expresses his intention well: paradoxically the grace of God is visible on this earth only in weakness, even if the communion with Christ is real in the present. But it is outside human control, because it is given by God. However, it should be noted that later (v.10) Paul will say that in weakness he is strong, i.e. he is even stronger than the Corinthians who similarly boast of the visions. In other words, in this world weakness has paradoxically more power than pure strength.

[6a] This takes up v.5a and emphasizes Paul's right to boast of his journey to heaven. Literally v.6a reads: 'Though I boast, I shall not be a fool (*aphron*), for I speak the truth.' The theme of being a fool refers back to II Cor.11.1,16,19, and II Cor.12.11 shows that Paul regards II Cor.12.1–10 as a compulsion to speak as a fool,[313] i.e. to commend himself, although the Corinthians should have commended him. To understand 'boast' better, we need to supplement it with either 'about the visions' or 'about something other than weakness'.

[6b] The phrase 'than he sees in me or hears from me' is enigmatic, and explanations therefore vary.[314] Does Paul mean that the Corinthians had not heard and seen any more details of his journey to heaven – and therefore there is no boasting? (Of course they have just heard something about it in the letter.)[315] What is probably meant is that the Corinthians' image of Paul is not to be based on such experiences of glory as Paul had, which cannot be verified, but on *their* experiences with him.

Paul claims that he can keep up with the 'arch-apostles' when it comes to visions (v.6a), but at the same time he emphasizes (and here an expression of modesty and a theological statement run into each other) the other characteristic of an apostle: this is first a life in weakness and persecution, which is made effective only by God's grace. There are external indications (*blepei me*) of this life like suffering and sickness. The other outwardly detectable characteristic is the proclamation of the gospel (*akouei ex emou*). (Cf. similar statements by Paul about the characteristics of his apostolate: I Cor.2.1ff.; 9.12–19; II Cor.4.10–13; 6.4ff.; Gal.4.13ff.; Phil.1.13f.,30; Rom.15.20.)

[7] The reference to 'and the abundance of revelations' is unclear. The words can be related to either v.6 or v.7: in the first instance the clause explains why someone could deem the apostle higher than he

or she would otherwise do on the basis of their own perceptions, namely (= epexegetical *kai*) because of the abundance of the revelations. If the phrase is to be referred to v.7, then it is perhaps an anacolouthon. Paul anticipates the key word around which the whole section revolves and links what follows (v.7b–9a) with what has gone before (vv.6–7a) by 'therefore' (*dio*).[316] However, the possibilities mentioned do not seem to me to require different interpretations of the statement. In terms of content there is hardly any difference. The word 'elate' provides a framework for the statement in v.7. This contains the interesting biographical detail that Paul was afflicted by an angel of Satan so that he did not exalt himself above others. Here we have a mythical description of an illness of Paul's.[317] The expression 'angel of Satan' presupposes that the angels which serve Satan are subject to him (cf. Matt. 25.41; Rev.12.9, etc.), and that the Satan, his angel and evil demons cause sicknesses (cf. e.g. Job 2.7 and perhaps also I Cor.5.5). (In I Thess.2.18 the Satan is connected with a hindrance to Paul's travel plans. There it does not necessarily have anything to do with an illness.) *Thus in Paul vision and illness*[318] *belong closely together.* The extraordinary revelations are accompanied by a sickness so that Paul does not exalt himself above others. The idea of self-exultation or exaltation is a Jewish notion (cf. Ezek.21.31; James 4.10; I Peter 5.6).[319] Those who exalt themselves will be punished or brought down. At this point Paul is evidently rationalizing (despite the mythological language [!]) the juxtaposition of revelations and sicknesses in his own person.

[8–9] These verses explain that the power which is expressed in these revelations will become even more powerful through the combination of vision and sickness. Verse 8 contains assured evidence for prayer to Jesus, which is otherwise only rarely attested in the letters of Paul (cf. I Cor.1.2, 'call on the name of the Lord', I Thess.3.11f.). The threefold prayer hardly goes back to Jesus' prayer in Gethsemane (Mark 14.32–42 par.) as a model, but reflects a current Jewish custom (cf. Dan.6.11) and/or expresses the urgency of the prayer (cf. Matt.7.7). Verse 9a contains the answer to Paul's prayer and in form-critical terms can be described with Hans Dieter Betz as a 'healing oracle',[320] even if a healing is refused.[321] It is the only word of the Lord which Paul cites in II Corinthians. One may assume 'that he received such an answer through a revelation, especially since revelations have been mentioned previously'.[322]

Probably the event described from v.8 on is similarly an ecstatic experience (audition, v.9a), which is still part of the same event as vv.2–4 or which for Paul has fused to become one event in the remembering. At least Paul understands both events, the 'ascension' and the interpretation of his weakness by the heavenly Christ, as related (in content). Bultmann objects to the view that behind v.9 there is an event analogous to that in vv.1ff. For want of the visual element he believes that this word of the Lord does not belong among the visions and revelations (12.1), and Jesus' saying in 12.9 ('My grace is sufficient for you . . .') is not unutterable discourse (12.4).[323] But here Bultmann is measuring first-century apocalyptists by rationalistic criteria. In apocalypses[324] the theme of unutterable words and a particular message can go together. Were Bultmann's view right, the apocalyptists would have had to remain completely silent, and this is not the case.

[9b] In this clause Paul once again paraphrases v.9a, now as a remark of his own. In so doing he accepts the word of the Lord as a meaningful interpretation of his situation.

[10a] This builds the bridge to the context (the peristases take up II Cor.11.24ff.) and v.10b ('for when I am weak, then I am strong') makes a weighty conclusion.

### The call vision and the vision behind II Corinthians 12

One important result of the previous section is the conclusion that in II Cor.12 Paul depicts a journey to heaven or a rapture which is combined with an audition and probably also a vision in which he saw paradise and the heavenly Lord. It resulted in, or was combined with, an illness.[325] That brings us to the point of attempting to identify the relationship between the call vision and the vision in II Cor.12.

Most exegetes antithetically contrast the call vision to Paul's other visions and also to the 'heavenly journey' of II Cor.12. Here are some examples:

Wilhelm Michaelis (as n.237): In so far as Paul says nothing in II Cor.12.1ff. of having seen the 'Lord' in his rapture and in so far as the passages in which he speaks of seeing the Lord always refer only to one experience, viz. that before Damascus, it follows that the plural in II Cor.12.1,7 must refer to other experiences of quite a different kind from the Damascus experience (98). 'However, one thing is certain: the

Damascus experience does *not* fall into the category mentioned in II
Cor.12.1 . . . If the Damascus experience belonged to the same category
as the rapture, Paul would quite certainly have *had* to begin with the
Damascus experience' (99). 'So Paul would not have described the
appearance before Damascus as *optasia*, as happens in Acts 26.19. At all
events the *optasiai* of II Cor.12.1 must have been of quite a different kind
and have had a different content from the Damascus event . . . At the same
time it is clear that for Paul himself the Damascus event cannot have had
the stamp of an ecstatic transportation' (99f.).

Friedrich Lang, *Die Briefe an die Korinther*, NTD 7, 1986: 'The apostle
makes a fundamental distinction between his call at Damascus and
ecstatic experiences which for him, like speaking with tongues (I
Cor.14.2), belong in the personal relationship of Christians to God and
are of no use for the edification of the community' (346).

Paul Althaus (as n.209): in the New Testament 'the later visions are
distinguished from the Easter appearances' (16). 'It is not the word
*ophthe* in I Cor.15 which is important but the manifest fact that
according to Paul in I Cor.15.5ff. the earliest community limited the
appearances which counted as testimony to Jesus' resurrection to those
mentioned by Paul and thus distinguished them from other events for
which the same word *ophthe* may have been used. Any attempt to indicate
that the distinction which is fatal for the vision hypothesis is secondary or
already the result of dogmatic reflection and thus to make it irrelevant for
the knowledge of the Easter events comes to grief on I Cor.15!' (20).

Against this Emanuel Hirsch already objected that Althaus spoke 'in
a systematizing way about historical things'.[326] For how can one
explain why one and the same word is used for matters which are
supposed to be fundamentally different? Furthermore, there is no
disputing the fact that in the visions of Jesus after the Damascus
event Paul experiences his encounter with the 'Exalted One' just as
really as on the first occasion. Just a little religious sensitivity leads to
the insight that the 'Damascus vision' and the 'heavenly journey'
narrated in II Cor.12 belong to the same form of experience,
although they are certainly not identical.[327] In terms of the
psychology of religion, however, 'the conversion vision and the
heavenly journey are two different events: in the first instance Christ
descended and "appeared" to Paul – here Paul ascends to the Lord in
heaven'.[328] However, both consist of a vision, and here II Cor.12 is
richer in that in it Paul sees not only the Lord but the whole of
Paradise with its inhabitants. Both events culminate in a hearing of
the Lord, but the content is different: 'Certainly for Paul in his new
calling the audition before Damascus was infinitely more significant

than that in paradise; but the latter was infinitely more holy, since its content was not anything *epigeia* (earthly), but probably exclusively *epourania* (super-terrestrial).'[329] The reason why Paul does not mention the Damascus vision in II Cor.12 may also be that it was already known to the Corinthians from Paul's preaching when he founded the community in Corinth, from oral personal tradition (cf. Gal.1.13,23) and from I Cor.15.8.

Here it is important that in the cases both of the vision reported in II Cor.12 and of the Damascus apperance an illness is part of the event (Acts 9.8/II Cor.12.7). According to the tradition preserved in Luke Paul became blind, whereas II Cor.12 does not allow any closer definition. Ulrich Heckel has recently identified the illness behind II Cor.12.7 as severe headaches ('trigeminal neuralgia') and connected it with the suffering which the apostle says that he experienced in Galatia (Gal.4.13).[330] If by comparison there is a genetic relationship between II Cor.12.7 and Acts 9.8 (which Heckel does not go into at all), the hypothesis of Paul's illness as hysterical blindness is all the more likely.[331]

### 4.1.3.5.4 *Paul's pre-Christian period*[332]

Paul's pre-Christian period, which lasted until he was around thirty,[333] had been characterized by a great zeal for the law (Phil.3.6), which expressed itself in the persecution of Christians (Gal.1.23). The reason for this lay in the proclamation of the crucified Messiah, the criticism of the temple and – closely connected with this – the *de facto* disregard of the Torah which came about in social dealings with Gentiles (Gentile Christians) as a consequence of 'Jesus' gospel of love', from the time of the Hellenists around Stephen onwards.[334] Saul actively persecuted Christians, whereas other Jews like 'Gamaliel' counselled waiting (cf. Acts 5.38f.). In other words, the preaching of the early Christians did not automatically provoke a persecution. Rather, the persecution came from a particular Jewish group to which Saul also belonged. (Later, Paul himself was to suffer persecution from this quarter [I Thess.2.15; cf. Gal.4.29].)

The sources tell us little about the change in Paul from persecuting Christians to proclaiming Christ, apart from the fact that it was the result of a sudden upheaval. Reference should be made to the passages analysed on 60ff. above and also to Gal.1.23 ('He who once persecuted us is now preaching the faith he once tried to destroy') as talk in the communities of Syria[335] about the sudden change in the persecutor of Christians.

The use of Romans 7 to understand the shift in Paul's life story which was once so popular has now been given up almost everywhere. In this chapter Paul describes the history of his ego and the rift in it before he turned to Christ. Three objections have been made to a biographical understanding of the ego since the classical 1929 work of Werner Georg Kümmel:[336] (a) The ego is stylistic form, as e.g. in the Psalms; (b) Romans 7 is to be understood in the context of Romans: in the form of a retrospect it gives a theological, not a historical, description of the pre-Christian ego; (c) in other passages like Phil.3.6 Paul does not give any indication of the split in his pre-Christian life.

As criticism of the first two points it has to be said that a biographical understanding is certainly not ruled out here. Indeed, a reference to the theological form of this retrospect does not as yet (or at least does not necessarily) rule out the historical question as to how far this theological interpretation of Paul's own biography has a historical nucleus.

The rejection of the third argument may be made in a discussion of the most recent major treatment of the pre-Christian Paul, by Martin Hengel.[337] Hengel thinks that Phil.3.6 indicates a quite solid self-confidence on the part of the pre-Christian Paul. 'No one who is afflicted by depressions talks like that. This unique confession shows that the young scribe Paul believed that he could live up to the high demands of perfect observance of the torah of a Pharisaic kind, without any qualifications' (79). Where are such statements headed? Evidently they *want* to leave the question raised in the dark. But a really historical understanding of the kind that Hengel in particular strives for in all his work[338] cannot rest content with this. A *historical* work has to investigate this statement of Paul in various ways: how far is the picture which the apostle paints here of his biography governed by the context of the argument in Philippians and its historical situation? What are Paul's interests here? What is he emphasizing (and why?)? What is he leaving out (and why?)? What possibilities do we have for knowing?

Hengel's reference to Phil.3.6f. takes too little account of the argumentative character of the text, in which the apostle was concerned to bring out his perfection in the fulfilment of the law (cf. Gal.1.13f.). Moreover one can be proud in awareness of one's nomistic achievements and at the same time unconsciously be coping with a conflict. So Hengel completely misses the more sophisticated possibilities.

The question arises whether at this point further exploration in terms of depth psychology can prompt historical reflections, despite Hengel's criticism that 'we just do not know enough to begin on the psychological sounding which is omnipresent today' (80).[339] For Hengel's own *interest* in this supposed impossibility becomes evident in the remark which immediately follows: ' . . . and it is good that that is the case' (ibid.).

This brings me to an attempt at an explanation in terms of depth psychology, which thinks explanation as important as understanding. It seeks on the one hand to increase our knowledge about the conversion of Saul and on the other to grasp its significance. As a theoretical model, one can use a psychodynamic approach which understands religion as a grappling with the unconscious. This model clarifies and identifies from a psychological perspective and at a secondary stage what has been implicitly recognized in the actual use of the historical method in connection with the phenomenon of Paul's conversion. (An awareness of method always follows the actual use of method.) In other words, an interpretation in terms of depth psychology continues a historical-critical understanding and contributes towards understanding Paul in terms of the context in which he lived. As Gerd Theissen has recently provided a crystal-clear discussion of the theoretical problems of psychological exegesis,[340] we can go by his account of the psycho-dynamic approach[341] here.[342]

The two classical approaches to psycho-dynamics were developed in the analytic psychology of Jung and the psychoanalysis of Freud. Jung found genetic predispositions in the expressions of the unconscious (in dreams, myths and poems) and called them archetypes. Archetypes are 'forms or images of a collective nature which occur practically all over the earth as constituents of myths and at the same time as . . . individual products of an unconscious origin. The archetypal motives presumably derive from patterns of the human mind that are transmitted not only by tradition . . . but also by heredity.'[343] At the centre of the doctrine of archetypes stands 'the archetype of the self, which grounds the striving for wholeness and self-realization' (Theissen, *Aspects*, 14). So Jung interprets 'religious symbols chiefly as the objectification of an archetypal tendency towards self-realization. Christ is a symbol of the self. In him the polarities of conscious and unconscious, of ideal and shadow, masculine and feminine are integrated in a comprehensive unity' (15).

By contrast, Freud's psychoanalysis understands Christ symbolism as a resonance of early childhood conflicts (17). Here Freud assumes a pre-Oedipal imprinting by parents who fulfil wishes and an Oedipal imprinting by parents who deny wishes (27). In early Christian religion an infinite trust in the heavenly Father is regressively renewed. On the other hand, the punishing Father emerges with archaic strictness and kills the Son. 'The "superego" is . . . the internalized voice of all normative systems of the culture of that period, that is, of all control mechanisms to which human beings can potentially react with absolutist readiness for activation' (21). 'Religion is confrontation with this archaic heritage – not only with the "father" but with all authorities, institutions and ideas with which that archaic readiness to react is bound up. For Paul, this readiness to react was connected with the "law", as the quintessence of the norms of his sociocultural world' (20).

The theories of Jung and Freud as symbols of goals and conflicts seem to stand over against each other with no possibility of reconciliation. But they are theoretical constructs, which need to be tested by an application to empirical historical evidence. For the fact is that Jesus is not automatically Christ in Jung's understanding, since in that case he would not have needed to live at all. Furthermore, we will need to guard against a monocausal application of the theories mentioned above.[344] To make the point once again – their value needs to be measured by whether they further and deepen an understanding of the text.

As I have already indicated above, the source texts indicate that the pre-Christian Paul was a committed, zealous persecutor of Christians. This vigorous reaction on Paul's part presupposes that the basic elements of the preaching of Christians had had a very strong effect on him. The encounter with Christians and their preaching and practice took place not only at a cognitive level but also at an emotional and unconscious one, as is probably true of all social and religious experiences. I shall now go on to attempt to show that behind Paul's vehemently rejecting, aggressive attitude to Christians there was an inner build-up in his person of the kind that numerous works of depth psychology have ascertained in other cases to be the basic motivation for aggressive behaviour; it is also something that has been described in art and literature. Is it too much to assume that the basic elements of Christian preaching and practice unconsciously attracted Paul? However, out of fear of his unconscious strivings, he projected them on to the Christians, so as to be able to attack them there all the more wildly.

Fanatics often suppress the doubt in their own view of life and practice.[345] If that is true of Paul,[346] his religious zeal was a kind of measure of his inner build-up, which was formally released in a vision of Christ. Perhaps we can say with Jung that Saul was unconsciously a Christian even before his conversion.[347]

> 'The fact that Christ appeared to him objectively, in the form of a vision, is explained by the circumstance that Saul's Christianity was an unconscious complex which appeared to him in projection as if it did not belong to him' (307). At the moment of the Damascus event 'the unconscious Christ-complex associated itself with Paul's ego' (ibid.). But because he did not want to see himself as a Christian, as a result of resistance to this, for a while he became blind. This blindness was psychogenetic, and in terms of experience an (unconscious) unwillingness to see. 'This resistance . . . was never entirely overcome, and occasionally it broke out in the form of fits which are erroneously explained as epileptic. The fits were a sudden return of the old Saul which had been split off by his conversion just as the Christ complex was before' (ibid).

The unconscious 'Christ complex' (presuming that there was such a thing in Paul) may have been formally brought to the boil by the Christians whom he persecuted. He wanted to find release by fighting an external enemy. That became his 'destiny'. And Saul became Paul.

What may we suppose the content of this Christ-complex to have been? First, it may have had to do with the law. Romans 7 is formulated in retrospect and describes the unconscious conflict which Paul endured before his conversion.[348] Secondly, this conflict could have been sparked off by the proclamation of the crucified Christ (a crucified figure could not be the Messiah), thirdly by the universalist tendencies of the preaching of the Christians whom he persecuted, and fourthly by Jesus' preaching of love, which was also handed down by the Hellenists. Oskar Pfister[349] conjectured that Paul was a hysteric with a marked gift for love of other people (26). He had that sense of anxiety, so frequent among hysterics, 'which in religious natures is amalgamated with a feeling of guilt and intensified the pressure of sins' (276). 'Jesus and the Christians called for love and only love. As a genuine hysteric Paul could not love completely before his conversion, and that is what made him suffer'

(277). 'When Paul approached Damascus, there was a catastrophic breakthrough of the long-suppressed longing . . . Paul fled from the painful situation into the other world of hallucination . . .' (279f.)[350]

*The crucial point here is that what he had desired unconsciously had become reality in a person.* Paul's ideal of Christ, first brought to the point of breakthrough by the preaching of those whom he persecuted, has a parallel in the activity of Jesus. At the same time the historical cross of Jesus gave Paul's image of Christ a previously unknown dimension. Paul may have also experienced the change from persecutor to preacher as an experience of life, as an experience of eternity, as liberation from the law and from sin. For all the themes which are addressed are contained in Romans 7. Here it is almost impossible to decide whether Paul could have said that in such a form immediately after Damascus. Like other visionaries, he reflected on his vision. But the problem behind Romans 7 is too 'loaded with experience' for it to have been conceived of and developed in an exclusively theoretical way. Now if it was a genuine conflict (possibly a conflict over a decision),[351] then historically it cannot be too far removed from the Damascus event.

## 4.1.3.6  I Cor.15.5a
### (The first appearance to Peter and the appearance to the Twelve)

#### 4.1.3.6.1  *The appearance to Peter*

The relationship of the appearance to Peter to that to the Twelve can be defined in two ways:

1. The thesis that the two appearances go back to one presupposes that *eita* has replaced an original *kai*. In that case Paul would have altered 'to Cephas and the Twelve' to 'Cephas, then to the Twelve', because of the other appearances which he intended to cite in sequence.[352] However, such a view is improbable (see below).

2. The assumption that the appearance to Peter was an individual appearance (i.e. without the Twelve) is supported by the wording of I Cor.15.5 and the following historical grounds:

Right at the beginning Peter was leader of the earliest community in Jerusalem. This may be concluded from Gal.1.18, according to which Paul went to Jerusalem three years after his conversion, to make the acquaintance of Cephas. How Peter attained this position is most plausibly explained as being the consequence of a legitimation by 'the Risen One'. I Corinthians 15.5 is a reflection of this and may be derived from a visionary event which is to be deemed historical.

Outside I Cor.15.5 there is no *clear* testimony to this event in the New Testament; that may be connected with the fact that the tradition of Peter as the first witness to the resurrection was *suppressed*.

Adolf von Harnack[353] describes the following stages of the development of the tradition in a way which I believe to be still valid today.

1. The suppression already begins in Luke, who has condensed a detailed Petrine tradition into the one formula 'he appeared to Simon' (Luke 24.34), which he inserted as an appendix to the Emmaus story. Furthermore, in Acts he usually has Peter appearing with John as his companion (Acts 3.1,3,4; 8.14, etc.).

2. The suppression is subsequently continued by the Gospel of John, in which the appearance to Peter is explicitly described as the third (John 21.14) – and thus not as the first.

3. The author of the First Gospel deleted the visions of both Peter and James and in their place inserted a vision of the women which he himself composed (Matt.28.16–20: for the reasons for this view see 130f. below), which is then followed by the apostles' vision (Matt.28.16–20). On this Harnack writes: 'This fact cannot be interpreted in any other way than that the author thus wanted to mediate between the followers of Peter and the followers of James by simply suppressing their claims. This is a process which is well known from later church history' (99f.).

4. According to John 20.11ff and the secondary conclusion to the Gospel of Mark (16.9), Mary Magdalene was the first witness of the resurrection, while Peter or Peter and John merely confirmed the empty tomb (John 20.3ff.). 'So here too James is completely suppressed, and Peter is not given adequate recognition' (99f.).

Nevertheless, outside the New Testament there is a reflection of the first appearance, in Ignatius, Smyrnaeans 3.1–2:[354]

> 'For I know and believe that he was in the flesh even after the resurrection. And when he came to those with Peter he said to them: "Take, handle me and see that I am not a phantom without a body." And they immediately touched him and believed, being mingled both with his flesh and spirit.'

Though it was said above that Peter was suppressed as the first witness of the resurrection, nevertheless there may still be remnants of an original christophany to Peter, namely in the texts Luke 5.1–11/John 21 and Matt.16.18–19. (However, given the state of the sources, the uncertainty factor is incomparably higher than in I Cor.15.5.)

## *Luke 5.1–11/John 21*[355]

Both pericopes, which may go back to an original resurrection story (for the reasons for this see 168 below), belong genetically together. The following motifs in them correspond:

   1. The unsuccessful fishing trip;
   2. Allusions to Peter's denial (cf. the confession of sins in Luke 5.8b and the threefold question of Jesus in John 21.15–17);
   3. The abundant catch (John 21.6; Luke 5.6);
   4. John 21.11 is parallel to Luke 5.10c (the motif of catching is associated with Peter);
   5. The call to discipleship in John 21.19 corresponds to Luke 5.11;
   6. The assessment of Peter is given by a saying of the Lord (John 21.17c/Luke 5.10c);
   7. Peter is the main figure in the narrative (after Jesus).

Given this comparison it can be pointed out that the second and the fifth point do not derive from the pericope John 21.1–14, but only from the context, and on 21.15–17 in particular it was observed that it cannot 'be regarded as originally old tradition. The precise imitation of the story of the denial betrays . . . later reflection.'[356] But on the one hand this judgment is questionable (see 169f., below) and on the other, given the other parallels cited above, it is very probable that through John 21 the pericope Luke 5.1–11[357] can be defined as a former Easter story. This is all the more likely since in its focus on Peter the Lukan version of the saying about being a fisher of men (Luke 5.10) requires 'compellingly the logion to be rooted in the Easter situation'.[358] For whereas Mark 1.17 relates only a promise of future appointment to be fishers of men, Luke 5.10 ('from now on') depicts the appointment itself, which follows immediately with this saying to Peter. Furthermore, Mark 1.18 contains a call to discipleship which at a *secondary* stage has been adapted to the circumstances of the life of Jesus, whereas Luke 5.10 has the call 'Do not fear!' The latter has hardly developed from Mark 1.18, but has its original context in this appearance story, which fits the Easter situation. Of course not every revelation scene is to be rooted in the

Easter situation. But there is a further important indication in the
fact that Luke 5.8b narrates 'a desperate confession of guilt on the
part of Peter, for which there is no occasion in the situation
presupposed in Luke 5'.[359]

Should Peter's denial of Jesus be deemed historical (see 95
below), then provisionally the significance of the historical event
underlying Luke 5 can be described as 'being forgiven profound guilt
and being appointed a witness and apostle of the living Lord'.[360] Cf.
also the view of Hans Grass: 'We may certainly not psychologize the
"Depart from me, for I am a sinful man" in Luke 5.8b . . . But there is
nothing against the assumption that the Easter story underlying
Luke 5 and John 21 contained not only the first appearance of the
Risen One but also a confession of guilt on the part of Peter, a
reconciliation and mission. At all events Peter's confession of guilt in
Luke 5.8b fits an Easter story better than the story of a calling.'[361]

Now it is sometimes objected against understanding Luke 5.8 as
the reflection of an encounter with 'the Risen One' that: (a) Peter's
reaction can be explained as religious reticence in the face of a
supernatural event. (b) The picture of the repentant sinner is
generally Lukan (Luke 7.36–50; 15.1–10; 18.9–14; 19.1–10).[362]
However, the first argument in no way excludes an Easter situation.
Furthermore, despite the Lukan terminology, what we have in Luke
5.8–10 is a revelation scene in which the lordship of Jesus[363] and the
sinfulness of Peter are in substance put in parallel. (This therefore
suggests the assumption of an underlying piece of tradition.)

So it is still best to assume that Luke 5/John 21 go back to the
tradition of a christophany; of course we are not as well informed
about its details as we are in the case of Paul, especially as both texts
have been formulated in their entirety from a later perspective (cf. the
redactional stylization).

### (b) Matthew 16.17–19

A further account of a first appearance of Jesus to Peter, again
formulated from a later perspective, probably underlies
Matt.16.17–19.

Rudolf Bultmann[364] already defended with good reason the
considerably antiquity of this passage. He writes: 'The community
handed down a saying of Jesus in which Peter is promised authority
in matters of doctrine or discipline' (138). That follows, he argues,
from the verbs 'loose' and 'bind' in v.19. The whole idea of v.18

points to earliest times: the 'community of which Peter is the authority will be saved in the end-time, when the powers of the underworld overwhelm mankind. Here the Palestinian community expresses its eschatological consciousness of being the eschatological community of the just. So the content of the verses no less than the language of v.17 that goes along with vv.18–19 shows the Semitic origin of the saying' (139f.).

Bultmann also thinks that the tradition of Matt.16.17–19 originally followed on Mark 8.17–30, but was broken off by Mark, who 'connected with this a polemic against the Jewish-Christian point of view represented by Peter from the standpoint of the Hellenistic Christianity of the Pauline sphere' (258, cf. Mark 8.32f.). One might also point out that Bultmann's theory goes very well with the observation of Harnack reported on p. 85f. above that the significance of Peter was suppressed in earliest Christianity, and the author of the First Gospel evidently relativized the special position of Peter in Matt.16.19 by Matt.18.18.[365]

Bultmann continues:

'The words can hardly have been formulated in any other place than in the earliest Palestinian community, where Peter was looked up to as the founder and leader of the community and the blessing of Peter was put into the mouth of the risen Lord. For it is doubtless the risen Lord who speaks in Matt.16.17–19, and if the supposition be correct, that Matt.16.17–19 is the original conclusion to the confession scene, it also indicates that the Easter experience of Peter was the hour when the messianic faith of the earliest community was born. Indeed, in that case the whole narrative would have to be designated an Easter story which was carried back into the life of Jesus (perhaps first by Mark). Just as John 20.22f. is a parallel to Matt.16.19, so the whole story of the Messianic confession has some parallels in the Easter story in John 21.15–19' (258f.).

This view of Bultmann's has dominated the debate since then. In my view it still holds the field, though Ulrich Luz[366] has recently advanced important arguments against it. He writes on Peter: 'The more one emphasizes his position of pre-eminence within the earliest church, the more difficult it is to understand how he could have gone away from Jerusalem and even at the time of the apostolic council have been only one . . . of several pillars in the building of the church (Gal.2.9)' (457). The saying in Matt.16.17–19 is in his view 'at most formulated as a retrospect on the completed activity of Peter' (458).

He gives the following reasons: (a) Eph.2.10; Rev.21.14; (b) the substantive parallel in John 21.15–17. As he goes on to say: 'Peter did not become the most important apostolic founding figure of the church exclusively as a result of his leading role. Of course it was important that Peter had the first appearance at Easter and played a central role in the earliest Jerusalem community. But it is astounding that there is no detailed report of the first appearance of Jesus to Peter in the New Testament and that the initial role of Peter as leader in the earliest Jerusalem community only becomes really important in the later Acts of the Apostles' (470).

*Criticism*: Luz takes too little account of *fundamental* changes in the Jerusalem community of the early period.[367] The 'substantive parallel' in John 21.15–17 can also plausibly be connected with the tradition of a first appearance (see below, 169f.). 3. The traditions Eph.2.10; Rev.21.14 mentioned by Luz are more formal and paler than the traditions claimed by Bultmann for a protophany, which seem alive. So Bultmann's verdict on Matt.16.17–19 remains.

From what has been said so far it has become probable that (as in the case of Paul) narratives about Peter's Easter experience were circulating in the communities. In contrast to Paul's case, they claimed to be accounts of a first appearance and evidently above all for this reason were 'chopped up' because of changing situations and the rivalry in the earliest Jerusalem community, and put in other narrative contexts. Nevertheless, the historical verdict may be expressed that Peter (like Paul later) heard and saw Jesus alive after his death.[368] With this vision was connected the task of mission and the leadership of the church and the granting of authority to forgive sins. How far the last three points were the historical object of the appearance or arose subsequently from Peter's interpretation is difficult to say with any certainty (see above, 66f.).

Now in the light of these statements one could break off the historical investigation and regard any further investigation as historically impossible and/or theologically illegitimate. However, the claim that it is theologically *illegitimate* is to be rejected with good reasons (see above, 9ff.). The situation is more complicated in the question of the historical *possibility* of further investigation, especially as the situation with the sources is incomparably worse than in the case of Paul. Here in fact the commandment of historical reason not to speculate where the sources give out must be observed.[369] On the other hand, the Peter traditions of the New Testament may not have been completely exhausted for the question of Peter's Easter vision. That is especially true of the tradition of a denial of Jesus by Peter, which is said to have taken place immediately after Jesus' arrest. Luke 5.8 in all probability already pointed to this tradition. If it should be historical, it would seem likely that Peter's denial of Jesus (*before* his death) and vision of Jesus (*after* his death) should be connected. This might possibly give us a deepened access to Peter's vision.

### 4.1.3.6.2  *The prehistory of the appearance: Peter's denial (Mark 14.54,66–72)*

Preliminary comment: it is generally agreed that the Gospel of John (18.15–18, 25–27) has no special tradition on the denial and can be left out of account here. This recognizes that the beloved disciple was inserted into the story redactionally in John 18.15f. (cf. below, 152f.).

### *Redaction and tradition*

Verses 54,66–72 refer back to the announcement of the denial (vv.26–31) and bring the fulfilment of the second part of Jesus' prophecy there (the first part [v.27] has already been fulfilled by the flight of the disciples). Verse 54, the beginning of the pericope of Peter's denial, has been prefaced to this by Mark in order to bracket it with the story of the hearing before the Supreme Council (vv.53,55–65). Verse 66a ('as Peter was below in the courtyard') takes up the thread broken off in v.54. 'Warming himself' (v.67) relates back to 'warming' in v.54. Verse 55 repeats the subjects from v.53 (sometimes varied). This interlocking produces an impressive contrast between Jesus' confession (Mark 14.62) and Peter's denial. The second evangelist already used an analogous technique in Mark 3.20–35 (vv.22–30); 5.21–43 (vv.25–34); 6.6–30 (vv.14–29); 11.12–25 (vv.15–19); 14.1–11 (vv.3–9).[370] The significance of the link between the denial and the hearing before the Supreme Council in Mark is clearly to provide a contrast between the confession of Jesus (Mark 14.62) and the threefold, i.e. total, denial by Peter. This contrast warns Christians to follow the example of Jesus in public confession. So the whole section has a paraenetic tendency as a result of this external redactional structure independently of the question of the detailed relationship between redaction and tradition.

Can clear characteristics of Markan redaction be identified in the text? Various authors think that Mark originally expanded the story of one denial to three. Often v.68 is regarded as the original denial. The second evangelist is said to have artificially triplicated the denial as in the redactional tripartite division of the Gethsemane pericope (Mark 14.32–42) and the mockery scene (Mark 15.16–32). Another argument in favour of this is provided by the threefold group of announcements of the passion (Mark 8.31; 9.31; 10.32–34), which is probably Markan, and the figure three in Mark 15.6–16 (Pilate's threefold question as to whether Jesus is to be released, vv.9,12,14). However, it is difficult to decide what part Mark played in shaping the last-mentioned scene. In general, we cannot completely exclude the possibility that even in the passages cited earlier, where the threefold repetition seems to arise from the redaction, there is a basic tradition, since three is a round number and may already have been chosen at the level of the tradition. It may therefore be almost impossible to resolve the question of the extent of Mark's shaping of the threefold denial with sufficient certainty; fortunately this has no bearing on the question of its historicity, which needs to be raised later.[371]

> There are clear traces of Mark's linking activity or typical Markan terminology in the following verses: v.66, 'high priest' (picks up the high priest in v.53); 'warming himself' (picks up the same verb from v.54); 'with the Nazarene' (for 'with' cf. 3.14; for 'Nazarene' cf.1.24; 10.47; 16.6); v.69, 'again', 'began'; v.70, 'again'; v.72, 'and immediately', 'he remembered' (cf.11.21), 'the word', cf. 9.32. The whole of v.72 relates redactionally to 14.30 (but the later could also be part of the tradition, if 14.27–31 formed a unity with the pericope about the denial [see 93 below on Eta Linnemann's thesis]).

*The train of thought in Mark 14.66–72*

Verses 66–68a portray the *first* denial. Peter is in the courtyard, and is recognized by a maid of the high priest who says directly to him that he too had been with Jesus of Nazareth (v.67b). Thereupon Peter replies, 'I neither know nor understand[372] what you mean' (v.68a). Strictly speaking this is a denial by Peter that he is a disciple and not yet a denial of Jesus. But since Peter's reply in v.68a at the same time rejects any knowledge of Jesus, the concrete denial of Jesus in v.71 is prepared for. Here the text aims at a cumulative effect: the questions to Peter become more intense and more oppressive, so that

he can no longer help himself with general remarks about not
understanding, but has to become *concrete*.

Verses 68b–70a portray the *second* denial, which takes place in
the courtyard. Again the maid sees Peter and now says to the
bystanders that Peter is one of the followers of Jesus ('this man is one
of them' [v.69b]). In contrast to the first denial, this one is not
elaborated, but only stated. That fits the fact that the maid only
'informs' the bystanders about Peter (and no longer addresses him,
as on the first occasion). The cumulative effect is achieved by the
increase in the number of people involved in the scene who press
Peter with the question whether he belongs to the Jesus circle. This
question from the bystanders to Peter is not actually described, but
presupposed, as Peter refers to it ('but again he denied it'). 'Again'
(*palin*) picks up the same word from v.69 and is used again in v.70,
probably to emphasize the chain reaction of question and denial.

Verses 70b–71 relate the *third* denial. The place where it takes
place is apparently the same as the first (the courtyard), but this is not
explictly mentioned. This time the bystanders, to whom the maid has
communicated Peter's identity at the second denial, take the
initiative: here 'of them' in v.70b is picked up from v.69. Thus the
second and third denials are closely related ('the bystanders' in v.7
picks up 'the bystanders' in v.69). The assertion of the bystanders is
supported by the fact that Peter (like Jesus) is a Galilean. First they
confirm what the maid has just (v.69b) told them, and this time they
address Peter directly: 'Certainly you are one of them'. The content
of this third denial of Peter is most firmly emphasized by cursing and
swearing: 'But he began to invoke a curse on himself and to swear, "I
do not know this man of whom you speak"' (v.71). Only now is
there a concrete denial of Jesus. In this way 14.30 (the announcement
of the denial) is first really fulfilled.[373]

Verse 72: this verse provides a close redactional link between the
denial in Mark 14.54f.,66–71 and the announcement of it in Mark
14.27–31. Just as Jesus in Mark can look towards the coming denial
of Jesus, so earlier he has known in advance about the betrayal by
Judas (Mark 14.18–21) and his own death and resurrection (Mark
8.31; 9.31; 10.32–34).

Even after the train of thought has been described, it is hardly
possible to answer whether the tradition available to Mark had three
elements or only one. All that is certain is that one tradition – albeit
one which cannot be marked out with any certainty – underlies it and
that the tradition of the denial once circulated in isolation, independ-

ently of the passion narrative, as the linking of the two is redactional (see above, 90).

*Excursus*

This theory needs to be defended or deepened by a critical discussion with Eta Linnemann.[374] The author questions whether Mark 14.27–31 is redactional and suggests that the announcement of the denial made there could have arisen earlier than the story of the denial (83). In her view, Mark 14.27–31 is 'an originally independent piece of tradition which arose for similar reasons to the "faith legend" of the announcement of the betrayal (viz. Mark 14.18–21), to which it formally corresponds' (85). She continues: 'As the story of the denial in v.72 presupposes an announcement of the denial and corresponds to Mark 14.30 in its formulation, it would seem most probable that what is presupposed in Mark 14.27–31 is to be found there. Accordingly the announcement of the denial is earlier than the narrative of the denial, and the one depends on the other. Once the announcement of the denial was made known, evidently a novelistic and paraenetical interest led to the denial also being narrated. Whether a particular interest in the figure of Peter played a part here is not completely certain to me. Of course the story of the denial is not a continuation of the announcement of the denial, but an independent pericope which merely presupposes acquaintance with it' (ibid.).

Criticism: 1. Peter's third denial can also be understood in another way: Mark deliberately shaped the prediction 14.30 from it (see above); 2. Mark 14.72 is a Markan link; 3. counter-question: What Sitz im Leben would a statement about the denial have? Here I am presupposing that Mark 14.30 cannot have been related by the community as a prediction of Jesus unless the announcement had been fulfilled.

So the position remains that the tradition of the denial, the precise extent of which can no longer be discovered, was originally handed down in isolation from the passion narrative and without a prediction. Before a new proposal is made about the origin of this tradition we must first also examine the relationship between the tradition of the denial and a tradition which deviates from it, one which occurs in Luke 22.31f.[375]

*The relationship between Mark 14.66–72 and Luke 22.31f.*

Bultmann describes Luke 22.31f. as traditional and 22.32b–33 as Lukan. 'Verses 33f. look out of place after vv.31f., since v.32 ended with a forward look to the great part Peter will play, whereas vv.33f. contain only the tragic obverse of that.'[376] With 'when you have turned again' (*epitrepsas*) in v.32b Luke is said to link the passage with the story of the denial in Luke 22.56–62. Bultmann goes on to say that the piece of tradition in Luke 22.31f. is important above all for two reasons: '1. It shows that some elements of the passion narrative also had a separate tradition. 2. Verses 31,32a evidently presuppose that in the "sifting" of the disciples all but Peter have fallen away; only his loyalty has not wavered. So this tradition does not know the story of the denial' (267). The image of the sifting of the wheat presupposes that not all the disciples have fallen away, but that a remnant has survived the 'sifting', and the statement of Jesus 'that your faith does not waver' virtually excludes any apostasy of Peter (288 n.1).

By contrast, Jack Finegan thinks that there is no tradition at all in vv.31f., but that both verses were shaped by Luke. Verses 31f. are said to be the Lukan interpretation of Mark 14.27; for Luke cannot allow the disciples to be 'scattered', with the result that he uses the picture that the disciples will be sifted like wheat. The presupposition of the image is said to be fulfilled when the faith of Peter is not finally lost, although he falls away, since then he nevertheless finds himself again.[377] However, the break which Bultmann aptly observed between vv.31f. and vv.33f. tells against Finegan's definition of vv.31f. as redactional.

Conclusion: There is a tension between the tradition of Luke 22.31f., which speaks of an apostasy of the disciples and a persistence of Jesus in the face of Jesus' passion,[378] and the tradition of a denial of Jesus by Peter. Günter Klein has concluded from this that the denial is not historical. For, 'if the denial were historical, then the earliest community controlled by Peter would have had to suppress it in favour of Luke 22.31f.'.[379] But that is only one possibility, which moreover knows too much about what the earliest community *must* have done. Furthermore, we cannot exclude the possibility that the tradition Luke 22.31f. wanted to correct an existing tradition of the denial. In addition it is conceivable that the tradition – despite the denial – wanted to affirm in retrospect 'that Peter in no way completely abandoned the cause of Jesus . . . but was in some way concerned to keep faith with it'.[380]

## The origin of the tradition of the denial

As I have already said, Günter Klein argues that Peter's real denial is not historical. Instead of this he gives a biographical interpretation of its threefold repetition and associates it with the changes of position which Peter had made in his career: first he was a member of the circle of the Twelve, then an apostle, after that a member of the college of the pillars and finally a lone figure.[381] But who could have interpreted this as *betrayal*? Moreover, where can we locate the opposition of Peter from which the anti-Petrine tradition of the denial must be derived?[382]

By contrast, it is better to revive the old proposal of Martin Dibelius that Peter himself told of his denial, 'though not in connection with his description of the Passion so much as in connection with his Easter experience'.[383] In addition to Dibelius one can point as a parallel to the way in which Paul's past and his present preaching of the gospel was reported. In Gal.1.23 it is said: 'He who once persecuted us is now preaching the faith he once tried to destroy.' The verse should be described as oral personal tradition which was current in the churches of Syria persecuted by Paul and which may have similarly been known in the churches which he had founded. Indeed Paul explicitly refers in the context of Galatians to the fact that the Galatians had heard of his way of life in Judaism (Gal.1.16). Similarly, the denial of Peter and his Easter experience were reported in a 'formerly-now' scheme. In both cases we evidently have personal traditions with a high degree of historical plausibility.[384]

## The denial of Jesus by Peter – a historical fact

Peter distanced himself from his master in Jerusalem after Jesus' arrest in order to save his life. In this he was like his fellow disciples, who had already taken flight previously (Mark 14.50).[385] Another disciple, Judas, had even co-operated in Jesus' arrest. Presumably there were considerable tensions in the group of disciples around Jesus after the decisive journey to Jerusalem. There were formal rifts. The saying about Satan (Mark 8.33), which is too sharp not to be authentic,[386] points to ambivalences in the relationship between Jesus and his 'first' disciples. There was a catastrophe and the togetherness was abruptly ended by the execution of Jesus.

*The Easter experience of Paul and Peter – a comparison*

If we return to the relationship between Paul's Easter experience and
that of Peter it has to be said: (a) both experience an 'original'
revelation, whereas all the other Easter revelations are dependent
revelations.[387] Peter's vision of Christ shaped all the other visions of
the exalted Lord in the circle of the disciples, with the exception of
the vision of Paul, who had not known Jesus and Peter at all in his
pre-Christian periods.[388] (b) For both, furthermore, the vision of
Jesus is indissolubly connected with the denial of Jesus or the
persecution of his community. (c) In both cases the guilt feeling is
replaced by the certainty of grace. (d) Both may have shared a similar
doctrine of justification, even if these did not completely correspond.
According to Gal.2.15f., in Antioch Paul had addressed Peter as
follows: 'We ourselves, who are Jews by birth . . ., yet who know
that a man is not justified by works of the law but through faith in
Jesus Christ, even we have believed in Jesus Christ . . .' (ibid).
Certainly Gal.2.15–21 does not contain what Paul himself said in
Antioch at that time (around 47 CE), for here the apostle is already
using Pauline terminology with a view to the current controversies in
Galatia. But his reference (v.16) to the *common* agreement over the
doctrine of justification needs to be noted.[389] (The 'we' of vv.15f.
includes Peter!) Paul was evidently in agreement with Peter from the
start that men and women are justified through faith in Christ and
not through the law; indeed this conviction had dawned on both of
them when they turned to Christ, in their 'Easter experience'. In this
connection we need to note the great proximity between the content
of I Peter and Pauline theology,[390] which is to be explained either by
the assumption of a common dependence on traditio-historical pre-
Pauline theology or by the thesis that in I Peter there is a later
Paulinism.[391] At all events I Peter 2.24 (' . . . that we might die to sin
and live to righteousness', cf. Rom.3.2f.; 6.11,18), the formula 'in
Christ' (I Peter 3.16; 5.10,14), which does not occur outside the
Pauline sphere, and the notion of joy in suffering (I Peter 1.3-8, etc.;
cf. I Thess.1.6; 3.3f.) indicate the nearness of I Peter to Paul's
writings. One explanation of this could be that some of the theology
of the historical Peter has been preserved in the pseudepigraphical
work I Peter.

Finally – and here I am considering Peter's Easter experience once
again by itself – this was brought about solely by Jesus. He had
formally lived out for his disciples the message of the boundless grace

of God – in word and deed. Human beings have nothing to show before God (cf. Luke 18.1–14). The word of salvation is for the poor (Matt.11.5) and the outcast (Matt.21.28–31; Luke 15.2–10; Luke 15.11–32). Jesus thus understands the notion of grace in all its depth, and that of sin, without parting company with the Judaism of his time. Where grace is understood in the power of its invitation, the notion of forgiveness is understood in unobtrusive simplicity. Peter had transgressed or sinned against Jesus by denying him. But under the impact of Jesus' proclamation and death, Peter, through an experience of the 'risen Lord', related God's word of forgiveness present in the activity of Jesus once again to himself, this time in its profound clarity. For where is forgiveness greater than where one has previously literally denied everything and rejected it (cf. Luke 7.36–50)? The message of forgiveness thus ran literally through the death of Jesus (we shall return to this at 181f. below).

### Peter's Easter vision – a piece of mourning

I shall now attempt on the basis of the story of Peter (his relations with Jesus and his denial of Jesus) and the fact of his vision of Jesus to depict what could have happened within him between Good Friday and Easter. I am concerned to trace this process as vividly as possible, going through it with the help of contemporary depth-psychological research into mourning, using this research in order to understand it and ultimately to explain what the presuppositions of Easter faith can be.

For Peter, in the drama of the situation of Good Friday and his denial, the world has collapsed. At Easter the word of Jesus, i.e. the word of Jesus' forgiveness, once again came to Peter, shattered and in mourning, despite his denial of Jesus and despite Jesus' death: he 'saw' Jesus. He experienced the word of Jesus as something living, as an encounter with the whole Jesus himself, in an image.[392] That Peter's situation can be described as one of mourning is evident from a comparison with reports by mourners, which occasionally also contain the element of the image of the presence of a beloved person who has died. Yorick Spiegel[393] cites some cases:

> 'The mourner hears the step of the dead person on the stair, hears the gravel crunch in front of the house and believes that the door is opening: "I saw Kay standing inside the house door. He looked as he always did when he came back from work. He smiled and I ran into his outstretched arms as I always used to do and leaned against his breast. I opened my eyes

and the image had disappeared." A mother who has lost a baby may hear
it crying when half asleep and rush to its bed before she realizes that it was
all only a wish' (171).

'Children who have lost a father or a mother very often report quite
vividly how they sit on the edge of the bed talking to them. Almost half the
patients whom Parkes had investigated reported similar disturbances of
vision. Often shadows are perceived as an appearance of the dead person'
(172).

'In addition to hallucinations and auditions there is almost more
frequently the feeling that the dead person is present. Parkes was told by
widows: "I still have the feeling that he is near, and that there is something
I should do for him or tell him . . . He is always with me. I hear him and see
him, although I know that he is only an idea"; "When I wash my hair I
have the feeling that he is there and cover myself in case someone comes
through the door." For some, the presence of the dead person is
particularly strong at his or her grave. In the novel by J. Agee mentioned
earlier there is a description of such an appearance of a husband killed in a
car accident; . . . the dreams about the dead person also belong to the
category of the mechanism of warding off the loss by breaking down the
controls over reality' (173).

A report is also cited which was sent to the journal *Schweizerischer
Beobachter*, in response to an enquiry in the paper. (The question
was whether readers had experienced dreams which later came true,
appearances of spirits, intimations, etc.) This report, by a woman,
runs:

'At the age of nine and a half I lost my father, I was constantly miserable
and wept for him for many years ... Then one Christmas Eve it
happened. I was already in bed, but wanted to go to Christmas mass. It
was time to get up again but I got severe stomach-ache and just had to lie
there. Soon afterwards the pains stopped again, but by then it was already
too late for the mass. So I stayed in bed. Then I heard the door open, and
gentle steps, accompanied by a strange knocking. I was alone in the house
and was quite frightened. Then the marvellous thing happened: my father
came to me, so beautiful, shining like gold and transparent like mist. He
looked as he had always done. I could clearly recognize his outline, then
he stopped in front of my bed and looked at me in such a kind way and
smiled. A deep peace came over me and I was happier than ever before.
Then he went away.'[394]

In psychoanalytical terms[395] one may say that thought can assume
archaic features in the drama of a situation of loss. The collapse of

the world of the mourner unleashes libidos and aggressive energies to a considerable degree (68). Often the question of guilt also takes on heightened significance in this regressive phase (71). Here there can be a breakdown of the controls of reality, since the unconsciousness cannot bear the loss of a beloved person and 'uses the very organs which play an essential part in the formation of the reality-principle to create a pseudo-satisfaction for itself' (171).

Judged in that way, however, the vision of Peter would be delusion or wishful thinking, indeed really an example of unsuccessful mourning,[396] because it abruptly cuts off the process of mourning. Here we come up against the same problem as when discussing Paul's conversion, and (*pace* Spiegel) we should guard against taking a one-sidedly reductionist course. Rather, it is necessary to see that in contrast to the 'normal' process of mourning, in the case of Peter it was not a pale[397] but a living and vital image of Jesus which took the place of the beloved dead person. However, one could connect this process with extreme wishes. The question is, though, whether such an explanation does not prevent an understanding (see below).

To further an understanding of Peter's 'mourning' and 'vision', reference should be made in this connection to investigations at Harvard into cases of mourning and the painful loss associated with them.[398] The researcher followed forty-three widows and nineteen widowers through the process of mourning and interviewed them at intervals of three weeks, eight weeks and thirteen months after the death of the partner. The aim of the work was to investigate what made it possible to work through mourning. Among other things three factors were mentioned which prevented mourning: 1. a sudden death; 2. an ambivalent attitude to the dead person associated with guilt feelings; and 3. a dependent relationship.

Applying this finding to the situation of Peter and the disciples,[399] we should note that all three factors which make mourning difficult apply to them: 1. the crucifixion of Jesus happened unexpectedly and suddenly;[400] 2. the relationship of the disciples to Jesus was marked by ambivalence and guilt feelings: Judas betrayed Jesus and then committed suicide; Peter denied Jesus and wept bitterly; 3. a dependent relationship of the disciples on Jesus can be seen in the fact that most had left their work and homes to be with him. The dependence was perhaps further intensified by the fact that the followers of Jesus represented a small religious group which had detached itself from its original social structures and thus had formally parted company with the outside world. Jesus was one and all to them. (Granted, these are conjectures, but they may have a historical foundation.)

Conclusion: the mourning hindered by the three factors mentioned was enormously helped in the case of Peter by a vision, indeed concentrated in a moment of epiphany. The mourning first led to a deeper understanding of Jesus, and this in turn helped towards a new understanding of the situation of mourning. Recollections of who Jesus was led to the recognition of who Jesus is. Seeing Jesus here included a whole chain of (potential!) theological conclusions.

### 4.1.3.7  I Cor.15.5b (The appearance to the Twelve)

There is no extended report in the New Testament of the appearance to the Twelve unless one connects parts of Luke 24 or John 20 with it (see below, 163). The following narrative appears in the Kerygma Petri from the beginning of the second century:

> 'In the "Preaching of Peter" the Lord says to his disciples after the resurrection: "I have chosen you twelve because I judged you worthy to be my disciples . . . And I sent them, of whom I was persuaded that they would be true apostles, into the world to proclaim to men in all the world the joyous message that they may know that there is (only) one God, and to reveal what future happenings there would be through faith in me, to the end that those who hear and believe may be saved; and that those who believe not may testify that they have heard it and not be able to excuse themselves saying, 'We have not heard.'"'[401]

The text certainly has no genetic relationship to the appearance to the Twelve and is wholly indebted to the theology of the unknown author, which is centred on the preaching of the one God and the mission of the twelve apostles to the whole earth. We might further ask whether the existing fragment is not part of a conversation between Jesus and his disciples after the resurrection, but this would similarly point to a later period.[402]

### 4.1.3.8  I Cor.15.6 (The appearance to more than 500 brethren)

*Preliminary comment*

I shall go on to give reasons for supposing that this appearance is a kind of foundation legend of the Christian community and can be

derived from the event which historically underlies Acts 2 (=
Pentecost).[403] We may start by reflecting that it is very improbable
that such an event before more than 500 people should otherwise
have left no traces. Moreover Paul emphasizes that those concerned
can still be asked questions about it; only a few of them have died. So
he presupposes that they have a function as witnesses corresponding
to his own, which is also significant for the Christians in Corinth.
Does that not tell in favour of the universal significance of this event
in early Christianity?

*Analysis of Acts 2.1–13: redaction and tradition*

The section can be divided into two parts: vv.1–4 describe speaking
in tongues, vv.5–13 a linguistic miracle.

Verses 1–4 contain many elements of Lukan language. The mode
of expression of vv.2f. is assimilated to the Sinai theophanies (cf.
Ex.19.16–19; Deut.4.11–12). For vv.3f. cf. especially Num.11.25.
At other places, too, Luke imitates the LXX. His hand may further be
seen in the sevenfold 'and' (listing items one after another) used in the
report. The following parallelization also suggests Lukan revision:

A    And suddenly a sound came from heaven (v.2)
A1   and there appeared to them tongues, distributed (v.3)
B    like the rush of a mighty wind (v.2)
B1   as of fire (v.3)
C    and filled all the house where they were sitting (v.2)
C1   and resting on each one of them (v.3).

Verses 5–13 are shaped by Lukan language; here the Lukan 'and'
(vv.1–4) is redactionally replaced by 'but' (vv.5,6,7,12,13).

Read straight through at the redactional level, the text reports a
linguistic miracle at the Feast of Pentecost after the death and
resurrection/ascension of Jesus. If the concrete detail 'Pentecost'[404]
already indicates tradition, similarly tensions in the text suggest
elements of tradition. We shall have to ask whether here Luke has
merely worked two traditions together or whether the disparate
elements go back to Luke's own construction, with which he
expands and transforms an existing tradition.

The event depicted in vv.1–4 takes place in a house (v.2: a
reference back to the upper room in Acts 1.13?); the one that follows
(vv.5–13) evidently in the open air.

Within vv.5–13 the list in vv.9–11 holds up the development and because of the many concrete details and its character as a list certainly derives from a source. As this material is well worked into vv.5–13 in both content and language, the whole section vv.5–13 may have been shaped by Luke at a sitting. Other indications strengthen this impression: vv.2–4 can stand independently, whereas vv.5ff. in the demonstrative pronouns of vv.6a and 7b presuppose the section vv.1–4. The accusation of drunken talk or babbling in v.13 does not fit very well with the miraculous gift of being able to speak in foreign languages which can be understood, and is probably the original conclusion to vv.1–4. The statement in v.4 that the disciples spoke in 'other tongues' is ambiguous. If we regard 'other' as redactional (and there is good reason to do so, because it was the only way in which the author of Acts could connect the miracle of the languages with the story of a glossolalia), then behind the miracle of languages as described in the present context of Acts there is a speaking in tongues corresponding to that in I Cor.14. In that case, vv.1–4 (and v.13) report the tradition, which evidently belongs with the concrete note of time, i.e. 'Pentecost', of an ecstatic experience of the disciples of Jesus (in a house?), and Luke was the first to interpret it in terms of a miracle of tongues.

In its context, the present section has the following function: the report of the disciples being filled with Holy Spirit translates Jesus' promise of Acts 1.8 into action. It is no coincidence that the subsequent speech of Peter (vv.14–40) begins with the outpouring of the Holy Spirit (vv.17–18). This is from now on a characteristic of being a Christian (cf. Acts 8.14–24; 19.1–7).

Along with describing the receiving of the Spirit, Luke's purpose may also have been to express the Pentecost event as a miracle of tongues. The Lukan conviction of the universal scope of Christianity underlies the equipping the members of the new movement with the languages of all other peoples by the Holy Spirit on the very day of the founding of the Christian religion.

*The historical nucleus behind Acts 2 as an appearance to more than 500 brethren*

Paul himself attests the phenomenon of glossolalic speech. He claims for himself in I Cor.14.18 that he speaks in tongues more than the Corinthians,[405] and in I Thess.5.19 ('do not quench the spirit')[406]

seems to give his community formal encouragement to glossolalic or
ecstatic discourse.[407]

Glossolalia[408] generally is incomprehensible ecstatic discourse –
in the world view of Paul, the language of angels (I Cor.13.1 [cf. II
Cor.12.4]), to which I Cor.14 provides a vivid parallel: glossolalia is
incomprehensible (vv.2,16,23), ecstatic (v.23)[409] speech, but it can
be translated, and if it is, its content is edifying (vv.4f.,26) and
instructive (v.19). Either the person speaking in tongues himself or
herself translates (v.13), or another member of the community
(v.27). For example, Paul has both the gift of speaking in tongues and
that of prophecy (vv.6,18f.). In general, glossolalia and prophecy
belong more closely together than appears at first sight. They are
regarded as a spiritual gift (I Cor.14.1), relate to divine secret
knowledge (I Cor.13.2; 14.2) and are both ecstatic phenomena (I
Cor.14.32: 'the spirits of prophets are subject to prophets').[410]
Glossolalia is translated, prophecy interpreted (I Cor.14.29; cf.
12.10).[411] In Palestinian Christianity there are comparable phenomena in TestJob 48–52[412] (these chapters, i.e. 46–53, are a genuine
part of the writing and in no way a secondary Christian interpretation[413]) and in the prophesying daughters of Philip (Acts 21.8f.). (I
presuppose that here glossolalic phenomena play a role.) So a similar
event is quite conceivable in Jerusalem, and the glossolalia reported
in the tradition underlying Acts 2.1–4 (13) is historically quite
plausible.[414] Probably this glossolalic event took place at the
Pentecost after the Passover when Jesus died,[415] and might be
identical[416] with the appearance to more than 500 brethren (I
Cor.15.6).[417]

The number 'more than 500 brethren' is to be understood as 'an
enormous number',[418] i.e. not taken literally. (Who could have
counted?) As the place of the appearance, 'the whole house' (Acts
2.2) is in any case suspect of being Luke's redaction;[419] there is no
contradiction here, so that the assumption of intermediaries in
handing down the tradition, to explain the tension between the
'more than 500' and the place of the appearance, 'in the house', is
superfluous.[420] Certainly it can be objected to the thesis of a genetic
connection between the two traditions behind I Cor.15.6 and Acts
2.1–11 that: 'The development from a christophany (viz. like I
Cor.15.6) to this theophany is unimaginable, especially as the Spirit
is not mentioned in the earlier version of the Easter
christophanies.'[421] But at any rate John 20.21f. is evidence of the
connection between christophany and the giving of the Spirit, and, as

has been demonstrated above, the features of the theophany have probably been introduced into Acts 2 at a redactional stage (the glossolalia may be regarded as a traditional substratum of the story).

In general the above objection fails methodologically, since it draws too far-reaching conclusions from the lack of any mention of the Spirit. For the decisive question is not whether the Spirit is explicitly mentioned at any point, but whether the the Spirit is essentially *presupposed and thought of* by the New Testament witnesses. And for historical reasons there can be no doubt about that.[422]

But there is no reason for a split into two traditions which are strictly to be distinguished – a christophany on the one hand (I Cor. 15.6) and the giving of the Spirit on the other (Acts. 2. 1–4) – since for Paul from the beginning Christ is identical with the Spirit. The presence of Jesus is actually experienced in the ecstatic event of Easter. Latently, and by the nature of the phenomenon, the identification of Christ with the Spirit is already given. Paul later conceptualizes it. So in I Cor. 15.6, at least in content the apostle's view is the same as that of Luke and/or the tradition which Luke has used in Acts 2.1–4: through an ecstatic experience, human beings become capable of testifying to faith.

New Testament scholars have long been agreed that Spirit and Christ in Paul[423] are at least partially identical.[424] This can be illustrated from a Pauline text.

In Romans 8.9 ('But you are not in the flesh, you are the Spirit, if the Spirit of God really dwells in you. Anyone who does not have the Spirit of Christ does not belong to him'), the Spirit of God and the Spirit of Christ are used as complete equivalents to describe what fills Christians. In the context of Rom.8.9f. the Spirit of God dwells in Christians (v.9), Christ is in Christians (v.10) and the Spirit of the one who has raised Jesus from the dead dwells in Christians (v.11). However, in thus binding the Spirit to God – just as he bound ecstasy to God in II Cor.12 – Paul is preventing any autonomy of those who bear the Spirit and thus understanding the gift of the Spirit as a sheer gift. That does not alter the fact that Spirit (of God) and Christ stand side by side in parallel and are ultimately identical (cf. also the way in which the formulae that appear in Paul's writings outside Rom.8, 'in Christ' [Gal.3.28 etc.] and '[in] the Spirit' (Gal.5.25 etc.] correspond).

'The Spirit works like a "power" in the very different forms which appear in the community and of which the apostle traces the emergence in himself. The visions and auditions indicate to the visionary that the Spirit is none other than the present Lord who continues to be at work in the community and makes his power known in the most varied ways. Only the one to whom the Lord himself has appeared in the Spirit, the one to whom the Lord speaks in revelations and visions, can utter the identification "The Lord is the Spirit". The Holy Spirit, the emergence of the power of the Holy Spirit in visions, revelations, healings, the discernment of spirits, driving out of demons, authority over evil beasts and over the elements is the form of the presence of the Lord in the intermediate period until his return.'[425]

The partial identity between Spirit and Christ in Paul indicated above confirms what I have been saying about the conversion/call of Paul, in which Paul saw Jesus as a pneumatic heavenly being. Against this it certainly could be argued that Paul never designates the Exalted One who appeared to him *explicitly* as *pneuma* or attributes the vision to the working of the *pneuma*.[426] But is not I Cor. 15 with its reference to the spiritual body of the Exalted One (v.45) an answer to the question of what figure of the Risen Lord Paul saw before Damascus?[427]

Furthermore, we can follow Ernst von Dobschütz[428] in referring to the connections between Spirit and Christ in Revelation and the Gospel of John: 'The apocalyptist introduces his writing as a revelation of Jesus Christ which God gave him to show his servants what would happen soon. But then it is "in the Spirit" that he sees all the visions. It is Christ who commissions him to send the seven letters in which the formula constantly recurs, "He that has ears to hear, let him hear what the Spirit says to the churches." Similarly the two notions also run side by side in the farewell discourses of the Gospel of John: the Lord promises to return to his disciples and to show himself to them (16.16ff.; 14.3,18f.,21,23,28), and on the other hand he promises to send the Paraclete to them in his stead (15.26; 16.7ff.; 14.16f.,26)' (34f.). 'So one must always keep in mind here the variation in the notions, which have not yet been forced into a formula' (ibid).[429]

Thus the question is not whether christophanies and experiences of the Spirit are identified in a theological, didactic way, but whether from a historical and phenomenological perspective, in the early period the experience of Christ was experience of the Spirit, and being moved by the Spirit was being touched by Christ. Those, for example, who follow Jacob Kremer in explaining the nearness of the Spirit to Christ by the fact that 'the Kyrios is at work in the church through the Holy Spirit',[430] and want to use that for an argument against the identification of the appearance to the more than 500 with 'Pentecost', overlook the fact that such a statement already has a theological and

didactic character and does not take account of the historical-
phenomenological level at all.[431]

Intermediary conclusion: the conjecture made at the beginning that
the appearance to more than 500 brethren is identical with the event
described by the substratum of tradition in Acts 2 may be said to be a
plausible one. In that case we would have an enthusiastic experience of
a great crowd of people, which was seen as an encounter with Christ.
Given the unusual character of such an event one may think it quite
possible that the act which Luke describes may be called the hour of
the church's birth. The locality would then be Jerusalem, because here
above all it was possible for so many people to meet – e.g. at a festival.

Precisely how are we to imagine and understand such an
appearance to 'more than 500 brethren'? There are no references to
the historical context similar to those that we have from their past in
the case of Peter and Paul to help us to understand. But perhaps
conclusions from research into mass psychology may help us here.

Gustav le Bon arrived at the following insight ninety years ago:[432]

People differ from one another most in intelligence, morality and
ideas, and least in animal instinct and emotions. Therefore the power
of the mass is the greater, the more its members resemble one another,
since the things in which they differ are for the moment put on one side.
They then possess a kind of communal soul in which the capacities for
understanding and personalities or the individuals become blurred
and the unconscious properties prevail (13f.). Le Bon further
observes: 'The masses are roughly in the position of a sleeper whose
capacity for thought has for the moment been removed, so that in his
spirit images of the most extreme vigour arise, but quickly vanish
away once reflection has a say' (43). Everything that stimulates the
imagination of the masses is said to appear in the form of a moving,
clear image which needs no interpretation (44).

Here one could say that the members of a mass have a formally
infectious influence on one another.[433] Le Bon cites the following
instructive example of this infectious influence:

> 'Before St George appeared to all the crusaders on the walls of Jerusalem he
> was first certainly perceived by only some of them. Through influence and
> transference the miracle thus proclaimed was immediately accepted by all.
> Thus there came about the process of collective hallucinations which are so
> frequent in history and seem to have classical characteristics of
> authenticity, as here we have appearances which were noted by thousands
> of people' (23f.).

Paul Wilhelm Schmiedel[434] refers with good reason to the mass visions of Thomas à Becket[435] and Savonarola[436] after their deaths as analogies to the appearance to the 'more than 500'. Here it should be evident that in the case of all the phenomena mentioned we have psychological facts, but that their significance and truth-content has not as yet been stated. Just as God's Word can appear in human speech without being absorbed in it, so too a psychological event may be the human context of an appearance of the divine Spirit. History or psychology and theology relate to each other, since they relate to different aspects of the one reality, but they cannot be reduced to each other. Here we are first of all concerned with the historical aspect.

*Conclusion*: The appearance before the 'more than 500' as a historical phenomenon can plausibly be represented as mass ecstasy which took place in the early period of the community. Given the nature of mass psychology, the stimulus towards it may have been provided by one or more individuals. Again that fits well with what has been worked out so far, namely that at least a first appearance took place to Peter (and the Twelve). Here we may pursue this notion just a little further: Peter saw the crucified Jesus alive (as did the Twelve). They also spoke of it, for example, at the next great festival (after the Passover at which Jesus died) in Jerusalem, the Jewish Feast of Weeks (= Pentecost), on which many festival pilgrims met. (Indeed it was such a festival which first made possible the appearance to a large number of people.) This preaching and the recollections of Jesus which were generally present formally led to religious intoxication and an enthusiasm which was experienced as the presence of Jesus, indeed as the presence of the Risen Christ as Peter had seen him. The appearance to the 'more than 500', at which those who had previously had visions were also present, brought together and confirmed all the previous individual experiences and thus gave the group an incomparable thrust.[437]

> There is no need to claim here that this is the only way in which the events may have taken place. But it is claimed that these reflections have developed a historical notion of the event which is appropriate to the sources and the conclusions that can be derived from them.

In retrospect, and with historical appropriateness, Luke spoke of this as the 'hour of the birth of the church'[438] and – similarly with theological justification – he interpreted the ecstasy as a capacity to speak comprehensibly in foreign languages, for the message represented by Jesus meant something to all people. Had there been no more than ecstasy and intoxication, Christianity would have had no chance of survival and could not have asserted itself. But also, theologically speaking, it would not have remained faithful to its task of addressing God's saving word to human beings in comprehensible language.

### 4.1.3.9 I Cor.15.7 (The appearance to James)

This appearance is described as follows in the Gospel of the Hebrews[439] in Jerome (c.347–419/20), *de viris inlustribus*, the first Christian 'literary history':[440]

> 'The Gospel called according to the Hebrews which was recently translated by me into Greek and Latin, which Origen frequently uses, records after the resurrection of the Saviour: And when the Lord had given the linen cloth to the servant of the priest, he went to James and appeared to him. For James had sworn that he would not eat bread from that hour in which he had drunk the cup of the Lord until he should see him risen from among them that sleep. And shortly thereafter the Lord said: Bring a table and bread! And immediately it is added: he took the bread, blessed it and brake it and gave it to James the Just and said to him: My brother, eat your bread, for the Son of man is risen from among them that sleep.'[441]

The text has the following peculiarities relating to James: (a) James is the first witness to the resurrection. (b) Already *before* Easter James belonged to the community. (c) The focal point of the text is the release of James from a vow, not the reality of the resurrection of Jesus or a christophany.[442] Perhaps here the vow is modelled on Peter's promise to go with his Lord to death (Mark 14.31). If James had fulfilled the vow while Peter was known to have broken it, the first testimony would emphatically have to be attributed to James. (d) However, little can be traced of any *direct* rivalry with other apostles or Peter (in the text) despite (c); indeed neither Peter nor other disciples are mentioned at all.

Thus the text is already a long way from historical reality: 'James no longer needs to fight for his position; his victory is complete. He has been recognized as the first and supreme witness to the Risen Christ, the most important bearer of the tradition, also and particularly over against Peter and the Twelve.'[443] James (and not Jesus) stands at the centre, and the fact that he was not one of Jesus' disciples during Jesus' lifetime is forgotten.

Furthermore, the attestation to the report is late. Its basis is a New

Testament tradition of the eucharist which 'has been transformed into a personal legend to glorify James'.[44] Apart from the fact that Jesus appeared to James, the text gives us no reliable information of any kind. Rather, the tradition in the Gospel of the Hebrews serves to enable admirers of James in the second and third generations to claim the first appearance for James rather than Cephas.[445] Similarly, in the Johannine circle the protophany is indirectly stated by the narrative to have been to the Beloved Disciple rather than to Peter (John 20.3–8), in that it is explicitly said that the Beloved Disciple beat Peter in the race to the tomb (see below, 152f.).

It follows from all this that the report of the Gospel of the Hebrews is to be understood exclusively in literary apologetic terms and has no genetic relationship to the historical vision of James (see above, 37).

Only vague conjectures are possible about the historical background to this individual vision, which represents a kind of conversion of James. Because of I Cor.15.7 it is certain *that* James 'saw' his brother. (By comparison the vision 'to all' the apostles completely escapes our knowledge and therefore is not discussed here.) But this could primarily have been within the framework of the vision to the more than 500 brethren, which would then have been followed by an individual vision. It should be noted that James had no religious link with his brother during Jesus' lifetime. The presuppositions for a vision were therefore different from those in Peter's case. (Therefore this vision is not the same as an original revelation, since Peter's vision was known to James and existed beforehand.) That James later became the leader of the earliest community has more to do with the fact that he was a member of the family. In antiquity people thought in terms of family politics (cf. especially also the significance of the family in the Hasmonaean dynasty). Scholars have rightly envisaged a kind of caliphate in early Christianity as well.[446]

The account in the Gospel of the Hebrews was subsequently developed into a narrative on the basis of other already existing traditions of appearances, and certainly does not derive from a report by James or his immediate followers.

## 4.2 Mark 16.1–8: The proclamation of the risen Christ at the empty tomb

Now that we have analysed the details of the sources connected with the resurrection traditions from the Pauline letters, it is time to investigate other reports in New Testament and early Christian texts which have not yet been discussed. We begin with the earliest narrative, Mark 16.1–8, and then go on to analyse the Gospels of Matthew, Luke and John.

## 4.2.1 *Introduction*

The present pericope is remarkable in a number of ways: the *first* problem that it poses relates to its position at the end of the Gospel. The question arises: how can a Gospel have ended with the statement 'for they were afraid' (v.8)? Now attempts have long been made to reconstruct the original ending to the Gospel of Mark. It is presupposed, in view of the fact that a variety of endings to the Gospel were supplied in the second century (see 26f. above), and that the parallels Matthew and Luke supplemented the Mark that they had before them, which extended as far as 16.8, that the original ending to Mark was broken off at a very early stage (through the loss of a page or by a deliberate excision). That would certainly solve the problem discussed here. However, in the face of all supplements, for methodological reasons, first of all we must make an attempt to understand the Gospel of Mark as it has come down to us in its present form, however many problems that may present. Speculations about lost parts may only begin if there can be no agreed interpretation of the parts which are certainly 'authentic'. Moreover, it is often forgotten that if a page was lost, it must have been lost from the very first copy. For the later the damage is supposed to have taken place in the process of tradition, the more we would expect that the authentic long conclusion to Mark would have been preserved.

The *second* problem lies in the content of what Mark reports. If the women did not obey the command of the angel, as v.8 says, how did the message of the resurrection then reach the disciples and Peter? On the other hand, it is certain that the Gospel of Mark was read by Christians. In that case, we have to conclude that even if there seems to be something historically wrong at this point, nevertheless the message as the author meant it may have been clear to the readers of the Gospel. In other words, the intention of the implied historical contradiction in v.8 must be noted in the context of the text as a whole.

Therefore, as we go through the text for the first time it is important to see what Mark wanted to say to his readers. At a second reading, on the presuppositions of the results of the first reading, we shall investigate the underlying tradition, and in a third reading any historical facts that it may be possible to reconstruct.

### 4.2.2  Redaction

[1] As in 15.42, a note of time introduces the story ('sabbath' takes up 'day before the sabbath' [15.42]). The note of time in v.1 is then repeated once again in v.1 (on the first day after the sabbath' [*mia ton sabbaton*]). The pronoun 'him' (*auton*) instead of 'Jesus' is not enough to suggest a genetic connection with the previous unit at the stage of the tradition (cf. Acts 7.54). Rather, 'him' at the redactional level indicates a close interlocking with the previous passage. The names of the women take up those from Mark 15.40 and 15.47. In all three cases Mary Magdalene comes at the head. Mark evidently thought that this was the same group around Mary Magdalene. As so far there had been no mention of these women disciples of Jesus in his Gospel, he adds in v.41 that they had already followed Jesus and served him in Galilee (cf. Mark 1.31). In addition he points out that other women, too, had gone with Jesus to Jerusalem. This gives rise to a hope among the readers that their loyalty to Jesus will be stronger than that of the disciples.[447]

Given the above-mentioned considerations on the function of lists of women, we must raise the question of the relationship between them in the history of the tradition. In the context, 15.40 gives the impression of being isolated. The confession of the centurion under the cross (15.39) is the climax, and the list of women (15.40) with an explanation (15.41) looks like a supplement. As Mark certainly formulated v.41, we might try also to derive v.40 from him and, following Ludger Schenke,[448] formulate the hypothesis that he derived the names from the tradition of Mark 16.1 and 15.47. The reason for this is that the mention of the three women by name in Mark 15.40 ('Mary Magdalene, Mary, the mother of James the younger and of Joses, and Salome')[449] agrees with Mark 16.1 and 15.47: Mary Magdalene, Mary and Salome. By contrast, the surnames of the Maries differ in 15.47; 16.1, which may point to independent traditions. (This confirms the above theory of the dependence of Mark 15.40 on the other two lists of women.) In other words, we have mentions of women in the tradition for both the passion story in 15.47 and the story about the tomb in 16.1. However, it is to be doubted whether the women from 15.47 were connected with the tradition of the burial of Jesus. Rather, Mark found their names in the passion tradition and put them at this point in order to make a better transition to 16.1–8.

'Bought' (v.1) takes up 'bought' in 15.46. The planned anointing recalls 14.3–9 (the anointing of Jesus by the [anonymous] woman[450] in Bethany). There she did it 'for the burial' (14.8). By again citing the motif of anointing from 14.3–9 in connection with the women, Mark frames the account of the passion with narratives which have similar motives. Other examples for such Markan frameworks[451] are: 1,21–28 to 6.1–6 (miracle); 6.30–44 to 8.1–9 (story of the feeding); 8.22–26 to 10.46–52 (healing of the blind); 15.40–41 to 15.47 (list of women).

[2] 'Tomb' relates to the same word in 15.46. With 'when the sun had risen'[452] cf. 'when evening had come' (15.42): nightfall had prevented the anointing of Jesus. The notes of time, 'very early' and 'when the sun had risen', are not in tension, as is sometimes said. Cf. the passages in Mark with a twofold indication of time: 1.32, 35; 4.35; 10.30; 13.24; 14.12, 30, 43; 15.42. That one could not buy unguents in the morning before sunrise does not disturb the narrator: the all-important thing is to get the women to the tomb.

[3] 'Stone' and 'door of the tomb' pick up the same words from 15.46. The question of the women about who can roll away the stone for them is answered by the next verse.

[4] The explanation that the stone was great heightens the magnitude of the act performed by the figure who appears in the next verse:

[5] He is a young man in a white robe who sits in the tomb. For the figure of the young man cf. II Macc.3.26,33 (two young men in splendid garments, who meet the temple robber Heliodorus) and Gospel of Peter 9.36: two young men descend from heaven in the splendour of light; for 'white' cf. Mark 9.3; Rev.7.13f. Matthew 28.2 then explicitly identifies the young man as an angel.

In the present context the young man in the white garments (cf. Mark 9.3),[453] unlike the young man of Mark 14.51, is of course a heavenly figure. (Thus in Tobit 5.14 the angel Raphael is called a 'young man'.) The whole scene is a kind of epiphany. The 'sitting on the right hand' gives the message of the young man emphasis and confirms it, as right is the correct, lucky side (cf. John 21.6 etc.) and as 'sitting' evidently expresses the authority with which the young man speaks (cf. Dan.7.9; Rev.21.5).[454]

Linguistically, the reaction of the women, their amazement (not at the empty tomb but at the angel), has Markan colouring. (The verb *ekthambein* ['amaze'] occurs in the New Testament only in Mark: 9.15; 14.33; 16.5, 6 [cf. also Mark 1.27; 10.24, 32].) So this passage is clearly a Markan theologoumenon leading to the theme which will stand in the foreground up to v.8.

[6] 'Amazed' (*ekthambeisthe*) takes up the same word from v.5. 'Jesus of Nazareth, who was crucified' refers back at the redactional stage to the passion narrative (Mark 14–15) and the predictions of the passion (Mark 8.31; 9.31; 10.34).[455] The message of the young man is that Jesus has been raised (*egerthe*). It corresponds to Jesus' own prediction: 8.31; 9.31; 10.34. The reference to the empty tomb ('he is not here') underlies the factuality of Jesus' resurrection. Cf. in 15.44 the emphasis on the factuality of his death. But in the narrower context the tendency of the text should be noted: the statement 'Jesus has been raised' comes first; 'only then does the empty tomb come into view: Jesus has been raised – he is not here – so the tomb is empty'.[456] Really the women do not discover the empty tomb at all. 'Nor can their amazement be attributed to this discovery, but only to the unexpected encounter with the angel.'[457]

At the same time, however, a warning must be given against an excessive readiness to dismiss historical arguments, since as Mark understands it, the empty tomb is a key piece of evidence.[458] In the understanding of Mark and the tradition, the resurrection of Jesus necessarily involves thinking of the tomb as empty.

[7] The verse contains the charge to the women to tell the disciples and Peter[459] that Jesus will go before them into Galilee. The young man continues: 'There you will see him, as he has told you.' This is an explicit reference back to Mark 14.28 ('But after I am raised up, I will go before you into Galilee'), which indicates the redactional character of both verses.[460] 'In the renewed reference to Galilee there is a deliberate recollection of the beginning of the proclamation and thus the beginning of the Gospel . . . So XVI.1–8 has the purpose not only of giving a meaningful conclusion to the passion narrative but at the same time of providing an adequate ending to the composition of the Gospel as a whole.'[461] Thus, as in Mark 10.32, Jesus' going before refers to the Christian way which has to be taken in his footsteps. Here Mark stands in the earliest Christian tradition, in which the 'way' has become a technical term for the Christian way (cf. Acts 9.2).[462]

The other two possibilities of interpreting v.7 are to interpret it in terms of the parousia[463] or as a symbolic understanding of Galilee as the 'land of the Gentiles, which is symbolic of the world-wide mission'.[464]

[8] The flight of the women recalls the flight of the disciples in 14.50. Their fear is described twice in the present verse (cf. the analogous duplication in Mark 1.32). It leads to their telling no one anything, which amounts to disobeying the command of the young man. This is matched by the failure of the disciples throughout the Gospel of Mark, so that Mark 16.1–8 is the last report of a failure of those who were with Jesus – this time the women.[465] 'The flight of the women from the tomb, despite the resurrection of Jesus, despite the revelation of the angel, is probably the deepest failure of disciples that the Gospel of Mark relates – and does so at the end of the whole text.'[466] The sentence 'for they were afraid' which concludes the Gospel is similarly Markan: compare only 9.6: 'They were full of fear.' Reference should also be made to Gen.18.15 LXX (cf.45.3) as an example of how 'for they were afraid' could stand at the end of a sentence and a story. Certainly Mark 16.8 is both unusual and surprising as the conclusion to a pericope and a Gospel, but it is quite conceivable (cf. Mark 16.51b–62 [Matt.14.33 differs] and the alteration of Mark 16.8 in Matt.28.8). Moreover v.8b is a reference back to the fear of the women, which has already been depicted in a vivid way. So 'it is hard to dispute that the text as it stands is probably understandable and displays an effective rhythm of language'.[467]

One can attempt to explain further the aim of Mark 16.8 as the deliberate ending to the Gospel of Mark.[468] According to Andreas Lindemann, Mark, 'by having the women – and the readers – experiencing Jesus' resurrection only through the word of the *neaniskos* makes it clear that this resurrection is in no way the subject of a factual report but the object or, better, the content, of proclamation directed towards faith.'[469] Or: if the women are silent, all that follows depends on Jesus showing himself.

Mark 16.1–8 is thus a meaningful end to the Gospel, in the way in which it vividly illustrates the kerygma of the cross and resurrection (v.6) which has been clad in the dramatic episode 16.1–8. Similarly, the whole Gospel can be understood as a demonstration of the kerygma (= proclamation as narrative).

### 4.2.3 Traditions

In the redactional analysis v.7 was defined as Markan[470] – although corresponding historical knowledge underlies I Cor.15.5 – and so was v.8b ('they were afraid'). Furthermore vv.3 and 4 may be a product of Mark's narrative skill, though of course that does not exclude the possibility of an underlying tradition. The date 'the third day' presupposed in v.1 certainly comes from the tradition. Here we cannot exclude the possibility that the date serves to justify the church's celebration of Easter (cf. Acts 20.7; Rev.1.10; I Cor.16.2 [?]). Behind the intention to anoint the body, which could be redactional and motivated by the account, there could be the tradition of a lamentation of Jesus by the women,[471] cf. Luke 23.27. One result of the analysis of the redaction was that the women (Mary Magdalene, Mary, Salome) belong in the tradition of the story about the tomb.

At this point we need to clarify two questions:

(a) Was Mark 16.1–8*[472] an element of a pre-Markan passion narrative?

(b) How can we define Mark 16.1–8* in form-critical terms?

On (a): The following reasons tell against Mark 16.1–8* being an element of a pre-Markan passion narrative and for the text being an originally independent unit: 1. In Mark 16.1 and 15.47 there are two different lists of women; 2. Mark 16.1 is a new beginning; 3. references to the Old Testament, which are frequent in the passion narrative, are absent from Mark 16.1–8; 4. Mark 16.1–8 and the story of the burial (Mark 15.25–27) do not fit well together. In the story of the burial, the burial of Jesus seems to have been completed. In addition, the intention of anointing the body which motivates the joureny of the women to the tomb on Easter morning (Mark 16.1) is in conflict with this, since such a plan presupposes that the body has not been anointed and therefore that the burial is only provisional.

Now occasionally it is asserted, with reference to the parallels between the Markan and Johannine passion narratives, that at the level of tradition Mark 15.24–27 was connected with Mark 16.1–8.[473] But there are good reasons for supposing that the Johannine framework is dependent on the passion narrative in the Gospel of Mark;[474] thus the assertion is unconvincing.

*Conclusion*: Mark 16.1–8* was not an ingredient of a pre-Markan passion narrative, but a small unit which Mark worked in at this point.

On (b): to the attempt to define Mark 16.1–8* more closely in form-critical terms it could be objected that for want of comparative material and because of uncertainties in the reconstruction of any earlier material, such an enterprise is *a priori* hopeless. But too often such scepticism is connected with approaches which no longer show any interest in real history – for whatever reason. 'Faced with a vapourizing of concrete history one should therefore almost insist on a form-critical analysis of the text.'[475]

In the form-critical definition of Mark 16.1–8* which now follows I shall primarily keep to the classical analysis by Rudolf Bultmann.[476] He regards v.7 as redactional (see above, 113) and the pre-Markan piece as isolated from the passion narrative. In terms of form he describes it as a 'quite secondary formation' (284), 'an apologetic legend' (290), as emerges from Mark 16.8 ('they said nothing to anyone'), a statement which 'can originally have referred only to the discovery of the the empty tomb and can "give an answer to the question why the women's story of the empty tomb remained unknown for so long"'[477] (285). 'The point of the story is that the empty tomb proves the resurrection: the angel has no significance in himself, but simply plays the part of the *angelus interpres*' (290). Bultmann describes the structure of the story as 'impressive: the wondering of the women, v.3, the sight of the rolled-away stone and the appearance of the angel, vv.4f., the masterly formulated angelic message v.6 and the shattering impression in v.8' (286).

It has been objected to Bultmann's analysis that the 'envisaged historical situation of such apologetic ... remains unclear'.[478] However, this does not make sense. Matthew 28.15 attests that at the time of the composition of the Gospel of Matthew (and certainly also before that) Jews showed an interest in where Jesus' corpse had been put, and of course a proclamation of Jesus as the Risen One virtually provoked questions about his body from opponents or unbelievers. The basis reconstructed above by Bultmann therefore connects the Christian proclamation of the resurrection of Jesus with its consequences, the empty tomb, and thus in a twofold apology provides a smooth answer for all possible critics: vv.3–6 defend the fact of the resurrection and v.8 the authenticity of what is reported in vv.3–6. Now it has also been objected against Bultmann's analysis that 'The status of women in the ancient world was such that a story fabricated as proof or apology would not be based on the testimony of women.'[479] But first, the bond between Mark and the material in the tradition must be emphasized. And secondly, in the tradition the testimony of the women is only brought into play very hesitantly, since v.8 ('and they said nothing to anyone') presupposes that it long remained unknnown.

In my view, other attempts to trace the riddle of the tradition behind Mark 16.1–8[480] have failed.

According to Ludger Schenke, the original narrative (Mark 16.2, 5–6, 8a) 'of the journey of the women to the tomb on Easter morning . . . is an aetiological legend connected with the empty tomb of Jesus which was known and venerated in the earliest Christian community in Jerusalem. This legend was the basis for, and was told at, a cultic festival of the community in memory of and in solemn celebration of the resurrection of the Crucified One at least annually on the memorial day of Jesus's resurrection, at sunrise in or at the empty tomb.'[481] But a cultic celebration at the tomb of Jesus is not supported by any other source. The tomb was evidently unknown. It was only 'rediscovered' 300 years later, when it was needed.

'The fact that the tomb of Jesus was unknown and that at first people had no relics does not seem to have disturbed anyone for 300 years. On the other hand, one can detect from the tremendous power of the Turin shroud what would have happened had the tomb of Jesus with all its magic properties in fact been known. However, no one seems to have missed it. Of course people had the legends about the tomb, and the vanished Jesus could be identified without further ado with the heroes and god-men of the pagan past who had similarly vanished without a tomb. The tomb was only "rediscovered" when it was needed. That it was found under a temple of Venus as the "cave of salvation" in the year 326 CE, as Eusebius reports in his Life of Constantine (III, 25–30), could hardly be misunderstood in the politics of religion. The background was again a magical one, as is confirmed by the first representations of the tomb of Christ which appeared in art around 400 CE: they also appear on ampullae of pilgrims, which probably served apotropaic ends.'[482]

According to Martin Albertz the tradition behind Matt.16.1–8 in truth goes back to a christophany. It already degraded the christophany to an angelophany under the influence of the list in I Cor.15.3ff., which contains no account of women as witnesses to the resurrection.[483] The correct element in this thesis is that the appearance of an angel had greater significance than Bultmann was ready to note. The narrative indeed has traits of an epiphany story, even if Albertz's thesis of the repression of a christophany by an angelophany is a secondary hypothesis and the probability of it therefore cannot be demonstrated.

Elisabeth Schüssler Fiorenza similarly regards Mark 16.1–6,8a as a resurrection story in which the early Christian confession, 'Jesus the Nazarene who was executed on the cross is raised', was first of all revealed in an appearance to the women disciples of Jesus.[484] However, that is not a definition of form but a summary statement meant to be historical (see further below, 143f.).

Nevertheless, we must ask whether Bultmann's view of the angel as an interpreting angel is enough. Indeed, the angel does not just interpret but at the same time proclaims, and the women are terrified at his appearance. The tension between the kerygma of the resurrection and the empty tomb is evident in the hiatus between the angel of the proclamation and the empty tomb, between the terror of the women at the angel (and his message) and their intention to anoint the body. However, this qualification does not alter in any way the correctness of Bultmann's general verdict on Mark 16.1–8*: it is an apologetic legend with traits of an epiphany.

In addition to the form-critical definitions above, we may also develop from the pericope a proposal about the history of the tradition. At the beginning is the kerygma (v.6) as it is confirmed by the writings of Paul (see above, 35f.). From there the narrative of the tomb develops with apologetic intent. It was not strange that women should have been the main figures in this legend, since the flight of the male disciples was an established fact. Now if the women were part of the passion narrative (cf. above, 110f., on Mark 15.7), because of the connection between death and resurrection in the Christian kerygma a need may also have been felt to relate how the women heard of the resurrection of Jesus. So on the basis of the kerygma an apologetic legend developed with women as recipients of the proclamation of the resurrection at the place where Jesus was buried.

That the creed of the death and resurrection of Jesus was connected with an appearance to Peter from the beginning follows indirectly from v.7. Here 'the disciples and Peter' appear in connection with seeing the risen Lord. That may relate to the old kergyma I Cor.15.1, in which Cephas and the Twelve are mentioned as the first witnesses to the appearance of the Risen Christ. (Note that v.7 has been inserted by Mark into the tradition, but earlier knowledge seems to have been preserved in the redaction.)

*Excursus: An analogy to the relationship between the appearance and the empty tomb from the history of religion*

In Book IV 14 of his *Histories*, Herodotus[485] reports the following about Aristeas of Proconnesus:

> 'Aristeas, they said, who belonged to one of the noblest families in the island, had entered one day into a fuller's shop, when he suddenly dropped down dead. Hereupon the fuller shut up his shop, and went to tell Aristeas' kindred what had happened. The report of the death had just spread through the town, when a certain Cyzicenian, lately arrived from Artaca (a harbour about five miles from Cyzicus), contradicted the rumour, affirming that he had met Aristeas on his road to Cyzicus, and had spoken with him. This man, therefore, strenuously denied the rumour; the relations, however, proceeded to the fuller's shop with all things necessary for the funeral, intending to carry the body away. But on the shop being opened, no Aristeas was found, either dead or alive. Seven years afterwards he reappeared, they told me, in Proconnesus, and wrote the poem called by the Greeks "The Arimaspeia", after which he disappeared a second time.'[486]

Herodotus is reporting a story from oral tradition ('they said'). What is analogous to the above definition of the death, location of the body and appearance of Jesus in this story is that despite the death, the body is not found where it was to be expected, and the dead person appeared to someone. Evidently supporters of Aristeas, who during his lifetime was perhaps a priest of Apollo, told this story after his death.[487] The primary thing was that he had 'appeared' to them. From that they inferred that his body could not be found. The story is a vivid example of how religious fantasy associates and draws 'conclusions'. How opponents possibly reacted to it may be indicated from Herodotus IV.94f. Herodotus reports about the Thracian tribe of the Getae, that they think that after death they go to the demon Zalmoxis. 'They believe that there is no other god than their own' (94.4). Now Herodotus has learned from the Greeks on the shores of the Hellespont and the Pontus that this Zalmoxis was a man, who deceived his fellow-countrymen as follows:

> 'The Thracians at that time lived in a wretched way, and were a poor ignorant race; Zalmoxis, therefore, who by his commerce with the Greeks, and especially with one who was by no means their most contemptible philosopher, Pythagoras, was acquainted with the Ionic

mode of life and with manners more refined than those current among his
countrymen, had a chamber built in which from time to time he received
and feasted all the principal Thracians, using the occasion to teach them
that neither he, nor they, his boon companions, nor any of their posterity
would ever perish, but that they would all go to a place where they would
live for ever in the enjoyment of every conceivable good. While he was
acting in this way, and holding this kind of discourse, he was constructing
an apartment underground into which, when it was completed, he
withdrew, vanishing suddenly from the eyes of the Thracians, who greatly
regretted his loss, and mourned over him as one dead. He meanwhile
abode in his secret chamber three full years, after which he came forth
from his concealment, and showed himself once more to his countrymen,
who were thus brought to believe in the truth of what he had taught them.
Such is the account of the Greeks' (95.2–5).[488]

The story is probably the reaction of opponents to the claims of
immortality advanced by Zalmoxis and his followers. There is a
similar criticism of Aristeas in the church father Gregory of
Nazianzus, who compares him with Trophonius and others who
hide in cells in order to deify themselves.[489] We may conjecture that
something similar was already said of him by his contemporaries, as
the above story against the followers of Zalmoxis indicates. And
finally it becomes clear why criticism of the empty tomb of Jesus was
not long in coming.

It seems to me that the thesis of Elias Bickermann must be
discussed once again.[490] He referred to the numerous stories from
Christian legends of the saints and Hellenism (including the story of
Aristeas related above), in which the empty tomb proved the rapture
of the person concerned. 'By contrast the resurrection is never
indicated nor proved by the disappearance of the body but exclusively by the appearance of the person who has come to life again'
(277). However, this sharp distinction may not help much for the
above narrative from Herodotus, in which Aristeas appears *and* the
tomb is empty. Moreover, according to the early Christians, rapture
or exaltation and resurrection are closely connected or even identical
(cf. Phil.2.6–11),[491] as Bickermann also stresses. For example, he
writes: 'Luke 1.33; Acts 5.31; John 3.10; 12.32, 34 ... also
occasionally use the word "exaltation" instead of "resurrection"
unconcernedly. For the one unconditionally presupposes the other
according to their faith' (281). Bickermann again sees correctly that
the first christophanies refer 'to the belief of the first disciples in the
immediate exaltation' (282). In the same passage he identifies this

with a rapture. However, there is a lack of clarity here, since raptures really presuppose not-dying,[492] whereas Jesus was exalted as the one who was crucified and dead. It was as such a figure that he appeared to Cephas (from heaven).

Bultmann was critical of Bickermann's article. But probably the disagreement between the two is only one of degree. Bickermann regards the story of the tomb as the story of a transportation to heaven and therefore puts it very early. Bultmann emphasizes its 'secondary apologetic character',[493] but this does not exclude the possibility that it was understood by Hellenistic Christians as Bickermann thinks. In other words, the disagreement is at the level of tradition, not over the history-of-religions question.

### 4.2.4 *Historical*

The visit of Mary Magdalene (with the other two women) to the tomb of Jesus on the day after the sabbath can hardly be said to be historical. Historical enquiry must be directed at the character of the underlying traditions. The source in our case is an apologetic legend with features like an epiphany which probably did not exist without the kerygma. Those who handed down these traditions 'concluded' from the message that the crucified one had risen that the tomb of Jesus was empty. The present story is as it were the product of a conclusion or a postulate. The story is first inferred from the 'dogma'.[494] Therefore in all honesty we can discover absolutely nothing from the story about what really happened in history.

## 4.3 The Easter stories in Matthew

### 4.3.1 *Introduction*

In his presentation of the Easter stories, in general Matthew bases himself on Mark's account and supplements this with two appearances of the Risen Lord (28.9f., to the women at the tomb; 28.16–20, to the eleven in Galilee), because the conclusion of Mark's Gospel (16.8) was as unsatisfactory for him as it was for Luke. Then he adds a story about the guards at the tomb which provides a framework for the narrative of the journey of the women to the empty tomb which follows Mark (for the question of its traditio-historical connection with Matt.28.2–4, see 129 below). I shall go on to investigate each of the units separately, combining the narratives about the guards at the tomb (Matt.27.62–66; 28.11–15). (They 'belong together like the two halves of a globe which, when fitted together, produce a perfect sphere'.[495]) First of all we shall look at the redaction, then at the tradition, and finally at the possible underlying historical facts.

### 4.3.2 *Matt.27.62–66; 28.11–15:*
### *The bribing of the guards at the tomb*

#### 4.3.2.1 Redaction

[62] The verse introduces the narrative with Matthaean vocabulary (cf. only 'gathered' in the Matthaean passion narrative: 26.3, 57; 27.17, 27; 28.12). The note of time 'next day' follows from the 'evening' of v.57. The 'Pharisees' appear only here in the passion narrative and reflect the real opposition in the time of Matthew. (The conflict with the official representatives of Judaism has become harsher than in the time before the Jewish War, cf. below on 28.13.) Strikingly, the session before Pilate takes place on the sabbath, not for historical reasons but because this is necessary for the narrative. The death of Jesus on the Friday and the resurrection or discovery of the empty tomb two days after his death, the day after the Sabbath, were given by the Markan tradition (cf. Mark 16.1).

[63] The high priests and Pharisees explicitly 'remember' in their speech to Pilate a saying of Jesus: 'That fraudster said, while he was still alive, "After three days I will rise again."' This is obviously not a reference to the predictions of the passion, where Matthew (16.21; 17.23; 20.19), contrary to Mark, which he had before him (8.31; 9.31; 10.34), each time alters 'after three days' to 'on the third day' (cf. I Cor.15.4), but to Matt.12.40: 'For as Jonah was three days and three nights in the belly of the whale, so will the Son of man be three days and three nights in the heart of the earth.' It keeping with that, Pharisees are present in the scene in Matt.12.38f., as they are in Matt.27.62. The divergent formula 'after three days' is evidently meant to recall this passage.

[64] The verse contains Matthaean linguistic colouring ('order'

takes up 'ordered' [27.58]). The Jewish leaders ask Pilate to have the tomb of Jesus watched: 'fraud' refers back to 'fraudster' in v.63. Verse 64c ('and the last fraud will be worse than the first') corresponds to Matt.12.45c: 'the last state of that man becomes worse than the first', i.e., if the disciples are left with their preaching of the resurrection, things will be even worse than they were with Jesus. (Note that Matt.12.45c is part of the scene which already underlies Matt.27.63.)

[65f.] These verses tell how Pilate yields to the request of the Jewish leaders. Then follows Matt.28.1–10, the pericope of the empty tomb and the appearance of Jesus to two women disciples (see below, 125ff.). After this, Matthew continues his account of the bribing of the guards by the tomb.

[28.11] 'While they were going' (*poreuomenon auton*) hangs in the air (surely a redactional seam). On the one hand the clause connects vv.10 and 11 in such a way as to suggest that vv.9f. and vv.11–15 took place at the same time. On the other hand, *poreuomenon* takes up 27.66 (*poreuthentes*). As is well known, *poreuomai* is a favourite word of Matthew's (cf. in the previous section 28.16,19). The watchers by the tomb themselves report to the Jewish leaders all that has happened, i.e. in fact about the resurrection of Jesus. So they know of this, just as it was clear to them that by his own testimony Jesus would rise after three days (27.63).

[12] The bribery of the guards recalls the bribery of Judas (26.15).

[13] This verse takes up 27.64. The soldiers are to spread the rumour that the disciples stole the body while they were asleep. But the Jewish authorities had already expressed this as their fear. Nevertheless, now that Jesus has really risen, they bribe the soldiers to spread this false information. (The anti-Jewish criticism here has intensified as much as in Matt.23.1–36, in comparison to Mark 12.37b–40 which he had in front of him.)

[14] This provides the necessary supplement for the soldiers' action. Should the governor hear that the soldiers have slept on watch – the watch had in fact been agreed with him (27.65) – the Jewish authorities would intervene with him on behalf of the soldiers.

[15] This verse concludes the story. The soldiers do what the Jewish authorities ask of them. The second half of the verse looks forward to Matthew's time: 'And this story has been spread among the Jews to this day.'

#### 4.3.2.2 Traditions

Verse 15b indicates that the tale of the theft of Jesus' body by the disciples was generally widespread among the Jews of Matthew's time and beforehand. Whether the details of the story told by Matthew are part of this is very questionable, since the portrait of the Jews is extremely negative and they even know of the resurrection of Jesus. In the middle of the second century, in his *Dialogue with the Jew Trypho*,[496] the apologist Justin also knows this Jewish claim (but does not mention the guards).

Hence the following history of the tradition is possible: Jews claimed that the body of Jesus had been stolen by the disciples. The Christians reacted *to this* with a story about the bribery of the guards at the tomb of the kind we have in Matthew – unless we are to assume that Matthew composed the whole scene.

Now on various occasions the theory has been put forward that the Jewish rumour virtually presupposes the recognition of the empty tomb.[497] We should not play off against that the 'temporal and spatial distance (viz. of the Matthaean text) to the historical situation',[498] since the conclusion from the empty tomb drawn in resurrection belief occurs very early in the Christian tradition. Certainly it is hard to understand how the (unbelieving) Jews could have come to think that the tomb had been empty otherwise than through this Christian tradition (at all events historical reasons can be ruled out, since Jesus did not have a regular burial [see above, 44f.]). In a similar way, the Jewish narrative of the rejection of Mary by her betrothed handed down by Origen (*Contra Celsum* I 28, 32), 'the mother of Jesus was rejected by the carpenter to whom she was betrothed because she had been convicted of adultery and had given birth by a soldier called Panthera' (*Contra Celsum* I, 32), pre-supposes the New Testament text Matt.1.19 and is not, say, an earlier tradition.

#### 4.3.2.3 Historical

Two historical judgments can be made on the facts:
  (a) The information about a theft of the body of Jesus is certainly historical, but not the theft itself, as Reimarus thought.[499] For the disciples did not know where Jesus was 'buried', and furthermore, because of their utter disappointment they would no longer have been in a position to perpetrate such a fraud.

(b) The tradition of the bribing of the guards cannot be taken seriously, because it too clearly has partisan features of Matthew or the Matthaean tradition. (The guards would have been convicting themselves had they confessed that they had slept at the tomb.)

### 4.3.3 Matt.28.1–10: The empty tomb and the appearance of Jesus to two women disciples

#### 4.3.3.1 Redaction and tradition

[1] This verse can be explained completely on the basis of Mark. The reason why only two women come to the tomb in Matthew (who are identical with those of Matt.27.61), whereas there were still three in Mark, is that here Matthew probably felt a tension between Mark 15.47 and 16.1 and smoothed it out accordingly. The women's intention in the Markan account, which is very striking – because it is unnecessary –, namely, to anoint the body in the tomb, and after three days at that, is absent from Matthew. The phrase 'to see the sepulchre' is to be explained as being influenced by Mark 15.47, since after the women have stayed by the tomb in Matt.27.61 (they 'sat opposite the sepulchre'), 'seeing the sepulchre' is quite remarkable.

[2–4] There is a tension between vv.2–4 and vv.5–8, where again Mark's account is a basis, for the tremendous events of vv.2–4 have no connection at all with the giving of the message in vv.5–8. Verses 2–4 depict the opening of the tomb by an angel from heaven, before whom the guards fall to the ground helpless, and in vv.5–8 the *message* of the resurrection is addressed by the same angel to the women, while what is narrated in vv.5–10 must have taken place while the soldiers were helpless. The fact that the guards were not terrified at the earthquake but at the appearance of the angel 'is the influence of Mark 16.5, where the women, to whom alone the angel appears, are terrified'.[500] By Matthew's insertion of vv.2–4 here the women indirectly 'are made witnesses to the very event of the resurrection ... in their presence, before their eyes, with the earthquake the angel descends and the stone is rolled away. The only thing that the evangelist does not mention is the emergence of Jesus from the tomb. He will have probably thought of it as having been

concealed by the dazzling splendour of the angel. (In the Eastern
view, light is the covering of the divine which blinds the eyes.)'[501]

## *The tradition behind Matt.28.2–4*

1. The event described in vv.2–4 has a parallel in the Gospel of Peter,
of which a lengthy fragment was discovered in 1886 in the tomb of a
Christian monk in Upper Egypt:

> 'The discovery was sensational. For up till then the existence of a Gospel
> of Peter was known from the tradition of the early church only by remarks
> made by Origen and Eusebius; however, they did not quote it, and this
> aroused the suspicion that they themselves had never read it. The only
> concrete thing that was known of it was the report of Eusebius (*Church
> History* VI.12) about Bishop Serapion of Antioch (c.200), who at first
> allowed the Gospel of Peter to be read in the church in the community of
> Rhossos at the request of its members, but after reading it himself banned
> it, explaining 'that while most of the Gospel is the true teaching of the
> Saviour, some commandments have been added'; that it was used by the
> heterodox; and that it especially supported the view of the Docetists.
> Serapion set down his criticism in a work from which Eusebius quotes.
> Since then the Gospel of Peter has been part of the Antilegomena.'[502]

The fragment (the whole of it is written in the first person, Peter is the
speaker [7.26; 14.60]) begins with the scene in which Paul washes his
hands. The hand-washing itself is not reported in the fragment, but it
can be inferred with some certainty from its beginning. Then follows
the request of Joseph of Arimathea for the body of Jesus, who in the
Gospel of Peter is called only 'the Lord' (2.3–5), the mockery (3.6–
9), crucifixion (4.10), inscription on the cross (4.11), dividing of the
garments (4.12), intercession of the criminal crucified with the Lord
for him (4.13f.), darkness (5.15), drinking gall and vinegar (5.16),
the last cry and death of the Lord (5.19), rending of the veil of the
temple (5.20), deposition from the cross (6.21), earthquake (6.21),
end of the darkness (6.22), burial (6.2f.), repentance of the Jews
(7.25), behaviour of Peter and the disciples (7.26f.), setting of guards
over the tomb (8.28–33), mass visit of the inhabitants of Jerusalem
to the tomb (9.34), resurrection (9.35–10.42), report of Pilate and
command to the soldiers to keep silent (11.43–49), the women and
the empty tomb (12.50–13.57), the return of the disciples to their
home (14.58f.), Peter, Andrew and Levi go fishing (14.60). Here the
fragment breaks off. On the basis of the parallels in the canonical

Gospels one can conjecture with some justification that there then followed an appearance of the 'Lord' by Lake Tiberias.

Now it has already been pointed out that after the opening of the tomb depicted in Matt.28.2 one really expects *as in the Gospel of Peter* the emergence of the revived body of Jesus:

> This is what Gospel of Peter 9.35–11.44 says of the resurrection: 'Now in the night in which the Lord's day dawned, when the soldiers, two by two in every watch, were keeping guard, there rang out a loud voice in heaven, [36]and they saw the heavens opened and two men come down from there in a great brightness and draw nigh to the sepulchre. [37]That stone which had been laid against the entrance to the sepulchre started of itself to roll and gave way to the side, and the sepulchre was opened, and both the young men entered in. [38]When now those soldiers saw this, they awakened the centurion and the elders – for they also were there to assist at the watch. [39]And whilst they were relating what they had seen, they saw again three men come out from the sepulchre, and two of them sustaining the other, and a cross following them, [40]and the heads of the two reaching to heaven, but that of him who was led of them by the hand overpassing the heavens.[503] [41]And they heard a voice out of the heavens crying, "Have you preached to those that sleep?", [42]and from the cross there was heard the answer, "Yes". [43]Those men therefore took counsel with one another to go and report this to Pilate. [44]And whilst they were still deliberating, the heavens were again seen to open, and a man descended and entered into the sepulchre.'[504]

In terms of source criticism (10.)41–42 must be regarded as secondary. This passage introduces (the journey of Christ to Hades and) the preaching to the dead (cf. I Peter 3.19f.; 4.6)[505] into the text.[506] (11.)44 has also been added later. The heavenly man is also needed for the discovery of the empty tomb (11.5–13.57).[507]

Grass asks a good question about Matthew's account: 'Were such powerful arrangements needed to roll away the stone and get rid of the guards so that the women could then see the empty tomb? Did Matthew think that the tomb was already empty before the angel or the earthquake opened it, as later church exposition in part assumed?'[508] We can hardly assume that. Rather, in the tradition of the angels used by Matthew the tomb opens so that the Jesus, now alive again, can get out.

A similar tradition underlies the *Ascension of Isaiah*[509] (AscIs). In a summary account of the fate of Jesus we read:

> III 13: 'that he was to be crucified together with criminals, and that he would be buried in a sepulchre, [14]and that the twelve who were with him

would be offended because of him, and the watch of the guards over the grave, [15]and the descent of the angel of the church which is in the heavens, whom he will summon in the last days; [16]and that the angel of the Holy Spirit and Michael, the chief of the holy angels, will open his grave on the third day, [17]and that the Beloved, sitting on their shoulders, will come forth and send out his twelve disciples, [18]and that they will teach to all the nations and every tongue the resurrection of the Beloved, and that those who believe on his cross will be saved, and in his ascension to the seventh heaven, whence he came.'[510]

Here, as in the Gospel of Peter and in the tradition presupposed in Matt.28.2, the idea is expressed that angels will open the tomb of Jesus on the third day and ascend with Jesus, brought to life again, into heaven. There is much to be said for supposing that the tradition is preserved in its purest in the Ascension of Isaiah (though this can also be because of the summary character of the notes to this effect) and that the Gospel of Peter and Matthew belong more closely together. For only in them do the guards play an important new role. (In the Ascension of Isaiah they are only mentioned.) The tradition underlying the Ascension of Isaiah is later than the tomb tradition in Mark, since the opening of the tomb by an angel (put in italics in the text), the emergence of Jesus and the ascension to the seventh heaven fuse the notion of the resurrection formally with the legend of the empty tomb (similarly the Codex Bobiensis, see below).

At this point two conjectures about the tradition behind Matt.28.2–4 need to be mentioned.

1. Within the framework of his understanding of the Easter event as a parousia event,[511] Hans Werner Bartsch attempts to reconstruct a christophany as the preliminary stage to the present appearance of an angel in Matt.28.2f. Referring to Rev.1.13–17; 18.3, Bartsch recognizes in Matt.28.2–4 an apocalyptic colouring: 'If we loosen ... the link with the legend of the empty tomb completely, it is not the angel of the Lord who descends from heaven to open the grave, but we have an account of an appearance of the Son of Man – Lord.'[512] He later continues: 'If we insert Peter as the first one to receive an appearance into the fragment of Matthew, something like the following account of an appearance results: "And behold, there was a great earthquake; for the Son of Man/Lord descended from heaven, and his countenance was like lightning and his face like snow. For fear of him I, Peter, quaked, and fell at his feet as one dead. But the Lord came and said, 'Do not fear'"' (ibid.).

*Criticism*: Matthew 28.2–4 cannot be regarded as an independent Easter tradition, since in terms of the history of the tradition it is extremely improbable that an angelophany should have developed from an individual christophany in the course of the tradition. Matthew would hardly have suppressed a tradition of the Easter experience of Peter; indeed in Matt.16.17–19 he explicitly emphasizes the pre-eminent role of this disciple. Rather, Bartsch's attempt at a reconstruction indicates the aporias we get into if we attempt to understand Matt.28.2–4 as an originally independent Easter narrative.[513]

2. Nikolaus Walter (see the previous note) thinks that the remnant of an Easter narrative has been preserved in Matt.27.62–66/ 28.2–4,11–15, which attests a third type alongside the narratives of the Easter appearances and the narrative of the discovery of the empty tomb, namely a narrative of the event of the resurrection itself. According to Walter this type includes not only the narrative of the Gospel of Peter but also the account in the Codex Bobiensis (= Old Latin translation of the New Testament from the fourth/fifth century) which has been preserved as a variant to Mark 16.3f.[514] The codex similarly inserts between Mark 16.3 and 16.4 an account of the event of the resurrection, taking up the women's question, 'Who will roll away the stone from the door?' It reads:

'But suddenly, towards the third hour, there was great darkness by day (?) over the whole earth, and angels descended from heaven, and they raised him[515] . . . into the glory of the living God and at the same time ascended with him, and immediately it was light (again). For those (women) came to the tomb, and when they looked in, they saw that the stone had been rolled away.'[516]

*Criticism*: Matthew 27.62–66; 28.11–15 are so clearly aimed at refuting the Jewish charge of stealing the body that it is difficult to combine these texts with Matt.28.2–4. At the level of tradition Matt.28.2–5, the Ascension of Isaiah and the addition in the Codex Bobiensis at Mark 16.3 have nothing to do with the guards, who are completely the contribution of Matthew (they are not even mentioned in the Codex Bobiensis). The extension of the Codex Bobiensis has a clearly secondary stamp and is an attempt to *improve* the text of Mark. That is possibly also visible in the fact that in connection with Mark 16.8 the codex – omitting 'and they said nothing to anyone' (v.8c) – then goes on to read: 'They told briefly to

Peter all that had been commanded them. And then Jesus himself
also (appeared and?) sent out through them (the apostles) the holy
and imperishable message of eternal salvation from the rising (of the
sun) to the setting.'[517] Now as numerous other witnesses have the
same short ending to Mark as the Codex Bobiensis, this need not
necessarily have anything to do with its reading of Mark 16.3f. cited
above.

Having discussed the question of the tradition behind
Matt.28.2–5, we can now return to the text of Matthew.

In vv.5–8 Matthew again follows the account of Mark with few
deviations:

[5] Parallel to Mark 16.6a.

[6] Corresponds to Mark 16.6b, where the statement of the
resurrection is derived from a prediction of Jesus. This is absent from
Mark, who a little later (Mark 16.7) derives the future seeing of Jesus
by the disciples from a prediction of Jesus. Matthew is probably
referring back to Matt.26.32.

[7] This has a parallel in Mark 16.7. However, the message is said
to be directed only to the disciples as a whole; Peter is not mentioned
by himself at all, as in Mark. In Matthew the content of the message
is the resurrection of Jesus; in Mark it is that Jesus is going before the
disciples into Galilee and will see them there. In Mark this is
connected with Jesus' prediction. Matthew turns it into a remark by
the angel, 'See, I have told you!'

[8] Here Matthew, in contrast to Mark (16.8: the women are
silent in fear), narrates that in fear (taking up what he found in Mark)
and in great joy the women want to communicate the message of the
angel to the disciples: 'Instead of the terror and fear of Mark's report,
in all that happens to them, as well as fear they feel great joy: they
immediately believe.'[518] This is not surprising, since previously
(vv.2–4) they have *indirectly* been made witnesses to the event of the
resurrection. That is a good preparation for the next episode (vv.9–
10), in which Jesus will appear *directly* to them.

[9-10] These verses have no parallel in Mark. They depict an
encounter of Jesus with the two women mentioned in v.1, who take
hold of his feet (cf. II Kings 4.27) and worship him (cf. later v.17).[519]
Jesus orders them not to fear and to tell his brethren (cf.
Matt.18.15f.; 23.8: the brotherhood of the disciples) to go to
Galilee, where they will see him.

There is much to be said for supposing that these verses do not go
back to pre-Matthaean traditions.[520] For apart from his greeting, the

risen Jesus does not say anything to the women at the tomb other than what the angel has already told them, 'Do not be afraid, go and tell my brethren to go to Galilee, and there they will see me' (v.10; cf. v.7). However, for Matthew's intention it should be noted that in vv.7f. we have 'brethren' rather than 'disciples':[521] 'It is not to a hierarchically-structured community that the universal mission is to be given, but to those who have experienced their solidarity in failure and are now reconstituted as the "brothers of Jesus". Such an explanation is further exemplified by the Matthean omission of the reference to Peter as separate from the disciples in 28:7.'[522] But at the same time it should be emphasized that even despite the mutual brotherhood of the disciples, with Jesus they have a teacher-pupil relationship (Matt.23.8–10).

Matthew relates the appearance of the risen Christ at this point so as to 'connect with the empty tomb not only an encounter with an angel but also an encounter with the Risen Christ'.[523] In John 20.1–18 this general tendency[524] has led to a scene which has been depicted vividly and with broad brush strokes,[525] whereas in the Lukan setting, because of Luke 24.22–24 only the appearance of an angel without any real christophany seems to have belonged to the tradition of the empty tomb.[526]

Another possible way of understanding Matt.28.9–10, which in my view is to be preferred to the previous one, is to regard the verses – despite the Matthaean vocabulary – as basically an independent piece which is not connected at all with the tomb of Jesus. As I explained on p. 28 above, C. H. Dodd noted that Matt.28.9–10; Matt.28.16–20 and John 20.19–21 have the same construction. The situation presupposed in each case is that the followers of Christ have been robbed of their Lord. This is followed by his appearance (Matt.28.9, 17; John 20.19), a greeting (Matt.28.9; John 20.19), his being recognized by the disciples (Matt.28.9, 17; John 20.20) and a commission (Matt.28.10, 19; John 20.21f.).

If this structural scheme is correct,[527] it means that at the stage of the tradition, Matt.28.9–10 is not necessarily about the women, as in its Matthaean context, but about the eleven (or twelve) or another group of disciples. It was Matthew who first made use of this narrative type at this point to provide a better transition between the story about the tomb and the concluding christophany.[528] In that case, however, the only possible recipients of the vision were the women, who on the basis of the previous narrative were the only ones to have been present (cf. Matt.26.56; 27.55, 61).

Be this as it may, at least on the basis of Matt.28.9f., the value of the tradition and thus the historicity of the appearance to women (or to Mary Magdalene) at the tomb of Jesus is virtually nil. We shall see below whether this verdict also applies to John 20.14–18.

### 4.3.4  Matt.28.16–20: The appearance of Jesus and the mission command

#### 4.3.4.1  General

At this point Matthew relates a further account of an appearance which has the same structure as that in 28.9f. (cf. above, 28). In general it is striking that the account of Jesus' own appearance is brief. It is expressed only by a meagre 'when they saw him'; here the reaction of the eleven is identical with that of the women in v.9 (they worshipped him). The emphasis here is not on the appearance itself but on the following words of Jesus (vv.18–20).

#### 4.3.4.2  Redaction[529]

[16] This describes the carrying out of Jesus' command in v.10. The 'mountain' is the place of the epiphany (cf.5.1; 15.29; 17.1).

[17] 'They worshipped him' takes up the same verb from v.9. 'Doubt' appears in the New Testament only in Matt.14.31 (Jesus as Peter sinks, 'O you of little faith, why do you doubt?') and may be redactional along with the 'fall down' which is often attested for Matthew (Matt.2.2; 4.9; 8.2, etc.).

For the doubt – in substance a motive which occurs often in the Easter stories, Luke 24.11, 25, 37f., 41 – cf. especially John 20.29.

First, the motif of doubt could be one aimed at bringing life to the narrative if one considers, for example, the way in which it is developed in the *Epistula Apostolorum* (= *EpAp*, which was composed in Egypt, a 'composite form consisting of letter, Gospel and revelation discourse'[530] from the middle of the second century. In it the women at the tomb receive the Lord's command to communicate to the disciples that the Master has risen: after that, in chs.10–12 (21–23) the Coptic version of the work reads as follows:

'Martha came and told it to us. We said to her, "What do you want with us, O woman? He who has died is buried, and could it be possible for him to live?" We did not believe her, that the Saviour had risen from the dead. Then she went back to the Lord and said to him, "None of them believe me that you are alive." He said, "Let another one of you go to them saying this again to them." Mary came and told us again, and we did not believe her. She returned to the Lord and she also told it to him. Then the Lord said to Mary and also to her sister, "Let us go to them." And he came and found us inside, veiled. And we doubted and he called us out. But we thought it was a ghost, and we did not believe that it was the Lord. Then he said to us, "Come, do not be afraid. I am your master whom you, Peter, denied three times; and now do you deny again?" But we went to him doubting in our hearts whether it was possibly he. Then he said to us, "Why do you still doubt and are you not believing?" I am he who spoke to you concerning my flesh, my death and my resurrection. That you may know that it is I, put your finger, Peter, in the nailprints of my hands; and you, Thomas, put your finger in the spear-wounds of my side; but you, Andrew, look at my feet and see if they do not touch the ground. For it is written in the prophet, "The foot of a ghost or a demon does not join to the ground." But we touched him that we might truly know whether he had risen in the flesh, and we fell on our faces confessing our sin, that we had been unbelieving. Then the Lord our redeemer said, "Rise up, and I will reveal to you what is above heaven and what is in heaven, and your rest that is in the kingdom of heaven. For my Father has given me the power to take up you and those who believe in me."[531]

Secondly, the motif of doubt addresses problems of Christians of the second and third generation, who no longer have any direct access to the original Easter experience. They can be found again in this form in the text, and are then more inclined to accept Jesus' answer to the question oppressing them.

[18] 'Came' is typically Matthaean language (4.3; 8.19; 9.28 etc.). There are numerous parallels in the redactional material to 'he spoke to them and said' (cf. only 13.3; 14.27; 23.1). In v.18b the notion of the enthronement of the Son of man (cf. Dan.7.14) is transferred to Jesus. For 'to me has been given' cf. Matt.11.27. The phrase 'in heaven and on earth' occurs as a whole or in part only in Matthaean special material (6.10; 16.19; 18.18) with the exception of Matt.9.6 (= Mark 2.10).

[19] 'Go' takes up 'they went' (v.16). For 'go' cf. 9.13; 10.7; 18.12; 21.6 etc.; 'therefore', 3.8; 6.8f.; 6.31,34; 7.12, etc.; 'make disciples', 13.52; 27.35.

The 'nations' (*ethne*) probably refers only to the Gentiles. Matthew is still too Jewish[532] to be able to include the Jews in the term 'nations', which in Judaism is reserved for Gentiles. His sharp polemic (ch.23) applies to the Judaism newly constituted by the Pharisees, which in this form no longer belongs among the nations.[533]

[20] This verse is full of Matthaean vocabulary: 'observe', 'all', 'command', 'and behold' (cf.28.9), 'end of the world'.

In this final section of his Gospel Matthew is answering the question of the basis of the Easter certainty and the overcoming of doubt. He points to the exclusive authority of the sayings of Jesus for the present. The preaching has become the preaching of the commandments of the Torah, rightly understood. The Easter vision,[534] which has become impossible in the Matthaean community, has been replaced by the word of the exalted Christ made present in preaching and in the gospel,[535] who is identical with the earthly Jesus (cf. what was said about 'worship' on p. 132 above).

At the same time we should follow Hans Dieter Betz in noting the implicitly anti-magical side of the end of the Gospel of Matthew:

'At many points in his Gospel Matthew indicates that the magical ingredients of the tradition were a theological problem for him. However, his solutions to this problem are basically different from those of Luke. To take up only this one point: for Matthew the one who appears is not a human being who has returned but the Risen Lord, who reveals himself through his concluding saying, "All authority in heaven and on earth has been given to me." . . . Already during his risen life Jesus was Kyrios and Son of God, so that the centurion could rightly say of the crucified Jesus, "Truly this was the Son of God . . ."(Matt. 27.54). In this light the concluding promise, which otherwise could be understood in magical terms, is no longer open to misunderstanding: "And lo, I am with you always, to the close of the age . . ." (Matt.28.20). The one who speaks thus is not a ghost, but the cosmocrator.'[536]

### 4.3.4.3 Traditions

Since vv.26f. have proved to be a Matthaean introduction, the question of the tradition arises primarily only for vv.18–20. Here three elements are visible:

1. Verse 18b: the exaltation of Jesus and the power bestowed on him with it (cf. Matt.11.27; John 3.35; Phil.2.9–11).

2. Verses 19–20a: the mission charge; presumably Matthew has replaced a command in the text that he had before him, 'preach the gospel', which was perhaps preserved in the secondary conclusion to

Mark (16.15),[537] with the invitation, 'make disciples' (cf. 14.52; 27.57).[538] The baptism 'in the name of the Father and of the Son and of the Holy Spirit' is striking because of its triadic formulation, since in the early period baptism was solely in Christ (Gal.3.27) or in the name of Jesus (I Cor.1.13; Acts.8.16; 19.5; cf. Did.9.5).[539] Probably here we have a baptismal formula with a liturgical character that has a parallel in Did.7.1, which reads, 'Baptize in the name of the Father and of the Son and of the Holy Spirit.'[540]

3. Verse 20b: Jesus' promise of his everlasting presence to the end of the world.

It is almost impossible to decide whether the three members were originally independent and were brought together by Matthew at this point or whether Matthew had already found them combined.[541]

In this connection the following point must be made: there is really no longer an appearance tradition in vv.18–20, although with his meagre 'when they saw him', Matthew is indicating that he wants to relate an Easter *story*. Rather, what we find here is Easter *theology*, which forces any vision that happened at the time to the side, or replaces it with words. In this way the scene remains open to the present. So what we have here is almost no longer an appearance but an enthronement of Jesus as Lord of heaven and earth, which here, as often, is directly connected with the resurrection, indeed is even identified with it. (Perhaps here it would be better to term the event an appearance of the enthroned Christ.) So the theme of authority as such does not serve to distinguish the Risen Christ from the earthly Jesus but virtually combines the two. The new element is the universal extension of the authority of the risen and the earthly Christ over heaven and earth. So the special feature is not just the combination of appearance and mission, but that of exaltation and mission to the Gentiles.[542]

### 4.3.4.4 Historical

The historical yield is extremely limited. It is true that Jesus appeared to (Peter and) the Twelve,[543] in other words that they saw him (I Cor.15.5), and then formed a community which proclaimed among its Jewish contemporaries the resurrection and exaltation of Jesus as the Messiah [?] and/or Son of Man [?]. That is the historical nucleus of the scene reported by Matthew. Whether this vision took place in Galilee, as the text indicates, remains uncertain on the basis of the previous passage, since Matthew has inferred 'Galilee' from Mark 16.7. But on the basis of general considerations (see 171f.) the location of this former 'vision' in Galilee may be historically correct.

In the closing scene Matthew and/or his tradition have concentrated later theological conclusions like the 'mission to the Gentiles', which were never drawn in such a way by the Twelve, but were so drawn already by Paul and the Jewish-Hellenistic Christians. Nevertheless it has to be said quite emphatically that these conclusions were already latent in the resurrection experience. (Religious language always means more than it says.) I shall be coming back to this.

## 4.4 The Easter stories in Luke

### 4.4.1 *Introduction*

In the preface to his Gospel the Third Evangelist has given us some information about his use of sources. He mentions 'many who have undertaken to compile a narrative of the things which have been accomplished among us' (Luke 1.1), and describes them as 'eyewitnesses and ministers of the word' (Luke 1.2). He himself has investigated everything (closely) from the beginning, in order to write down everything in order, so that 'Theophilus' (and consequently any friend of God) to whom he writes will be confirmed in the reliability of the teaching in which he has been instructed. Two of the sources which Luke presupposes here are well known, the Gospel of Mark and Q, although he does not mention them explicitly, but makes use of them tacitly.

As becomes clear in the foreword, the notion of fulfilment dominates Luke-Acts. This leads the author among other things to transpose what he finds in Mark. Thus for example he puts Mark 6.1–6 (Jesus in Nazareth) at the beginning of Jesus' activity (Luke 4.16–30) and strengthens the parallel between 'scripture' and the life of Jesus. In this sense the Lukan theology of proof from prophecy is also a main concern of Luke 24.[544] On the other hand an interest in the materiality of the resurrection seems to be developing, out of a subsidiary apologetic concern (see further below). 'Luke has brought together the different Easter stories which he took over from the earliest Christian tradition by interweaving them and putting them under the Leitmotiv of the Easter message which he often stresses: in Jerusalem . . . the sacred history is being fulfilled which had to be fulfilled in this way and not otherwise. The risen Christ is the Messiah of Israel, the saviour of the world, the Lord of his church.'545

## 4.4.2 *Luke 24.1–12: The empty tomb and the proclamation of Jesus' resurrection*

The Lukan sense of the pericope and the basis of its tradition can probably best be discovered by a comparison with Mark. Small details apart, the text diverges from Mark at the following points.

1. The women saw the tomb of Jesus (Luke 23.55) and prepared spices (*aromata*) and oil for anointing (*myra*) the evening before. They rested during the adjacent sabbath in accordance with the commandment (Luke 23.56). In Mark the women only saw (from afar) where the body of Jesus had been laid (15.47). They bought spices to anoint the body *after* the sabbath (Mark 16.1). Luke 24.1 does not explicitly mention the intention to anoint the body. But the women brought the balsam in the early morning: 'Since according to Luke the women had already prepared their spices on the day of the burial, they can hasten to the tomb even earlier. Their coming as early as possible in the morning attests the magnitude of their love and worship.'546

2. The names of the women are mentioned by Luke only at the end of the pericope (v.10), by Mark already at the beginning (v.1).547 The names of two women agree in Luke and Mark: Mary Magdalene and Mary the (mother) of James. Salome (Mark 16.1) does not appear in Luke but Joanna does; she had already been mentioned in Luke 8.3 as the wife of Chuza. (Presumably she came from there and is redactional here.) In addition Luke mentions the other women who had accompanied Jesus – here, too, he is probably thinking of Luke 8.2–3.

3. In Luke the women do not worry about who will roll away the stone for them (Mark 16.3 differs), but, as in the Markan account, they find the stone rolled away from the tomb and enter it (Mark 16.4/Luke 24.2f.).

4. The next remark, 'they did not find the body of Jesus',548 has no parallel at this point in Mark, where it is the young man, having given his message of the resurrection, who points to the empty tomb.

This shift of accent, along with the observation that Luke 24.3 explicitly mentions the *body* of Jesus (see above, Luke 23.55),[549] indicates a stronger stress on the empty tomb and the bodily resurrection.

5. In Luke two men meet the women (in Mark a young man [16.5]) in dazzling apparel (Luke 24.4); they recall the two men ('in white robes') of Acts 1.10 (cf. Luke 9.30, 32).[550]

6. The message of the young man in Mark ran: 'You seek Jesus of Nazareth, who was crucified. He has risen, he is not here; see the place where they laid him' (16.6). In Luke 24.5b–6a this becomes: 'Why do you seek the living among the dead?' He is not here, but has been raised.[551] (On v.5b see the question expressing a similar reproach in Luke 2.49; Acts 1.11).

7. Luke 24.6b–8 differs *considerably* from Mark 16.7. In Mark (and similarly Matt.28.7), the women are charged to tell Jesus' disciples and Peter that they are to *go to Galilee*, where they will see Jesus, as it has been told them. By contrast in Luke (in Lukan language)[552] the two men refer the women back to a saying which they had been given *earlier in Galilee*, that the Son of Man had to suffer and rise again on the third day (Luke 9.22; cf. 9.44; 18.32f.).[553] It should be noted that only Luke 9.22,44 was spoken in Galilee and that women are not thought of as having been explicitly present at these prophecies. For the 'must' (*dei*), cf. 142 below on Luke 24.26.

8. In Mark the women are silent despite their charge; in Luke they are convinced and, without having to be told, share the message of the resurrection with the eleven and all the rest (v.9), but meet with unbelief (v.11).[554]

*Excursus: The text-critical problem of Luke 24.12*[555]

Verse 12 (and parts of vv.3a and 6a) is missing in the significant manuscript Codex Bezae Cantabrigiensis and in some manuscripts of the Old Latin translation.[556] For internal reasons it has continually been judged secondary, namely as a post-Lukan insertion on the basis of John 20.2–10.

The main reasons for the interpolation theory are:
1. The sometimes word-for-word agreements between Luke 24.12 and John 20 (the historical present 'he sees' in Luke 24.12 and John 20.5 is particularly striking).
2. Verse 12 speaks of 'Peter', v.34 of 'Simon';

3. Verse 12 does not fit well into the context of Luke 24, where there is mention of 'some' who went to the tomb (v.24).

Counter-arguments:

On 1: The parallels could also be explained by the use of a common tradition or source. But the historical present 'he sees' in Luke 24.12 remains a problem. However, at the same time the Lukan language should be noted in Luke 24.12: 'rise again', 'wonder', 'what had happened'.[557]

On 2: The form 'Peter' is more frequent in Luke (Gospel 17 times; Acts 52 times). 'Simon' goes back to the earliest tradition.[558]

On 3: Tensions in the context can also be explained from the use of tradition. Contrary to divergent views,[559] Luke 24.24 can be regarded as a reference back to v.12 with a generalizing plural.

Conclusion: Contrary to some textual evidence, Luke 24.12 is probably an original element of the Gospel of Luke (like v.6a and 'the Lord Jesus' in v.3), although it is difficult to make the secondary omission of v.12 plausible.

There is a further question: from where did Luke (or his tradition) get the report of a visit of Peter to the tomb? (That is, presupposing that Luke did not know John 20.) The following answer suggests itself: Luke (or his tradition) knows the tradition of the appearance of Jesus to Peter (cf. Luke 24.34) and similarly the tradition of the visit of the women to the tomb. Both are combined in Luke 24.12, and added where they belong, at the end of the women's visit to the tomb. The 'logic' of this combination is as follows: if the tomb was empty and Jesus appeared to Cephas, then he must have previously inspected it in order to convince himself. The author of this combination will have been either Luke himself[560] or – more probably – one of the traditions which he used.[561]

Now as we know, there is a parallel to Peter's visit to the tomb in John 20.3–8. Either this passage presupposes a knowledge of Luke 24.12, or Luke and John are using a tradition of this visit to the tomb which is common to both of them. Now in both cases it has become clear that the tradition which appears in Luke 24.12 is a development of the tomb tradition of Mark 16.1–8, working in the tradition of the first appearance to Peter.[563] So the tradition behind Luke 24.12 is a secondary formation and therefore without historical value for the question of the 'resurrection events' (I shall be returning to the problem on p. 156 below).

## 4.4.3  Luke 24.13–35: Jesus meets the two disciples on the Emmaus road

### 4.4.3.1  Structure

The present 'narrative of the disciples on the Emmaus road, shaped with especial love'[564] is constructed as follows:

13–16: Exposition: two disciples meet Jesus on the road from Jerusalem to Emmaus;

17–27: Conversation on the way;

28–31: Meal scene;

32–35: Return from Emmaus to Jerusalem.

### 4.4.3.2  Redaction

[13] 'And behold' is a Lukan introduction (see most recently 23.50); 'of them' links the narrative with the preceding pericope; 'that very day': according to Luke all the resurrection scenes take place on one and the same day.

[14] This refers back to 'all these things' of v.9, the reports of the women. The disciples did not believe in them (v.11). Nevertheless Peter had inspected the tomb and was amazed.

[15] The two disciples, too, keep worrying about what has happened and what the women have told them. They talk about it and discuss it between themselves (cf. Luke 22.23 with Acts 6.9).

[16] Their eyes were kept from recognizing him (so that this does not happen right at the beginning of the encounter).

That is the end of the exposition. The resolution will consist in their eyes being opened (v.31). But before that can happen, the two, and thus the readers, are to undergo a recognition process. It begins with the conversation on the way in vv.17–27.

[17–19] Jesus begins – in real Lukan fashion (cf. Acts 8.30; 9.4, 10, etc.) – with a question which opens the dialogue, namely about what the two disciples have been talking about on the way. The note about their sorrow is emphasized by the pause in the external scene (they remain at a standstill), which heightens the tension. In the twofold exchange of a question from Jesus (v.17) and a more allusive counter-question from a disciple, Cleopas, casting some blame (v.18), a further question from Jesus and a first brief piece of information (v.19), it finally becomes clear that they were talking about Jesus himself, who is said to be 'a prophet mighty in deed and word before God and all the people'. Verse 19 is completely shaped by Luke. The Greek word for 'before' (*enantion*) occurs in the New Testament only in Luke (Luke 1.6; 20.26; Acts 7.10; 8.32 [= Isa.53.7]). According to Luke 7.16; 9.8, 19 and indirectly according to Luke 7.39, Jesus is called prophet by the people. For the phrase 'mighty in words and deeds' see Acts 7.22. However, we might ask why the two disciples describe Jesus with a christological title (prophet) which is not central to Luke elsewhere. The answer is that Luke is attributing to the disciples who are caught in incomprehension a christology which is later to be corrected (v.26). So v.19 still produces a tension (like v.18 previously), which looks for resolution.

[20] This describes the death of Jesus in a Lukan way: the Jews crucified Jesus (cf. Acts 7.51–53 and the exoneration of Pilate in Luke's passion narrative).

[21] This points back to the original but disappointed hope of the disciples that Jesus would redeem Israel (cf. Luke 1.68; 2.38; Acts 1.6).

'The reference to the disappointed hope of the disciples in 24.21a is to be seen as a redactional bridge against the background of the expectation of redemption expressed in chs.1 and 2. Indeed it is not only passages like Luke 1.68 . . . and 2.38 which are picked up in 24.21. We might also think of statements like 1.3–33,68–79; 2.10,14, 31f. The salvation that God has prepared for his people comes to fulfilment in the *egeirein*, in the "raising" of his Messiah (cf. Luke 1.69). The character of this event as fulfilment is particularly important for Luke. Thus he interprets it with the words, as God "spoke by the mouth of his holy prophets from of old" (1.70).'[565]

The hope is manifestly superseded through the creation of a church of the Gentiles (see the end of Acts). Through the note of time 'on the third day', Luke makes a link back to the chronology of the Easter stories and in vv.22–24 paraphrases what has been reported so far:

[22] This links up with the story of the visit of the women to the tomb, which has been told previously.

[23] This repeats their vision of the angel and the message to them that Jesus is alive (there is a link to v.5: 'Why do you seek the living among the dead?').

[24] This links back to v.12, where the word 'some' generalizes the visit of an individual, Peter.

[25] This introduces the development of the previous faith of the disciples – first of all through a reproach by Jesus (which has some similarity to the reproach of the angels to the women made in Luke 24.5–8): 'And he said to them, "O foolish men, and slow of heart to believe all that the prophets have spoken!"'

[26] This verse specifies that the suffering of Christ is necessary and in accordance with the scriptures (v.27; cf.v.25). That corresponds completely with Luke's notion of salvation history (cf. also Luke 24.6b, 44), the course of which is thought of as happening of necessity at every moment.[566]

Here Luke emphasizes in particular the paradoxical fact that the Christ destined for glory had to suffer:

> 'What really caused offence in the fate of Jesus was not the fact that the Jewish authorities had made his activity fail. What really caused offence was his death . . . His "suffering" (i.e. his death) demonstrated that people were wrong about his person.'[567]

'Enter into glory' evidently has the function of a statement about the resurrection and not about the exaltation. 'In the account of the angels at the tomb it is stated only that these had said that Jesus *is alive* (24.23; 24.6f. differs). Here as in v.26 Luke quite evidently avoided a precise formulation of the resurrection message, for reasons of narrative technique.'[568]

[27] This expresses the conviction found throughout Luke's work that there is mention of Christ in the books of Moses and in the prophets (cf. Acts 8.35), but does not cite any particular passage.

[28] The destination has almost been reached. Jesus' intention to go on increases the tension. (The Lord wants to be asked, and then it is certain that he will stay.[569]) Now, where everything is moving towards the climax, the recognition of Jesus by the two disciples, Jesus cannot go on and disappear.

[29] Accordingly, the two disciples urgently ask Jesus to stay (cf. Rev.3.20).[570]

[30] Jesus breaks bread at the common meal, blesses it and gives it to them. The many verbal allusions from v.30 on to the eucharistic words in Luke 22.19 indicate that here Luke is thinking in terms of the eucharist.

[31] Their eyes are opened and they recognize him. So their 'blindness' of v.16 is removed. What Luke wants to convey is that communion with Jesus is experienced in the eucharist. Once that is

clear, all has been said: Jesus can vanish (cf. v.31b). The explicit statement that the one who appears vanishes is typically Lukan: Luke 1.38; 2.15; 9.33; Acts 10.7; 12.10.

[32] In retrospect the disciples recognize that their heart was already burning within them when Jesus opened the scriptures to them on the way.[571]

[33] Now the two disciples can return to Jerusalem, to the eleven and the rest (as the women did in v.9).

[34] Before the two disciples can tell the eleven what they have just learned, they are told: 'The Lord has risen indeed and has appeared to Simon.' This as it were spoils their scene. Here as in other passages (Acts 8.14ff.; 11.1, 22) Luke makes room for a Jerusalem perspective. He corrects his tradition at this point and establishes the first appearance to Peter.[572] Now the second part of the statement, that Simon is one of the eleven, is puzzling in terms of a literal historical understanding. How can the eleven make such a statement 'neutrally'? So we have to ask what Luke wants to communicate to his readers with this verse. Answer: the experience that the two disciples and all the members of Luke's community have at the eucharist, namely that Jesus is present there, is confirmed by the earliest Christian confession that Jesus has risen and appeared to Simon. In other words, all the other Easter experiences rest on the earliest Christian creed. Moreover in Acts Luke will depict Peter as the leader of the earliest community (cf. Peter's speeches in Acts 2.14–40; 3.12–26) and portray the Jerusalem church as the earliest community of which the Lukan community is a descendant.

Elizabeth Schüssler Fiorenza[573] sees things differently. She writes: 'The Lukan stress on Peter as the primary Easter witness must be situated within the early Christian discussion of whether Peter or Mary Magdalene is the first resurrection witness' (51).[574]

Criticism: 1. The sources for the 'contest' between Peter and Mary Magdalene are relatively late (Gospel of Thomas, logion 114; Pistis Sophia; Gospel of Mary),[575] and cannot directly be projected back into the time of Luke.

2. Luke (24.10) explicitly says against Mark (16.8) that the women are the first to attest the message of the resurrection. The dismissive reaction of the apostles to the message of the women (Luke 24.11) hardly plays down the role of the women as those who proclaim the Easter message.

3. In terms of form criticism, a distinction must be made unconditionally between the 'attestation of the resurrection' and the 'appearance of the Risen Lord'. Because Schüssler Fiorenza does not do this, she can write the impossible sentence: 'The early Christian confession that "Jesus the Nazarene who was executed on the cross was raised" is, according to the pre-Marcan resurrection story of Mark 16.1–5,8a, revealed in a vision first to the Galilean women disciples of Jesus' (139).[576] In form-critical terms, the story of an appearance is rather different from a confessional formula. For both to stand side by side in a 'pre-Marcan resurrection story' is an indication of a secondary composition. After all, the confession did not drop down from heaven, but arises from human experience. Here we have to ask further questions and recognize that the tradition worked over by Mark (Mark 16.1–6,8a), to which Schüssler Fiorenza refers, presupposes the 'earlier' experience of Peter.

4. The real point concerns the historical reconstruction. Schüssler Fiorenza thinks that in Jerusalem, after the death of Jesus, on the basis of visionary-ecstatic experiences the women disciples came 'to the conviction that God had vindicated Jesus and his ministry. They, therefore, were empowered to continue the movement and work of Jesus, the risen Lord. They probably sought to gather together the dispersed disciples and friends of Jesus who lived in and around Jerusalem – women disciples like Mary, Martha of Bethany, the woman who had anointed Jesus, the mother of John Mark who had a house in Jerusalem, or Mary, the mother of Jesus, as well as such male disciples as Lazarus, Nicodemus, or the "beloved" Disciple. Some of these women probably also moved back, very soon, to Galilee, their native country. Such a reconstruction of the events after the death and resurrection of Jesus is historically plausible, since it might have been easier for the women of the Jesus movement to go "underground" than the men' (139). However, we are given no basis in the sources for such wide-ranging assertions.

[35] This sums up Luke's understanding once again: the two disciples relate what has happened to them on the way (viz., that the scriptures have been opened to them) and that they recognized Jesus in the breaking of the bread.

### 4.4.3.3 Traditions

Verse 34 is tradition (for the reasons see 26 above) and – from a form-critical perspective – is perhaps to be described as an ancient cry of Easter jubilation (see below, n. 110).

The redactional analysis made above has shown that the Emmaus story is a unit which at all points is shaped by Luke's theological profile.

So a reconstruction of the tradition faces great difficulties, although it is certain that Luke worked with material which already existed. As a test one could take out all the references to the context of the story to see whether the result is the plausible outline of a tradition. What is then left is a story which Hermann Gunkel has paraphrased like this: 'Here Christ appears unknown, as a wanderer – the role that the deity loved from of old, in simple human form, for example clad as a traveller to wander among human beings – and reveals his mysterious divine being at particular points; but as soon as he is recognized, he disappears. This outline of the story is very similar to *the earliest naratives about the appearance of the deity*; in style the story could be put in Genesis.'[577] If we presuppose such a legend[578] as the earliest stratum, we could distinguish from it the eucharistic tradition in vv.28–31, which may have been added at a secondary stage. However, possibly this was already associated with the earliest tradition.[579]

### 4.4.3.4 Historical

First of all it should be emphasized that v.34, the appearance to Simon, is the earliest element of the present pericope, since it is in harmony with the creed already received by Paul around 33 CE (see above, 38).

Individual elements of the pericope are beyond doubt old: thus possibly behind the name Cleopas (v.18) lies the Lord's cousin Clopas, whose son Symeon became a follower of James (Eusebius, *Church History* III.11; IV.22.4).[581] In that case, in this story we would have the reflection of the appearance of Jesus to a relative of the Lord which may go back to the earliest period. It is also worth noting that in John 19.25 one of the women at the cross is called 'Mary, (the wife) of Clopas'.[582]

The place Emmaus might also go back to historical knowledge.

'A stadion is 192 metres, so that the road to Emmaus must have been 11.5 kilometres long. But this geographical detail cannot easily be understood. Granted, since the Middle Ages reference has been made to a place Emmaus (El Kubebe), 11 kilometres north-west of Jerusalem. But none of the early church traditions mentions this place, and moreover excavations have produced only very scant remains from Roman times. So the identification of El Kubebe with Emmaus will have been made only in the Middle Ages, so that pilgrims could be shown a place the site of which corresponded precisely with the information in the Gospel of Luke. Now in the first century CE there were two other places with the name Emmaus. One of these two villages was only 6.3 kilometres from Jerusalem. Because the emperor Vespasian settled war veterans here, it was renamed as a colony and today is called qaloniye. However, in early Christianity people did not think of this Emmaus, but of another village of the same name, though this is 23 kilometres from Jerusalem. This place, which for a time was also called Nicopolis, is still called amwas. However, to get there one has to travel 120 rather than 60 stadia. So one of the two villages called Emmaus lies too near to Jerusalem and the other too far away for us to be able to state with any certainty which place the evangelist Luke was thinking of.'[583]

At the end of the analysis of the Emmaus pericope it should be stressed that a purely historical enquiry produces only meagre results and that the value of the narrative lies elsewhere than in history. Rather, its author gave it the task that Aristotle assigned to poetry. In his view, 'the poet's function is to describe, not the thing that has happened, but the kind of thing that might happen, i.e. what is possible as being probable or necessary . . . the statements of poetry are of the nature rather of universals, whereas those of history are singulars' (*Poetics* 9).[584] So we can learn virtually nothing which is specifically historical from the Emmaus story proper, but a good deal about the general character of Christian faith.

### 4.4.4  Luke 24.36–53: Jesus' appearance to the (eleven) disciples

Preliminary comment: the section is composed of three parts: following G.Lohfink,[585] vv.36–43 should be described as a recognition scene (= narrative), vv.44–49 as instruction of the disciples (= discourse of Jesus) and vv.50–53 as the farewell (narrative). The parts will be treated separately.

### 4.4.4.1  Luke 24.36–45: Recognition scene

Preliminary comment on the text: v.36b ('and said to them "Peace be with you"') and v.40 ('And when he had said this, he showed them his hand and his feet') are not contained in the Codex Bezae Cantabrigiensis (= D). But they might be part of the original text. The copyist may have thought that the greeting in v.36 came far too early, since in the following section the disciples were still afraid and terrified. He evidently thought v.40 superfluous.

### 4.4.4.1.1 *Redaction*

[36] 'As they were saying this' is a Lukan link between what follows and the previous scene: 'he stood among them' is Lukan in language.

[37] 'But they were startled and frightened', 'see' and 'Spirit' (for the content see similarly Acts 12.8) derive from Luke, as does

[38] 'in your hearts'.

[39] With Jesus' invitation to the disciples to see his hands and his feet in order to recognize his identity, this gives a *first* demonstration (whether the disciples did this is not said, but is presupposed): the invitation to touch him and see him is the *second* demonstration of the resurrection of Jesus. The risen Jesus is no spirit[586] (a resumption of v.37), but consists of flesh and blood. Given such realism, one can hardly avoid seeing here an opposition to docetism. Evidently in this verse Luke is combatting challenges to the bodily reality of the resurrection of Jesus as Ignatius, To the Smyrnaeans 3.2, does at the beginning of the second century:

'For I know and believe that he was in the flesh even after the resurrection. And when he came to those with Peter he said to them: "Take, handle me and see that I am not a phantom without a body." And they immediately touched him and believed, being mingled both with his flesh and spirit.' (For the question of a genetic relationship between this passage and the present text see the next section.)

[40] This is a variation on and intensification of v.39. It probably comes in its entirety from Luke.

[41] The introductory Lukan absolute genitive matches the introduction to v.36: for the construction with the absolute genitive and 'still' see Acts 10.44. The disciples are half won over by Jesus (for 'wondered', cf. Luke 24.12 [of Peter when he sees the empty tomb]). The *third* demonstration which now follows is meant to remove any doubt. Jesus asks whether the disciples have anything to eat (v.41b).

[42] They give him a piece of broiled fish.

[43]  He eats it before their eyes and thus proves that he is neither a spirit nor an angel. Angels do not eat (cf. Tobit 12.19), but human beings do. The narrator so much takes the probative force of this last demonstration for granted (thus already the *eti de* in v.41) that he does not even have to emphasize that the disciples are convinced. Acts 1.4; 10.41 say that the risen Jesus later ate with his disciples. By stressing the physical reality of the risen Jesus Luke evidently wants to strengthen the certainty of his readers, as he has announced in the preface (Luke 1.3–4).

Hans Dieter Betz has rightly emphasized that Luke, 'who understood something about Hellenistic religion, as Acts above all shows, . . . inserted this very vivid narrative here in order to avoid the magical-demonic conclusion that he feared. For him the expedient is that the person who appears there is the risen *Jesus* with his body of flesh and bones. The crude materialism which people have constantly noted in the narrative thus in no way simply arose from naive popular belief, but theologically, with the deliberate intention of repressing the rival magical and demonological interpretations.'[587]

### 4.4.4.1.2 Traditions

That there is an underlying tradition is shown first by the tensions with the preceding Emmaus story (despite the previous encounter of Jesus with the Emmaus disciples and with Jesus, the disciples are afraid), and secondly, the parallel traditions in John 20.19–23[588] and Ignatius, To the Smyrnaeans 3.2 (for the text see above, 147).

More than thirty years ago, Helmut Koester[589] gave such illuminating reasons for the independence of the Ignatius text from Luke 24.36–43 that my remarks below will follow him closely:
Luke 24.39 and Ignatius agree word for word in Jesus' invitation to the disciples, 'touch me and see'. 'In the statements which follow in each case the suspicion that this is only a ghost is rejected; however, this does not happen with the same words . . . Both reports are followed by a demonstration . . . In each case, at the end it is reported that the Risen Christ ate with the disciples' (46).
The difference in the reports is as follows: there is nothing of 'those about Peter', who in Ignatius include the Risen Lord, in Luke, where there is only the general presupposition of a group of disciples (Luke 24.37; cf. v.33). 'In Ignatius there is no mention of the fear of the disciples and Jesus' going in' (Luke 24.37–39). The way in which the Risen Christ eats with

them is mentioned only briefly, whereas Luke gives a detailed account. Ignatius stresses twice more than Luke the bodily appearance of Jesus, and following that on each occasion his spiritual nature. Finally, here too we have the most striking deviation of Ignatius from the account in Luke, namely the statement 'I am not a phantom without a body' (47).

The dependence of Ignatius on Luke at this point is only seemingly supported by the verbal correspondence mentioned at the beginning in Jesus' invitation to the disciples to touch him and see them. For words of Jesus are 'more faithfully preserved . . . than, say, the framework of such a narrative' (47). The possible theory that Ignatius has replaced 'spirit' (Luke 24.39) with the expression 'phantom without a body', is also improbable, since the expression is 'in no way characteristic of his terminology' (48). 'The statement "I am no phantom without a body" must have already stood in Ignatius's source. Now that means that Luke cannot have been the direct source for Ignatius' (ibid). Koester then reflects 'whether the account in Ignatius could not derive from a preliminary form of Luke's account in which there was still a note deleted by Luke that Jesus appeared "to Peter and those with him"' (49).

The tradition underlying Luke 24.36–43 is the story of an appearance in which the risen Jesus appears to his anxious disciples in bodily form. The focus is the fleshly, physical form of Jesus after the resurrection. What is presupposed is a discussion in the community of the nature of the corporeality of the risen Christ as we find it in the Johannine communities (cf. John 20; I John) and in its beginnings also already in the Pauline community of Corinth (I Cor.15). Accordingly this is a secondary formation – probably of the second generation, which no longer had any connection with the key witnesses to the 'resurrection of Jesus'. It is a well thought out composition which in three progressive steps (see the preliminary comments) documents for the disciples the fleshly nature of the risen Christ.

### 4.4.4.1.3 *Historical*

For the reasons given above, there is no genetic relationship to the primary witnesses of the 'resurrection' of Jesus. The historical yield is virtually nil.

That also applies to the whole section Luke 24.36–53, especially as it is clear that the following verses are shaped through and through by the outline of Luke's work and his theology.

#### 4.4.4.2 Luke 24.44–49: Instruction of the disciples

This section is a redactional composition:

[44] Jesus refers in retrospect to what he has said to the disciples. The main content is explained further by the second part of the verse. Just as Jesus already gave proofs from scripture during his lifetime, now he also does so after his resurrection.

[45] Jesus discloses to the disciples the meaning of the scriptures as he already did in the Emmaus story (cf. esp.v.27). The content of this disclosure is then made specific in the following verse in the form of a proof from scripture.

[46] This verse corresponds to Luke 9.22, Jesus' prophecy that he would suffer and rise again on the third day.

[47] This directs attention towards the future and the task of the disciples. Part of the proof from scripture is that in Jesus' name 'repentance and forgiveness of sins should be preached in his name to all nations, beginning from Jerusalem' (cf. Acts 2.32f., 38; 3.15f., 19; 5.28–32; 10.39, 43).

[48] This corresponds to Acts 1.4. The prophecies about receiving the Spirit are fulfilled in the narrative in Acts 2.

#### 4.4.4.3 Luke 24.50–53: Farewell

The concluding account of the ascension is wholly the work of Luke.

[50] The section has a parallel in Acts 1.9–11, where the ascension takes place from the Mount of Olives (v.12); here by contrast it is from Bethany (v.50). However, that must not prompt the erroneous thesis that the two scenes are rival traditions. Luke knows from Mark 11.1 that 'Mount of Olives' and 'Bethany' are geographically close together or are identical as place names. So the use of Bethany instead of Mount of Olives can be a variation.[590] In that case the scene would be redactional. For the blessing see the verbal parallels in Lev.9.22 (cf. Sir.50.22).

[51] For the disappearance of Jesus see the comments on Luke 24.31. Some text witnesses and the original reading of Codex Sinaiticus do not contain 'and was carried up to heaven'. Referring to this evidence, Wilhelm Michaelis thought that the only account of the ascension handed down by Luke is in Acts 1.4ff.[591] However, one could just as well conjecture, conversely, that 'and was carried up to heaven' was omitted to harmonize Acts 1.9 with Luke 24.51.[592]

[52] 'Return' is Lukan in language, 'great joy' takes up the same motif from v.41.

[53] The presence of the community in the temple is in accord with Lukan theology: the twelve-year-old Jesus remains in the temple (Luke 2.46), as does the early community (Acts 2.46; 3.1, 4, 52). In form-critical terms, v.53 is a brief summary, which has parallels in Luke-Acts (Luke 1.65f., 80; 2.20, 40, 51f.; Acts 1.14, etc.). In general, in any case we may attribute the last sentence to the evangelist, because here the author's intention is most to be expected.[593]

## 4.5 The Easter Stories in John

### 4.5.1 Introduction

John contains the greatest number of Easter stories in comparison with the Synoptics.[594] On the one hand that can indicate that the Gospel was composed at a later period of time when traditions were flowing more richly than in the early period. However, the reverse conclusion is possible in principle. In that case one must assume that in the very earliest period numerous traditions were circulating which have been collected together in the Gospel of John, whereas the Synoptic Gospels did not preserve these and represented a later stage. So such general reflections cannot help us further; the only help will come from detailed analyses of the text. Investigation of the Johannine corpus so far resulted in the demonstration that in at least one instance a tradition used there was of a considerable age (John 19.31–37), whereas John 20 already often proved to be a later product. We shall see what else emerges from a detailed investigation.

On a point of terminology, it should be noted that the work of the evangelist 'John' (= author) is termed 'redaction'. For the special problem of John 21 and the terminological question associated with it, see 165 below.

## 4.5.2 *John 20.1–8: The visit of the two disciples to the tomb and the appearance of Jesus to Mary Magdalene*

### 4.5.2.1 Redaction

[1] This corresponds to Mark 16.2, 4a. The question 'Who will roll away the stone for us from the door of the tomb?' (Mark 16.3) can be omitted, because the purpose of the visit is not given. However, the construction in v.1b has greater similarity to the parallel Luke 24.1f. As in Matt.28.1, Mary Magdalene is mentioned as subject. In the Synoptics, in contrast to John several women go to the tomb (Mark 16.1, three; Matt.28.1, two; Luke 24.1, more than three; cf. Luke 8.2f. and Luke 24.10). Mary Magdalene's early visit to the tomb is an expression of her love, which may be the reason for her visit anyway. The body of Jesus has already been completely buried (John 19.40) so that she does not need to worry about it.

[2] This verse depicts how Mary rushes to Peter – evidently without first looking into the tomb. The verse motivates the interlude which has been newly inserted, the race between Peter and the Beloved Disciple to the tomb that is developed in vv.3–10. The plural 'we do not know' does not necessarily require several women to have been to the tomb, because of John 3.2; 14.5. Perhaps this is an 'inauthentic plural which is also customary elsewhere in ancient speech'.[595] But possibly the plural does reflect several women, since in v.13 (cf. v.15) the singular appears when Mary Magdalene's lament is repeated word for word.

Verses 3–10:

This section has a close parallel in Luke 24.12, the text-critical originality of which was argued for above, and in Luke 24.24.

Hans Windisch acutely observed: 'It is noteworthy that while the first Easter story, the race of the two disciples to the tomb, is rich in actions which prompt performance, it does not contain any conversation, or indeed a single word, a feature for which it is unique in the whole Gospel; it is thus a piece of *pantomimic* narrative, which moreover serves apologetic ends.'[596] Its main motive 'is beyond doubt the rivalry of the two disciples, and, connected with that, the emphasis on the Beloved Disciple',[597] to whom the 'other disciple' in v.3 may be a reference.

Already in 13.23–25; 18.15–16;[598] 19.26–27, 35, the author inserts into the passion narrative this person who is meant to guarantee its authenticity. At the same time he represents the ideal disciple of Jesus. In comparison to the generally recognized position of Peter, the Beloved Disciple embodies the proximity of the Johannine community to Jesus; i.e., the other disciple becomes an unassailable authority (cf. John 14.6). Here the rivalry between the Johannine community and the mainstream church community is evidently reflected in the race of the two disciples to the tomb. The other disciple first sees – if only from outside – the cloth (v.5), and then v.8 explicitly states that (in contrast to Peter[599]) he came to believe. However, this is in tension with v.9: according to this verse he still must have failed to understand, which applies implicitly only to Peter. Therefore v.9 is either a gloss or an element of the tradition which explains the unbelieving reaction of Peter (and his companion, cf. Luke 24.12: Peter wonders at what has happened). In that case the author inserted v.8 without completely removing the tension with v.9. The faith of the Beloved Disciple would then be a fully valid testimony to the resurrection of Jesus even independently of an understanding of scripture and the empty tomb with the linen – not as a divine miracle, but in the sense of a dispensing with any proof (John 20.29),[600] even from scripture.

Yet another possibility for understanding v.9 is to see the verse as belonging to the immediate past and translating *edeisan* as a pluperfect: up until then – namely until what is depicted in v.8 – they had not yet understood the scriptures. *Now* things are different at least with the other disicples.

Because of his love (or the love of Jesus for him), this other disciple hastens more urgently than Peter towards Jesus, just as because of this he also stayed by the cross to the last, cf. John 19.26. In v.7 the rolled-up cloths are evidence of the impossibility of a tomb-robbing, since this would have been done in great haste, and it was difficult to fold up the linen cloths carefully. So this must be something other than a body snatching. The author of the Fourth Gospel is opposing Jewish slander in a different way from the legend of the guards at the tomb (Matt.27.62–66; 28.11–15). (Thus in the Johannine understanding the empty tomb almost became a complete testimony to the resurrection of Jesus, although Peter does not [yet] believe, even if the Beloved Disciple does.[601])

[10] *pros hautous* = home (cf. Num.24.25). 'The disciples' refers to Peter and the 'other disciple'. There is no question of

saying more about their discovery because of the section after next, vv.19–23.

[11] This verse picks up the broken threads of v.2. The join is rough. In v.2 Mary is not standing even at the tomb, and the two disciples play no role for her. 'In vv.11ff. she stands at the grave, as if the events recounted in vv.3–10 had not happened.'[602] That she 'stooped' (towards the tomb) takes up 'stooping' from v.5. Mary Magdalene mourns Jesus (cf. John 16.20) and weeps.[603] She has not yet gained the knowledge of the other disciple.

[12] This has a parallel in Mark 16.5. In the present text the motives of the angel and the tomb have been fully transformed. That there are two angels corresponds to Luke 24.4, so there could be a genetic relationship betwen the two texts.

[13] 'They have taken away my Lord' picks up the same phrase from v.2.

[14] For the incomprehension of Mary Magdalene cf. Luke 24.16: 'But their eyes were kept from recognizing him'; John 21.4: 'The disciples did not know that it was Jesus.'

[15] The address by Jesus to Mary Magdalene, 'Woman, why are you weeping?' is identical word for word with the address of the two angels to Mary Magdalene in v.13 (cf. how the message of the angels and the message of Jesus correspond, in analogy to Matt.28 7 and 10).[604] Mary's reply is shaped by a misunderstanding (cf. John 7.35; 8.22, but see the preliminary ignorance of Peter [13.17] and the disciple [John 16.18]), but also shows her love for Jesus, whom she still wants to care for in death.

Whether we should seek the Sitz im Leben for the gardener scene in Christian grappling with Jewish polemic[605] is an open question. It may also have been developed directly for the following point.

[16] 'She turned round' picks up the same verb from v.14. The verse depicts the recognition scene (see Luke 24.30), which is introduced by the mention of Mary's name. Cf. John 10.3, 'The shepherd knows his sheep and calls them by name,[606] and when they hear his voice they know him.' 'What it was that made her recognize him is not to be asked in this supernatural happening. We can only ask what deeper meaning the narrative has . . . Perhaps we may also add: the naming of the name tells a person what he or she is; and to be known in such a way leads a person to the encounter with the Revealer.'[607] In form, Mary's reaction 'Master' ('*rabbouni*') surpasses the address 'Sir' ('*kyrie*') from v.15, which was directed to the 'gardener'. It appears elsewhere in the New Testament only in

Mark 10.51, and is equivalent to the address '*rabbi*',[608] which occurs in the Gospel of John with reference to Jesus more frequently than in the other Gospels. In John 1.38 '*rabbi*', like '*rabbouni*' in John 20.17, is appropriately translated '*didaskale*'.

[17] 'Do not hold me, for I have not yet ascended to the Father' indicates that Mary is still subject to a possible misunderstanding.

The command can be understood in different ways:

1. No contact has taken place, nor is it to take place (perhaps because the Lord has not yet ascended to the Father and contact could prevent him from doing this).
2. Contact takes place, but is to be ended (perhaps because Jesus has not yet attained real heavenly corporeality).
3. The words have a transferred meaning and the question of contact or non-contact is open, to the degree that the Risen Lord can be touched at all (cf. the faith of the other disciple in John 20.8).

One can also combine one or more of these possibilities with a symbolic understanding, as e.g. Lindblom does. He renders the text as follows: 'Do not cling to me, for I am not yet ascended to the Father, but I am in process of ascending to him . . .'[609] 'Mary's effort to cling to Jesus serves . . . as a symbol for the anxiety of the disciples at having to part from Jesus.'[610]

The way in which the recipients of the message are addressed, as '(my) brethren', is striking. The expression '(my) brethren' appears in the same context of an instruction of the Risen Lord in Matt.28.10 and probably denotes members of the Christian community (cf. Matt.18.15; I John 2.9–11, etc.; III John 3). At any rate, such a use in John is singular, apart from 21.23. On the other hand, with 'the disciples' (v.18) the author is interpreting '(my) brethren' from v.17.

The content of the charge in v.17c ('Say to them, "I am ascending to my Father and your Father, to my God and your God"'), which certainly derives from the author, has a parallel in John 16.28b: 'I am leaving the world and going to the Father' (cf. 16.5, 10; 13.33; 14.4, 12, 28). But now the talk is no longer only of the Father of Jesus but also of the Father of the disciples, of Jesus' God who is also their God. The author means to say that through the departure of Jesus his Father becomes the Father of his followers. 'The real Easter faith therefore is that which believes this; it consists in understanding the offence of the cross.'[611]

[18] This verse narrates the execution of Jesus' command to Mary Magdalene: she tells the disciples (as Jesus' brethren), 'I have seen'

the Lord, which does not really fit Jesus' command. As the statement
sounds formal and corresponds to I Cor.9.1, the author wants if
possible to give Mary Magdalene emphatic legitimation with it. On
the other hand it contains the fulfilment of John 16.16–19.

### 4.5.2.2 Traditions

On vv.3–10: The report of a visit to the tomb by Peter (he virtually
repeats the experience of the women from Mark 16.1–8) proves to
be a piece of tradition, which has a parallel in Luke 24.12. This piece
of tradition is the foundation for the author's composition
describing the race between Peter and the Beloved Disciple.

On vv.10–18: In origin, the tradition is an appearance story,[612]
which at a secondary stage the author has linked with the story of the
tomb known from Mark[613] and into which he has inserted vv.3–10.
(Whether John uses the Markan report directly, or a related
tradition, or a tradition influenced by Mark 16.1–8 makes no
difference here.) In so doing he may have reduced the two women
given by the tomb tradition to one: Jesus appears to Mary
Magdalene. However, she only recognizes him when he has addressed her by her own name, just as the Emmaus disciples first
recognize Jesus by his gesture in the breaking of the bread.

The epiphany story is a recognition narrative. Its form is
Johannine throughout (cf. v.17 and the parallel between the address
to Mary in v.16 with John 10.3), but the nucleus may go back to the
independent tradition of a christophany of Jesus to Mary
Magdalene, even if we can no longer reconstruct its wording.
However, old Palestinian colouring may shine through in the
addressing of Jesus as *rabbouni*, even if it is unclear whether this is
attached to the tradition of an appearance of Jesus to Mary
Magdalene. The artistic *form* of the recognition narrative suggests
that it is late in date, if the form does not go back in its entirety to the
author.

According to C. H. Dodd, 'this pericope indefinably has something first-hand about it . . . At all events it stands alone.'[614] But this
is not sufficient reason for revising the above verdict. Like the
Emmaus story it is of later origin and is totally indebted to reflection,
even if one must immediately add that in religious language,
elements of the original can be contained even in late interpretation.
Similarly, for example, in Jesus' great 'I am' discourses the Gospel of
John is also historically remote from the historical Jesus. But who

would dispute that at the core of these discourses at least an essential part of the message of Jesus is contained or has been preserved?

A traditio-historical connection between this tradition and Matt.28.9f. is possible only if Matt.28.9f. derives from a christophany to women – and there are good reasons for disputing this.

Reference should further be made to a proposal by C. H. Dodd. He understands 'my brethren' in John 20.17 literally and puts the appearance to Mary Magdalene in the same strand of tradition as that to which the christophany to James the brother of the Lord (I Cor.15.7; cf. I Cor.9.5) belongs.[615] In my view this theory, which is attractive at first sight, is improbable, since in early Christianity 'brothers' denotes members of the Christian community (see above, 131). The fact that John 2.12 distinguishes physical brothers and disciples is hardly an argument in favour of '(physical) brothers' being tradition in John 20.17. But it must be explicitly conceded that questions remain open at this point.[616]

### 4.5.2.3 Historical

It remains to be asked whether the historical conclusion that Mary was the first to see the risen Jesus can be drawn from the fact that there is the independent tradition of a christophany to Mary Magdalene in the Gospel of John. At any rate the following view which is advanced in favour of this conclusion can be ruled out *a priori*:

> The isolated role of the women in Mark 15.40–16.8 suggests that 'after Jesus there was a phase in which the men among the disciples lost courage and women began carrying on the work'.[617] Susanne Heine has already rightly objected to this: 'The fact that the women watched the crucifixion from afar (viz. Mark 15.40) . . . does not tell us anything about Mark 16.1–8.'[618]
>
> Cf. also Schottroff's thesis that the power to proclaim gave the women 'a vision in which they were called to be proclaimers of the message of the power of life over death'.[619] The probability of that could be demonstrated only on the basis of an analysis of the tradition.

Now Mary Magdalene was certainly a follower of Jesus, indeed he had healed her of seven evil spirits (Luke 8.2).[620] Furthermore, we can conclude historically from her name Magdalene (= from Magdala, a place on the west side of Lake Genessaret), and the way in which her person is attached to the passion narrative that she took part in the fateful journey to Jerusalem along with Jesus and others. Nevertheless, the tradition of an appearance of Jesus to Mary Magdalene is evidently relatively late.

I Cor.15 has always been seen as as an important objection to attaching any great age to the tradition of a christophany to Mary Magdalene. Hans Grass has observed on this:

> 'All reflections as to whether Paul perhaps did not mention the women in first place because in the view of antiquity a woman was not a witness in her own right are superfluous. It would also have been remarkable had Paul been prevented by this view of the position of women from mentioning them when the Gospels no longer had any inhibitions here.'[621]

However, there needs to be more differentiation in the presuppositions than Grass advances: thus the reports in the Gospels of John, Matthew and Luke which he has in mind are quite different. Whereas in John and Matthew Jesus first appears to a woman (or two women), this is not the case in Luke. Furthermore there is no universal ancient view that women are incompetent witnesses. (That women were not allowed to give testimony was the case only in ancient Judaism.[622]) Finally, reference should be made to the difference in the form and function of I Cor.15.3–8 (a *list of witnesses*) and the *narrative* in the First and Fourth Gospels. (In addition cf. the denial of the 'right to speak' to women in the context of I Cor.15; I Cor.14.33–36.) So it would not have been inconceivable for Paul to have deleted Mary Magdalene as a witness to the resurrection had such a tradition been known to him. Accordingly I Cor.15 has lost much of its probative force against a possible first appearance to women or Mary Magdalene. We cannot therefore exclude the possibility that in I Cor.15 Paul has omitted the tradition of a first appearance to Mary Magdalene (and other women). However, this possibility does not automatically make Mary Magdalene or the other women who were friends of Jesus the first witnesses to his resurrection. The decision has to be made on the basis of the early Christian texts themselves.

So we may ask whether the tradition of an appearance to Mary did not arise in the Johannine circle and was then shaped by the author: he is fond of talking about individuals (cf. 165 below on Thomas [John 20.24–29] and the parallels mentioned there) to concentrate theological insights on them in a story. In that case it would only be from this Johannine narrative that the figure of Mary found her way into Gnostic texts, for which she plays a great role:

> Cf. Gospel of Philip 55b: 'The S[aviour lov]ed [Mar]y Mag[da]lene more than [all] the disciples, and kissed her on her [mouth] often. The other [disciples] [ ]. They said to him: "Why do you love her more than all of us?" The Saviour answered and said to them: "Why do I not love you like her?"'[623]

This saying displays a clearly Johannine colouring, in that Mary Magdalene to some degree occupies the role of the Beloved Disciple, which we know only from the Gospel of John. The kiss on the mouth is to be understood entirely within the framework of the Valentinian Gnostic ceremony of the bridal chamber, 'a form of the ritually shaped "redemption" . . . It is regarded as the "Holy of Holies" and ranks above the other sacraments.'[624] Cf. also the Second Apocalypse of James from Nag Hammadi, Codex V, 270:

> (James on Jesus): 'And he kissed me on the mouth (and) embraced me, saying: "My beloved! See, I will reveal to you what [the] heavens did not know – nor their archons . . . But now, stretch out your [hand]! Now, embrace me!" Immediately I stretched out my [hands] – and I did not find him as I thought. But afterwards I heard him saying: "Understand, and embrace me!" Then I understood, and I was afraid; and at the same time) I rejoiced with a great joy' (56.14–57.21.)[625]

The kiss on the mouth and the embrace could indicate a kind of 'Beloved Disciple conception'. 'While the probability of direct influence from John has not yet been demonstrated, a few other circumstances point at least to an affinity of motives: the invitation to embrace Jesus is misunderstood by James; what is meant is not a physical but a pneumatic embrace (57.13ff.); the same kind of thing happens with the so-called Johannine misunderstandings.[626] More-over there are some parallels in language and style (cf. the reference to the hour which is now come: 63.24f.; John 17.1). James is brought into a particularly intimate relationship with Jesus, since all three of these honorific titles – righteous, brother and beloved – are used by Jesus himself (48.22; 49.8f.).[627]

Cf. also Gospel of Philip 32: 'There were three (women) who kept company with the Lord at all times: Mary his mother, ‹his› sister and Magdalene, who is called his companion. His sister, his mother and his companion were all called Mary.'[628] The Gospel of John also evidently underlies this, for only there (John 19.25) is it said that Mary the mother of Jesus was present under the cross. The notion of Mary Magdalene as the companion (*koinonos*) of Jesus recalls the close connection between Simon and Helena,[629] and is to be understood against the background of Gnostic notions of syzygies in which Sophia is the consort of Jesus.[630]

Yet another feature characterizes the picture of Mary Magdalene in the Gnostic text, her opposition to Peter. For Mary this theme appears very clearly in the Gospel of Mary,[631] the Gospel of Thomas (logion)[632] and the Pistis Sophia.[633] But here too this rivalry may be caused by the tension between the Johannine conception of the Beloved Disciple and Peter.

According to Susanne Heine, Mary Magdalene is not mentioned in the earliest texts on the resurrection like I Cor.15 and Luke 24.34 because here 'christophany and leadership function . . . are closely connected . . . She is not the leader of a community, and as a result of the first institutional conflicts over authority within the developing Christian communities she fades into the background. But that does not exclude the possibility that she had spiritual authority as a follower of Jesus and a pneumatic personality.'[634] But even this verdict, so carefully arrived at, may be too optimistic for the early period, for the reasons mentioned. As far as the passion of Jesus is concerned, while the tradition of Mary Magdalene is historical, her role as first witness to the 'resurrection' cannot be confirmed. Nevertheless, Susanne Heine is quite certainly right in the following comment.

'In any case Mary Magdalene has a theological symbolic significance. The conflict between the mainstream church and Gnosticism attests that the question of the role of women in the communities was an integral part of this battle. Mary Magdalene does not stand for the emancipation of women – that would be an anachronism – but for the fact that receiving the Spirit, receiving grace from the Redeemer, faith and the handing down of this faith in proclamation and teaching, together with all the community functions which go with it, are not limited to men.'[635]

*4.5.3 John 20.19–23: The Risen Christ before the disciples*

### 4.5.3.1 Redaction and tradition

[19] The note of time takes up that in v.1. Whereas there it was early in the morning, now it is the evening of the same day (Sunday). Otherwise there is no connection with the previous narrative. There is no reference either to the message of Mary (v.13) or to the scene with the disciples at the empty tomb (vv.3–10). That suggests a basis in tradition for the present scene. 'For fear of the Jews'[636] appears similarly word for word in John 7.13; 19.38; cf. 9.22. The motif of fear in the parallel pericope Luke 24.36–43 appears in v.36 as a reaction to the appearance, and this may be original. In it, the redactional formula 'he stood among them'(v.36) corresponds to the phrase in the present verse 'he stood among them', which thus corresponds almost word for word. It may be explained from a use of the Gospel of Luke, especially as there are not two verbs of movement in the finite form combined with 'and' in any other narrative passage in John. Furthermore, 'among them' is unusual in John. The appended greeting ('and he said to them, "Peace be with you"') similarly goes back to Luke because of the word-for-word correspondence with Luke 24.36b.

[20] The demonstrative showing of his hands and his side (= taking up John 19.34) is remarkable at first glance, is done for no recognizable reason,[637] and in literary terms is probably governed by Luke 24.40. Perhaps this is meant to emphasize 'that the Risen Lord and the Crucified are one'.[638] The verse goes on to prepare for the next scene (vv.24–29) in so far as the disciples do not need to touch Jesus to believe, but Thomas will ask to. Verse 20b depicts the reaction of the disciples ('when they saw the Lord' corresponds to 'I have seen the Lord' [v.18]). The motif of the joy of the disciples recalls Luke 24.41. The parallel can again be explained from a literary relationship.

[21] The further greeting (after the first one from the tradition [v.19 end]) shows a redactional seam). The author repeats the greeting of peace and touches on the mission of the disciples (cf. John 17.18). 'There is no mention of an introduction to scripture in Luke 24.44–46 and the command to engage in mission no longer has the character of a detailed mission charge.'[639] That the saying about mission has been *formed* by the author does not mean that 'the motif of the sending of the disciples by Jesus as such was first introduced by

the evangelist into the report of his source',[640] since I Cor.9.1 and Gal.1.15f. suggest the possibility that a 'type of appearance account which . . . culminates in a mission charge from Jesus . . . seems to be relatively old'.[641] However, the linguistic form of the charge can no longer be reconstructed.

[22] There are parallels in the history of religion and in the Old Testament[642] to the breathing on the disciples, and it has an animistic character. It is unexpected after the sayings about the Paraclete (14.16; 16.7, 13; cf.6.39), which are stamped with a personalistic understanding of the Spirit.

> 'Evidently here the evangelist, perhaps using an earlier report as a basis, is making a concession to popular views, which is allowed to stand as such and must be spared any attempt to adapt it to views which are expressed elsewhere . . . And in v.23 he speaks for the only time in his book of the forgiveness of sins, which does not fit his view of Christianity but rather is an adaptation to the ideas of the community or to the material from which he is working.'[643]

The absence of an article before 'Holy Spirit' is striking in the phrase 'receive Holy Spirit'; it is unique in the Gospel of John, but has a parallel in Acts 2.4.

[23] The expression 'forgiveness of sins' is, as I have already remarked, unique in the Fourth Gospel (but cf. I John 1.9; 2.12) and may, like the previous verse, go back to traditions (e.g. Luke 24.47).

The closest parallels to the authority spoken of in this verse are Matt.16.18f.[644] and 18.18 and Luke 24.7 (this passage has been used here).[645]

## Summary of the analysis of the tradition

In general it may be said that the tradition used here presupposes Luke 24.36–49.[646]

The material which may be presumed to underlie it contained an undated report about a sudden appearance of Jesus to his disciples. The disciples were terrified. Jesus invites his disciples (perhaps as a reaction to their doubt) to touch him and gives them the Spirit with an archaic gesture of breathing on them, sends them (into the world?) and at the same time promises them authority to forgive sins.

#### 4.5.3.2 Historical

Simply because of the dependence on the Lukan account we can rule out the possibility that the traditions come from an eye-witness report. Nevertheless the tradition seems old and in parts 'authentic'. That applies to the combination of 'seeing' and 'being sent' and 'seeing' and 'being filled' with Holy Spirit. This pneumatic event, which can also be read out of Paul's primary account, forms the historical nucleus of the tradition of John 20.19–23. (There can be original elements even in later material.) Would it be going too far to see here (along with Luke 24.36–43) a reflection of the appearance to the Twelve? However, the fleshly objectification of Jesus is a secondary addition and unhistorical (v.20). The original seeing of the Easter witnesses was a seeing in the spirit and not the seeing of a revived corpse.

### 4.5.4 *John 20.24–29: Doubting Thomas*

#### 4.5.4.1 Redaction

This story is unique among the Easter stories. Thomas is not known elsewhere as an Easter witness and his stubbornness is also unique (cf. v.25b). The present story is in tension with the previous story, since according to vv.21–23 *all* the disciples except Judas, and this must have included Thomas as one of the Twelve, were given the authority to forgive sins.

[24] This verse explains why the appearance to Thomas is taking place or had to take place. Thomas was not present when the coming of Jesus described previously (vv.19–23) took place. Apart from the four lists of the Twelve (Mark 3.18; Matt.10.3; Luke 6.15; Acts 1.13), Thomas[647] appears in the New Testament only in the Gospel of John (11.16; 14.5; 20.24; 21.2) and in the present pericope. Here he appears as a typical representative of doubt (cf. Matt.28.17; Mark 16.11, 13, 14; Luke 24.11, 25, 38, 41). In the early Christian period numerous works appeared under his fictitious authorship: cf. only the Gospel of Thomas,[648] the Book of Thomas[649] and the Acts of Thomas.[650]

[25] 'We have seen' takes up '(they) saw' from v.20 and 'and I saw' from vv.18f. The second part of the verse ('Unless I see in his hands the print of the nails, and place my finger in the mark of the

nails, and place my finger in his side, I will not believe') depicts a crass materialism as the condition of Thomas's faith. The demand to be able to put a hand in Jesus's side refers back to John 19.34a. The use of nails in the crucifixion of Jesus appears elsewhere only in the Gospel of Peter 6.21 and probably goes back to Ps.21.17 (LXX), which reads, 'They pierced my hands and my feet.'

[26] The note of time 'after eight days' puts the further meeting of the disciples, like the first, on a Sunday. Verse 26b repeats v.19b word for word. Jesus comes to his disciples, although the doors are shut, and greets them.

[27] This verse takes up v.20 and corresponds exactly to Thomas's wish from vv.25f. For touching as a means of being convinced of the reality of the body of Jesus and the identity of his personality cf. Luke 24.39–43 and further Epistula Apostolorum 11f. (for the text see 132f. above). But the appended invitation ('do not be faithless, but believing') indicates what really counts.

[28] Thomas does not accept Jesus' offer. He exclaims 'My Lord and my God' (cf. John 10.30), and with that comes to believe. 'That confession is wholly appropriate to him who has risen; going far beyond the earlier confession "My Master" (v.16), it sees in Jesus God himself.'[651] (At the same time it also addresses the readers who can see here, as in the confessions of Simon [John 6.68f.] or Martha [John 11.27] a model for their own faith.) There is no longer any need for touching, since the word of Jesus creates faith in Thomas.

[29] This verse also speaks in a reproachful tone (for the form cf. John 1.50) only of Thomas's seeing (and not touching) and states generally in a beatitude[652] that what matters is not seeing but faith.[653] This is not far removed from Matt.28.16–20, where 'the message of the Risen One and obedience to this word is the way to the overcoming of doubt'.[654]

The reproach made to Thomas evidently affects all the other disciples, since Thomas, too, has not asked for any other proof than Jesus has voluntarily offered the others. ' . . . the doubt of Thomas is representative of the common attitude of men who cannot believe without seeing miracles (4.48) . . . fundamentally it ought not to be the sight of the Risen Lord that first moves the disciples to believe "the word that Jeus spoke" (2.22), for this word alone should have the power to convince them'.[655]

The Thomas pericope represents, in terms of the history of the tradition, a late stage of the early Christian Easter stories. It has no genetic relationship to the earliest Easter events. Apparently an anti-docetic interest can be seen in it (as in the Johannine letters, I John 1.1; 4.1f.; II John 7 and also Luke 24.39–43). Because of its secondary reference to John 20.19–23 it is easiest to regard it as a secondary construction of the author,[656] who by means of it gave independent expression to the motif of doubt or concentrated and individualized the widespread motif of doubt in a special story.[657] This is also suggested by the similarity in the structure of the Thomas pericope to John 1.45–51[658] and the evidence that individuals often play a special role in the Gospel of John (Nicodemus [John 3.1–9], Mary and Martha [John 11.1ff.], Philip and Nathanael [John 1.43–51], the woman of Sychar [John 4.7ff.]). [659] Therefore we can follow Anton Dauer in drawing this conclusion:

'The evangelist has attached to the figure of Thomas the theme of the unbelief of the disciples, its overcoming through an encounter with the Risen Lord and the treatment of the problematical question of the value of such faith.'[660] Here he transfers the motif of doubt which he evidently removed from John 20.19–23 into the present story.

### 4.5.5 *The Risen Christ by the Sea of Tiberias*

#### 4.5.5.1 Introduction

This chapter has clearly been attached to John 20 at a subsequent stage, as emerges for the following reasons:

1. 20.30f. is explicitly the conclusion to a book.
2. 21.24f. introduce the Beloved Disciple as the author of the whole Gospel, while there are no references whatsoever to this author in chs.1–20.
3. John 21 sometimes has different language from John 1.20. Cf. especially *paidia* (v.5) as an address to the disciples and *adelphoi* (v.23) as a designation of Christians.[661]

However, this finding does not amount to any preliminary decision about the age of the traditions contained in John 21. Still, in contrast to John 20 we are to regard the author as the one who composed John 21. (He is not necessarily identical with the author of John 1–20, though that cannot be excluded.)

We shall now go on to investigate first the redaction, secondly the tradition (this step includes a discussion of the relationship between the traditions that we have brought out and other traditions of the resurrection), and thirdly historical elements in the traditions.

#### 4.5.5.2 John 21.1–14: The appearance of Jesus by the Sea of Tiberias

##### 4.5.5.2.1 Redaction

[1] This verse corresponds to v.14 and comes from the author ('he revealed himself' [twice] in v.1 takes up 'was revealed' in v.14). In both verses John 20 is presupposed. 'For the third time' (v.14) describes the appearance narrated in John 21.2–13 as the third. In that case 20.19–23 would be the first and 20.26–29 the second appearance to the disciples. (The appearance to Mary Magdalene [20.11–18] is evidently not counted as it was not an appearance to disciples [plural].)

[2] This begins with a list of the people involved: 'Simon Peter' refers back to 20.2, 'Thomas who is called the twin' to 20.24. For Nathanael cf. John 1.45–49. The additional mention of the sons of Zebedee may go back to tradition, as they are not mentioned elsewhere in the Gospel of John. By contrast the two other disciples who are not described further because of the reference back in 'his disciples' to v.1 are redactional. All in all, then, we have the number seven, which has symbolic value. It stands for the future church (cf. also the seven churches in Rev.2–3).[662]

[3] This is the concentrated narrative of an unsuccessful fishing trip. Peter resolves to go fishing, the disciples in v.2 want to come too, the plan is carried out and the failure noted. (There is a close parallel in Luke 5.5, 'We have toiled the whole night and caught nothing.') Here it is striking how the six disciples are subordinated or attached to Peter (Peter makes the decision and the disciples follow).

[4] The note of time, 'as day was breaking', follows on from 'that night' in v.3. The story of a failed fishing trip becomes the story of an appearance of Jesus. Like Mary Magdalene before them (John 20.14), the disciples do not recognize Jesus (Luke 24.16). There is no longer any differentiation between Peter and the disciples.

[5] The familiar address 'children' (*paidia*) appears elsewhere only in I John 2.14, 18. Jesus's question about food expects a negative answer. The Greek word for food (= *prosphagion*) is often synonymous with 'fish'. The author is already thinking of the meal

described later, for which bread is needed as well as fish, and sees to it that the necessary fish have to be caught in what follows (v.6; cf. Luke 24.41). But according to v.9 there are already fish on the fire (so there was no need to catch any more). 'This inconsistency is most easily explained by supposing that the author wants to connect the story of the catch of fish and the report of the appearance (to which the meal belongs).'[663]

[6] This contains Jesus' command to the disciples to cast the net on the right side. They obey him and 'were not able to haul it in, for the quantity of fish' (cf. the precise parallel in Luke 5.4–6). The failure noted at the end of v.3 becomes an abundant success because of a saying of Jesus and the way in which it is obeyed (similarly Luke 5).

[7] Redactionally this is an interlude involving the Beloved Disciple and Peter, which has been inserted. As in John 20.8 it is emphasized that the Beloved Disciple recognizes Jesus before Peter. So he surpasses him a further time (thus also later in 21.20–23). When Peter learns that it is the Lord, after casting off his upper garment he immediately throws himself into the sea to swim to Jesus. This action expresses his great love for him (cf.v.15).

[8] This is about the other disciples (who are dragging the great catch of fish ashore) and explains why Peter could leap into the water (and swim to Jesus): they were only a hundred yards off shore.

[9] This brings together the catch of fish and the (Lord's) meal.

[10] Fish from the abundant catch are to be part of the meal, although there were already fish there (v.9). In this way the traditions of the catch and the appearance are closely interwoven.

[11] Peter again takes a central role in the story. It is he alone who drags the net and 153 fish to shore. This emphatic information about the number of the fish and the fact that the net did not break on the one hand stresses the miraculous character of the event (cf. John 6.13), and on the other calls for further interpretation. Perhaps for the redactor the net is a symbol of the church and the large number of fish expresses its universality. Here – as in Matt.16 – Peter again seems to be the guarantor of this church.

[12] The first part of the verse with Jesus' invitation to breakfast is in tension with the second part of the verse. What has the statement that no one dared to ask Jesus who he was to do with Jesus' invitation to have a meal, especially as it is said in the next clause that they knew that it was the Lord? Here there is a remarkable tension between the disciples' wanting to ask and their alleged knowledge. It is caused by

the redactor, who already in v.7 had established the identity of Jesus (only Peter had heard of it).

[13] The introduction of the sentence with 'Jesus came' corresponds to the beginning of 20.18 ('Mary Magdalene came'). The gesture of dividing the bread and the fish recalls John 6.11. At any rate the gestures of Jesus explain that the Risen Lord is present (cf. Luke 24.30). The disciples now no longer need to ask the question for which according to v.12 they did not have the courage.

[14] See above on v.1.

### 4.5.5.2.2 *Traditions*

(a) Verses 2–4a belong to the tradition of a catch of fish which, as Luke 5 shows, was connected with an Easter narrative of a call of Peter. However it must be emphasized that John 21 contains the tradition of a fishing trip that was at first unsuccessful.

(b) Verses 4b, 12–13 are the tradition of an Easter appearance.

### 4.5.5.2.3 *Historical*

On (a) Cf. 86 above on Luke 5/John 21.

On (b) The tradition is late (see what is said above 140ff. on the Emmaus story). The eucharist is understood as a symbol of encounter with the Risen Lord.

### *Appendix: On Rudolf Pesch's thesis:*[664]

Pesch has investigated the relationship between Luke 5.1–11 and John 21.1–14 and attempted to show (a) that the tradition of the story of a catch of fish in Luke 5 is genetically connected with the tradition of the story of a catch of fish in John 21 and (b) that this is *not* an Easter story.

Criticism: (a) is generally apt and largely underlies the remarks made above (though unlike Pesch, I regard John 21.7 as redactional); (b) is to be challenged since the narrative is *a priori* focussed on the post-Easter mission; thus it is primarily the account of a call and only secondarily a miracle story, for which in any case in Pesch's view no parallels can be adduced from the history of religion.[665]

### 4.5.5.3   The Risen Christ and Simon Peter

#### 4.5.5.3.1   *Redaction*

[15–17] The section vv.15–19, a conversation between Jesus and Peter, has an integrated structure. Jesus asks Peter, the son of John, three times whether he loves him.[666] In vv.15,16 the verb used is *agapan*, in v.17 *philein*. Peter answers three times: the first twice he says, 'Yes, Lord, you know that I love you (*philo se*)', the third time: 'Lord, you know everything, you see that I love you' (*philo se*). (Just before this it was said that Peter was grieved that Jesus had asked him the third time – apparently the first answer had not been enough.) The reaction to Peter's answer is on each occasion followed by a command by Jesus to his disciple: v.35 end, v.16 end, v.17 end. It betrays artificial shaping. The verb in the first and third commands is identical ('feed [*boske*] my lambs/sheep'), as is the object of reference ('sheep') in the second and third requests: the question generally is Peter's position of leadership in the church. Is it chance that Peter is to do what according to John 10 Jesus himself does? At all events, a deliberate literary shaping of the text by the author emerges from the careful construction.

[18–19] These verses shape the third dialogue by Jesus prophesying the death of Peter on the cross. Here the disciple is being singled out in a special way (see also v.19, 'glorify God'). Then in conclusion follows the invitation, 'Follow me'; i.e. the third command, 'Feed my sheep', is supplemented by the invitation to personal discipleship of Jesus, which (because of vv.18–19a) is a call to discipleship leading to martyrdom. Here there is a manifest reference to John 13.36 and it is said that only now is it possible for Peter to become a disciple of Jesus since despite his denial he has received forgiveness of sins. In other words, Peter is rehabilitated.

#### 4.5.5.3.2   *Traditions*

The last observation shows how the redaction wanted the meaning to be understood. The denial of Jesus by Peter has been 'overcome' by the repeated commissioning of Peter. Here the threefold structure of the dialogue is perhaps an imitation of the denial of Jesus by Peter which is also narrated three times in the Gospel of John (18.17,25–27).

It is sometimes inferred from this that there is no old tradition in the present pericope. Cf. the view of Lyder Brun, that John 21.15f. 'cannot be regarded as original tradition. The precise shaping of the story of the denial betrays . . . later reflection.'[667]

Rudolf Bultmann takes the opposite view. According to him, 'taken by itself, it provides no hint of a relation to the account of the denial. Surely the denial and the repentance of Peter ought to have found mention! And nothing like an absolution is expressed in the statement of Peter.'[668] Here Bultmann regards the tradition in vv.15–17 as a variant of the commissioning of Peter as it appears in Matt.16.17–19 and Luke 22.32. But can we rule out the possibility that the redaction suppressed a connection in the tradition betwen the commissioning and the denial?

If the hypothesis developed on 95f. above about the origin of the story of the denial is correct, the present text could be a reflection of the connection between denial and experience of grace as originally reported, all the more so since this is also probable in the basis common to Luke 5 and John 21.1–13. However, it has to be conceded that such a thesis cannot be developed from an isolated consideration of the text.

### 4.5.5.3.3  Historical

At all events, the tradition underlying John 21.15–17 derives from the recollection of a protophany of Jesus to Peter from the earliest post-Easter period.[669] In the fact of the appearance, the vision of Peter which corresponds to it and his commissioning to preside over the community of Jesus, it is certainly historical (cf. the remarks on Matt.16.17–19, see above, 87ff.).

### 4.5.5.4  John and the disciple whom Jesus loved

The section once again (after 20.3ff.; 21.7) illuminates the relationship between Peter and the Beloved Disciple.

### 4.5.5.4.1  Redaction

[20] Since it is said that the Beloved Disciple is (already) following Jesus while Peter only receives the invitation in v.9, the Beloved Disciple is once again given a spiritual superiority. The verse consciously refers back to the scene at the Last Supper (John 18.15).

[21–22] Since Jesus had prophesied the crucifixion of Peter in v.18, Peter asks him about the destiny of the Beloved Disciple. The author picks up a saying current in his community that the Beloved Disciple would not die before the return of Jesus and seeks to explain its real meaning. For that he uses a conversation between Jesus and Peter. Jesus tells Peter that it is no concern of his whether the Beloved Disciple remains alive until he himself come again. Rather, Peter is to follow him (an endorsement of the call to discipleship in v.19 and the pre-eminence of the Beloved Disciple over Peter).

[23] This verse corrects the expectation of the Johannine community about the survival of the Beloved Disciple by explaining this assumption as a misunderstanding. Jesus did not prophesy this, but only presented it as a possibility. The fact that a false expectation about the survival of the Beloved Disciple had to be corrected is to remove all doubt about the historical existence of this disciple.

To sum up: the conversation in vv.20–23 between Peter and Jesus is meant to clarify two points:[670] (a) The authority promised to Peter has gone over to the Beloved Disciple (Peter has to die a martyr's death, while the Beloved Disciple remains). (b) Despite his death the Beloved Disciple remains the guarantor of the Johannine community, since in v.24 he is regarded as the author of the Gospel of John. Conclusion: the present section goes back in its entirety to the author. So we need not investigate the question of the traditions used or their historical content.

## 4.6 Retrospect

In the last chapter we analysed all the early Christian texts on the resurrection, starting from the kerygmatic tradition (I Cor.15). As a conclusion to this investigation and to some extent in order to deepen it, we need (a) to recall some overarching perspectives and (b) to seek some criteria for the still unresolved controversy over the place of the first appearance.

(a) The clear result of the analytical part is that the traditions of the appearance and the tomb originally did not have anything in common. The earliest appearance did not take place at the tomb, and the tomb tradition is already a response to Jewish questions about the disappearance of the body, which goes hand in hand with the Christian assurance of the bodily resurrection of Jesus. As time went on, the traditions of tomb and appearance were brought increasingly closer together, so that the nature of the original appearance becomes almost unrecognizable. But through Paul we can gain some idea of the original event.

(b) Where did the original appearance take place, if not at the tomb of Jesus in Jerusalem? Taking everything together, most arguments suggest Galilee. Certainly a *direct* flight of the disciples there is improbable for a number of reasons (see above, 95) but no one has been able to give a plausible explanation of how the Galilean appearances could have come into being after the Jerusalem appearances unless the disciples had been present there. Here recollections of their historical time with Jesus in Galilee may in retrospect have shaped the formation of the appearance stories.

# 5  The History and Nature of the Earliest Christian Belief in the Resurrection

According to the evidence of all the New Testament Gospels the Roman prefect Pontius Pilate had Jesus crucified on a Friday – probably around 30 CE. The group of male disciples who had come up from Galilee to Jerusalem with him for the passover abandoned him in flight either before or at the arrest; after initial hesitation even including Simon Peter, one of the Twelve, who had a pre-eminent position among Jesus' disciples. By contrast, women followers of Jesus, who had also travelled with him from Galilee to Jerusalem for the passover, stayed with the Master longer.

The motives for the execution of Jesus by the Roman Pilate are clear. He saw him as a political troublemaker, who had to be put out of action politically. Evidently Jesus was falsely accused of being a political agitator by elements of the Jerusalem priesthood who were hostile to him, in reaction to his eschatological and messianic activity, which perhaps included a claim that he was identical with the coming judge-Son of Man. How far a disciple (Judas) was also involved in this – probably for other motives – need not be discussed further here.

The trial, execution and death of Jesus took place on one and the same day. This was followed by the sabbath, which in that year coincided with the first day of the feast of passover.[671] This presented the Jews with the problem what to do with the body of Jesus, since according to Jewish custom it was against the law to leave a dead body on the cross overnight (Deut.21.23) and moreover on a sabbath, which in addition coincided with the first day of the feast of the passover. At all events, the Jews were given permission by Pilate to take the body of Jesus down from the cross. Either the Jews entrusted Joseph of Arimathea with putting Jesus in a tomb, or Jews unknown to us buried the body at a place which can no longer be identified. That settled matters for the relevant Jewish authorities and Pilate, in whose view Jesus of Nazareth was only one of many Jewish messianic pretenders.

Women followers of Jesus kept as near as possible to him in his last hours, even if they could not avert his fate. They certainly included Mary from the Galilean fishing village of Magdala (whom Jesus had cured of a serious illness [Luke 8.2]).

No one knows what Jesus felt in his last hours. The words attributed to him during the trial and on the cross are certainly later creations. Nor, for example, can it be said that he really collapsed inwardly, as is often suggested,[672] though the opposite cannot be said either.

So Good Friday ended in silence as in a dark cave, and thus the torch lit by Jesus was evidently snuffed out in an ice-cold way. However, not long after the death of their master on the cross and the return of the disciples to Galilee a new spring unexpectedly dawned. We do not know precisely when this happened. That it was on the third day, i.e. on the Sunday after the sabbath, can be ruled out above all because the breakthrough took place in Galilee and the disciples cannot have got back there in one or two days (and moreover during the sabbath). But not long after the Friday on which Jesus died, Cephas saw Jesus alive in a vision which also had auditory features, and this event led to an incomparable chain reaction. If Cephas had seen and heard Jesus, the content of the vision (and the audition) was passed on to others. The news went round like lightning that God had not abandoned Jesus in death, indeed had exalted Jesus to himself and that Jesus would soon be appearing as Son of Man on the clouds of heaven.[673] That created a new situation, and the Jesus movement embarked on a tremendous new beginning. Now the women and men around Jesus could go back again to Jerusalem and there take up the work which their master had left uncompleted, and call on both the people and the authorities to repent. (Perhaps the present was understood as the very last reprieve that God had given.) The first vision to Peter proved formally 'infectious',[674] and was followed by others. The group of twelve which had been called into being by Jesus during his lifetime was carried along by Cephas and also saw Jesus. And probably at the feast of weeks which followed the passover at which Jesus died, there took place that appearance to more than 500. Women, too, were now among those who saw Jesus. Indeed when opponents on the Jewish side objected and asked where the body of Jesus was, it could immediately be reported that the women had found the tomb empty and later that Jesus had even appeared to the women at the tomb.

We cannot underestimate the explosive dynamic of the beginning. So in addition the physical brothers of Jesus (cf. I Cor.9.5) were caught up in the whirlpool, and went to Jerusalem; James even received an individual vision – that James who had not thought much of his brother during Jesus' lifetime (Mark 3.21; John 7.5).

We should reckon that the events mentioned (apart from the 'discovery' of the empty tomb and the appearance of Jesus there) took hardly more than six months. Here many things were going on side by side. In addition to the experience of the risen Christ in the present the following elements of the development can be clearly grasped historically: (a) in the breaking of the bread the assembled community immediately relived for itself the fellowship with the Messiah Jesus who had been so wretchedly executed and had now been all the more powerfully endorsed; (b) the recollection of Jesus' activity and his word immediately came alive; (c) 'the eschatological-messianic word of scripture present to their minds, here above all the messianic songs of the psalter, which people had long known off by heart' were now sung 'as psalms of present fulfilment, to the glory of the exalted Messiah-Son of Man'.[675]

The movement achieved a new stage when Greek-speaking Jews joined it in Jerusalem. That may already have happened at the feast of weeks following the passover at which Jesus died, when people from all countries were in Jerusalem and heard of Jesus. At all events, the message of Jesus spread into areas outside Jerusalem and attracted the attention of the Pharisee Saul. He went into action in a way which was at first to prove extremely successful, and suppressed the new preaching until he too was overcome by Jesus and saw and heard him. With this event an outer point is reached in the earliest Easter faith, although Jesus kept appearing in the subsequent period. Paul's calling was not recognized by many in Jerusalem, but also as a result of his missionary success, at a later stage he could achieve a temporary accommodation with some of the people there. Three years after he had seen (and heard) Jesus he visited Cephas in Jerusalem and learned from him further details of the preaching and activity of Jesus.[676]

Doubtless one or other point of this historical outline of the earliest Christian belief in the resurrection needs to be corrected. The reason for this is not only the relatively meagre amount of source material, but also the nature of the event itself. 'During these momentous months of the beginning, which are so obscure to us but which shone out so splendidly for the disciples, many movements and discoveries alongside and with each other and sometimes confusingly "through each other" were possible. The encounters with the Risen Christ formed a complex knot along with the formation of the earliest exaltation christology; but we can no longer neatly untangle the individual strands and put them in chronological order, especially as the world of ideas of the first disciples, shaped by eschatological enthusiasm, did not correspond to the rules of our analytical method.'[677] However, there is no gap here, nor anything of the kind, as is often said,[678] but the beginning of a religious enthusiasm[679] with its own dynamic. The oldest history of early Christianity runs almost logically (see below), and at any rate it would be over-hasty to say, as is often done, that the resurrection of Christ, as earliest Christianity proclaimed it, was something absolutely new.[680] Such a view is over-hasty in its systematizing and is evidently looking for a metaphysical anchor instead of first discovering the individual facts and then looking at them from its level of experience, transposing them into a historical sequence.[681]

At this point the question arises: 'What was the nature of the earliest Christian belief in the resurrection?' The central point is that it was said of the the crucified Jesus of Nazareth that God had taken him to himself or exalted him, in other words that God had put himself at the side of Jesus, which was unexpected after Jesus' death on the cross. To that is attached the conclusion that God speaks to human beings in the crucified Jesus. Because Peter had this experience as his guilt feeling was broken through, it is certain, *first*, that the experience of the crucified Jesus is directly connected with the forgiveness of sins. In other words, the experience of the forgiveness of sins is an essential point of the earliest Christian Easter faith. *Secondly*, the earliest Christian Easter faith is the experience of the overcoming of death, i.e. the experience of life which from then on is at work in the community as Spirit. This life was seen as present in a vision; real eternal life was experienced here and now, the future as present. To this degree, *thirdly*, the earliest Christian Easter faith is also an eternity faith and as such an end faith.[682] Time and eternity have become one, but in such a way that the heart looks into eternity (Emanuel Hirsch). So eternal life has become the life of human beings. These three essential characteristics also relate to Paul – as 83f. above show – and were concisely summed up by Martin Luther in the Small Catechism: 'Where there is forgiveness of sins, there too is life and blessedness.'[683]

The three core points of the earliest Christian Easter faith were put in different frameworks of theological ideas. First, the resurrection of Jesus was understood as the beginning of the general resurrection of the dead (cf. I Cor.15.20: Jesus as the firstfruits of those who sleep), then that God has exalted Jesus to himself (Phil.2.9), or even in a combination of both statements (I Thess.1.10). But the issue is not these different theological ideas; even without them the content of the first experience has become clear.

A further point needs clarification: as is well known, a wealth of different narratives were in circulation about the encounter with the Risen Christ, which have been analysed above. How do these relate to the original Easter experience? In the analysis it has proved that all are in some way removed from the real Easter situation and historically speaking no longer contain primary reports. But some express in narrative form the content of the original Easter experience: the forgiveness of sins (John 20.19–23; Luke 5/John 21), the experience of life (John 20.11–18), the experience of eternity (Luke 24.13–31). Others represent Jesus in the flesh and in this respect are even more remote from the Easter situation, though we must immediately add that the Easter experiences in the Spirit, say of the Pharisee Paul, necessarily contain pre-existent material features because of the world view: the heavenly body of Jesus (and of Christians) is a body which is pneumatic and imagined in material form, even if it has been changed. However, that does not in any way alter the fact that the original experience of a visionary kind happened in the Spirit, in rapture (I Cor.15.6; cf. Rev.1.10), and that the Gospel narratives mentioned above have little to do with the Pauline conceptual material. (According to Paul 'the Risen Christ' did not eat, he was not with his disciples for forty days; Jesus entered God's presence directly at the moment of his death [cf. Luke 16.22; 23.43]; he was exalted directly from the cross to God).[684]

Now one could make the criticism that the main points of the earliest Christian belief in the resurrection depicted in this way are an expression of wishes, in other words a projection. This argument of a reductionist hermeneutic which locates the centre of the meaning of faith as it were behind the backs of those who convey it has beyond question some degree of justification and must be

looked at seriously. At any rate this argument is more honest than
the claim of a conservative hermeneutic that behind the resurrection faith stands the testimony of divine revelation which tolerates
no questions.[685] That happens even in Hans Grass's book, truthful
though it is: he speaks of an objective resurrection vision and
connects this, in contrast to subjective visions, with revelation[686]
(cf. similarly Theodor Keim's thesis of a 'telegram from
heaven').[687] In this and other cases scholars know *a priori* what
needs to be proved or to be shown to be probable, and questions
are not asked at the decisive point.

The objection to reductionist hermeneutics is closely connected
with the concept of symbol which underlies it. Thus for example
according to Sigmund Freud symbols are concealments of unconscious, suppressed wishes.[688] But the question is whether symbols
do not contain more, all the more so since the positivistic
philosophy which underlies the reductionist hermeneutic takes no
note of spiritual, artistic and religious content and such a form is
now no longer advocated by any perceptive contemporaries. Thus
Paul Tillich understands symbol in a different way, in the framework of Schelling's idealistic philosophy.[689] First of all he distinguishes symbols from signs and metaphors, but also from dream
symbols, 'which in reality are symptoms' (3). For clarification he
calls them 'representative symbols', which display five characteristics:

The first and fundamental characteristic of all representative symbols is
their property of pointing beyond themselves . . . The second characteristic of all representative symbols is that the symbol participates in the
reality of that to which it points . . . This notion leads to the third
characteristic of all representative symbols: they cannot be invented
arbitrarily (4). The fourth characteristic of representative symbols is
their power to disclose dimensions of reality which are usually concealed
by the domination of other dimensions. One could also add a fifth
characteristic of representative symbols: their power to build up and
order, and their power to divide and destroy . . .'(5).

Now of course it should be noted that this does not yet say anything
about the truth of the resurrection faith of the first Christians,
which perhaps is to be understood symbolically. (Tillich regarded
the resurrection as a symbol which shows 'the New Being in Jesus
as the Christ as victorious over the existential estrangement to

which he has subjected himself'.[690]) But the attack of a reductionist hermeneutic can for the moment be warded off by the indication of another possible (and plausible) understanding of symbol. Now at last we get to the heart of the matter.

# 6 The Resurrection Faith of the Earliest Community and Ourselves – or: Can We Still be Christians?

We can no longer understand the resurrection of Jesus in a literal sense, i.e. in a bloody way, as the philosopher Kurt Hübner[691] has recently proposed (only we *must* regard the cross in a bloody way), for historically speaking we do not know the slightest thing about the tomb (was it empty? was it an individual tomb at all?) and about the fate of Jesus' corpse: did it decay? At any rate I regard this conclusion as unavoidable. But even today, or again today, quite a few people are attempting to avoid it by either claiming a historical periphery to the resurrection,[692] deliberately going beyond everything that is otherwise historically probable,[693] or putting the resurrection of Jesus in the framework of a conception of universal history and thus understanding it as a historical fact – in an eschatological sense (as Panneberg does). In my view all these approaches are really apologetic manoeuvres to evade history. Here the historical question is demoted to a question which is marginal compared with theology, theology is claimed in solemn exaggeration as the better history, or the concept of the historical is completely transformed into that of the eschatological and thus elevated into the speculative sphere. However, this immense apologetic concern itself shows that the historical question is one of the decisive questions which expects *answers* in our time.

What is correct about the statements mentioned above is that Christian faith, understood in the traditional sense,[694] has to or had to speak in this or a similar way. But the literal statements about the resurrection of Jesus mentioned above have lost their literal meaning with the revolution in the scientific picture of the world.

'The physical emergence of the Risen Christ from the tomb, the bodily ascension to a particular place which is called the throne of God and the bodily return to judgment form a single necessary sequence in which no member can be altered without everything breaking into pieces . . . Where is he, if he really emerged from the tomb through a divine resuscitation into a transfigured healthy human body which is now different from the old body that existed before the crucifixion only by the addition of some miraculously extra properties? He is said no longer to have been seen after a period of forty days, and death is said to have had no more power over him. We can see that the ascension as a bodily process becomes necessary, and with it also the spatially limited throne of God and the bodily return. But nowadays the bodily ascension into a heaven in which God's throne stands, and the bodily return from this heaven accompanied by angelic hosts, is impossible for us, because according to our knowledge of the cosmos there is no such heaven. So we must simply regard these notions as images of the ineffable if we want to find anything serious in them at all.'[695]

Then the critical consideration of the earliest Easter stories produced a completely different result from that recently presupposed by a theory with a supernaturalist orientation. So if the traditional notions of the resurrection of Jesus are to be regarded as finished and need to be replaced by another view, the question immediately and inexorably arises: are we still Christians? At the end of his life David Friedrich Strauss thought that he had explicitly to say no to this question, because for him the elements of the Christ myth had dissolved and not much more could be said of Jesus than his enthusiasm.[696] At this point I shall not discuss this further except to comment that international critical New Testament research has clearly arrived at a historical minimal consensus in respect of the historical Jesus.[697]

Now already various comments have been made above that through the Easter faith Peter was fundamentally led to a better understanding of the Jesus whom he knew. The experience of the unlimited grace of God which Peter had had in personal acquaintance with Jesus was made irrevocable at Easter.[698] Furthermore, Easter resulted in a continuation of Jesus' practice of sharing meals. In other words, Easter led to an experience with Jesus which strengthened the old one. Finally, our historical reconstruction led to the insight that the structural characteristics of the Easter experience indicated above, of the forgiveness of sins, the experience of life, the experience of eternity, are contained in the words and story of Jesus. So we have to say that before Easter, everything that was finally recognized after Easter was already present.[699] In between, however, lay the bloody event of the cross. Through the cross – to the judgment of faith – Jesus showed himself alive to the disciples. Here it is clear that no one can prove historically that Jesus deliberately took the cross upon himself, but this cannot be refuted either. Faith recognizes in the cross of Jesus the acceptance of death as an act of life.[700] It recognizes the deepest and most mysterious 'Yes' of God, where the heart first of all perceives nothing but the 'No'. It sees an absolutely hidden eternity, an absolutely hidden grace and never-failing offer of freedom where the neutral observer sees only the death of Jesus on the cross. However, faith no longer looks at history as one looks at nature, but in constant dialogue with it while being affected by it. The necessary historical distance is preserved, and at the same time the personal attitude of hearing and seeing is included.

Now that also means that traditional faith is not really robbed of any of its content provided that we ask critically enough – with all our heart and with all our soul – and do not regard historical research as a threat to our faith. David Friedrich Strauss's remark that it was the deluded belief in the resurrection which helped the proclamation of Jesus to its unprecedented success (see 9f. above)[701] is therefore too meagre in this generalized form since, to state it once again, the sayings and history of Jesus already contain within themselves all the characteristics of the earliest resurrection faith, so that the earliest witnesses, purged by the cross, were saying, sometimes in another language, the same thing as Jesus.[702] Therefore to the question 'Can we still be Christians?' the answer has to be a confident 'Yes'. And the further question whether the *extra nos* is guaranteed is to be answered with an emphatic affirmative, because Jesus is not an invention or a projection: 'We are Christians because, in the human Jesus, we have met with a fact whose content is incomparably richer than that of any feelings which arise within ourselves – a fact, moreover, which makes us so certain of God that our conviction of being in communion with him can justify itself at the bar of reason and of conscience.'[703] The man Jesus is the *objective* power which is the enduring basis of the experiences of a Christian (cf. 47). Through Jesus we are 'first lifted into a true fellowship with God' (60). Jesus grasps me, makes me bow down, exalts me and makes me blessed, loves me, through all the strata of the tradition. He is the ground of faith. (The statement that he is risen, whatever it means, and e.g. statements about the future of Christians as notions of faith for which there is no epistemology are to be distinguished from this ground of faith [345–9].)[704] However, it also has to be said that historical proofs alone are not enough. 'Jesus is a person who encounters us through historical mediation, a person who like all living persons is not bound to time in what one can perceive of their doing ... all certainty in the personal relationship ends up in relatively doubtful material which can be disclosed only through interpretation.'[705]

So it is here on the historical Jesus, as he is presented to me by the texts and encounters me as a person through historical reconstruction, that the decision of faith is made, not on the risen Christ as I would have liked him to be,[706] or as for example he is accessible archetypally to all human beings as a symbol of the self.[707] However, I *believe* that this Jesus was not given over to annihilation through death,[708] and the notion of his being with God, his exaltation, his resurrection and his life follow almost automatically from our communion with God – but in constant relationship to Jesus' humanity – without, however, it being possible to make statements about his present being. He is hidden from us as the Exalted One; only God is manifest. We must stop at the historical Jesus, but we may believe that he is also with us as one who is alive now.[709]

If, to sum up, the man Jesus as the ground of faith is the clue to God in our life, and notions of faith arise from the communion with God which is opened up as a result, then in conclusion the question can be asked: What do you think about probably the most important idea of faith, the hope of resurrection? To put it concretely, What do you think about your own future, about your own death?

As is well known, for a long time a wide-ranging discussion has been in progress as to whether insights into life after death are possible through parapsychology, occultism or other experiments.[701] Whether these approaches are accessible to general experience and whether from a philosophical perspective they contribute anything to a possible knowledge of what is beyond the earthly[711] remains to be seen. First of all, at any rate only a few fragmentary notions seem to remain of the notion of another world which Martin Luther could still paint so broadly,[712] if anything has come down at all. One commonly gets the impression that modern Protestant theoogy leaves no hope at all of 'resurrection' for the individual.[713]

But two things must be said here.

*First*: This point will be stated in close connection with Emanuel Hirsch, whose work most encouraged me in writing the present

work and indeed first gave me the courage to open up the theme that
has been discussed once again from the beginning. He writes:[714] 'In
its more precise images and notions our thought is always dependent
on data from experience of the world which now do not allow
conclusions towards the transcendent . . . Self-critically we have to
note that we can understand eternal life, which opens up with death
to the one standing in belief in redemption, only poetically and in
similes, in images and words' (219). 'As all knowledge bears within
itself an inner relationship to its limit, it would destroy itself if it were
not ready to honour intimations of something beyond the conscious
world which transcend knowledge. The interpretation of the mystery of death through belief in an eternal life is such an intimation'
(221). 'Wherever Christian belief in redemption is expressed, beyond
the person of the believer it also becomes a power against the
demonic nature of slavery to this world which today threatens to
make so many people – including theologians – defenceless against
practical atheism' (222).

*Secondly*: the unity with God experienced in faith continues
beyond death – that is the insight of faith which, as it talks of this,
takes on features of praise. It comes to consummation in God while
still in the night of death – 'there is nothing to think about *beyond*
such faith . . . it makes no sense also to ask what events will follow in
the beyond'.[715] Understood in that way, the Christian faith seems
reduced almost to a minimum by comparison with former ties, but as
a result it has also become elementary. It is no harm that from now
on – to follow Carlyle – Christians should live by the little that
they really believe, not by the much that they take pains to believe.
That is a great liberation, which already bears within it the germ of
the new.

# Notes

1. Cf. only Hans Conzelmann, *An Outline of the Theology of the New Testament*, 1969, 187f. and passim. Note Conzelmann's further explanation at another point, in a conversation: 'It is quite meaningless to ask whether the resurrection is a historical fact, whether it is an event in space and time. All that is significant is that the Crucified One is not destroyed, that he is there, in the way explained at the end of the Gospel of Matthew: "I am with you always, until the end of the world" . . . It is important that he is the Lord, that the world stands under the determination of the cross. For the Risen One is the Crucified One. Only as such is he there for us to see. Mark 16.6, "He is risen, he is not here", is true, and so is John 20.29, "Blessed are those who do not see and yet believe." That is the miracle, and the rule for all other miracles. If that is clear, then one can indeed say "He is risen", independently of one's faith. The faith which I have not given myself tells me that the Risen One is at work before me, but also that one cannot bear witness to or see the Risen One other than in testimony to him' (in Werner Harenberg, *Jesus und die Kirchen. Bibelkritik und Bekenntnis*, 1966, 189f.). But one may ask back: in that case, how has Jesus risen independently of my faith? Cf. Gerhard Bergmann's legitimate question, *Alarm um die Bibel*,⁴1965. Thought of in this way, does Jesus himself live at all? He would be as dead as Goethe.

2. Rudolf Bultmann, *Theology of the New Testament* 2, 1955, 45.

3. Willi Marxsen, *The Resurrection of Jesus of Nazareth*, 1970, 126f.

4. Exceptions prove the rule. Thus the works of Bultmann's pupil Hans Conzelmann on Luke are prompted by a theological sympathy towards him, as Luise Schottroff was able to demonstrate (ead., *Befreiungserfahrungen. Studien zur Sozialgeschichte des Neuen Testaments*, TB 82, 1990, 344–89).

5. To quote Bultmann again: when *Der Spiegel* asked whether Jesus had risen in the same way as Goethe, he replied: 'One can say that Jesus has risen in the same way as Goethe if one regards the person and work of Jesus as a phenomenon of intellectual history. For in intellectual history the persons and works of great men continue to have an influence, and that is also true of Jesus. But if one understands Jesus as an eschatological phenomenon, and that means – according to Rom.10.4 . . . as the end of world history, in so far as its course is open to an objectifying consideration, then his present does not consist in his influence on intellectual history, but it comes about only on

occasion in Christian proclamation and in faith . . . In that case, to believe in the resurrection of Jesus means to allow oneself to be encountered by the proclamation and to respond to it in faith (in Harenberg, *Jesus und die Kirchen* [n.1], 209f.).

6. I would refer to my own explicit attempts to work through the theology of Bultmann and his pupils critically: *Early Christianity according to the Traditions of Acts: A Commentary*, 1989; 'Die Religiongeschichtliche Schule und ihre Konsequenzen für die Neutestamentliche Wissenschaft', in Hans Martin Müller (ed.), *Kulturprotestantismus. Beiträge zu einer Gestalt des modernen Christentums*, 1992, 311–38.

7. Otto Weber, 'Die Treue Gottes und die Kontinuität der menschlichen Existenz' (1952), in id., *Die Treue Gottes und die Kontinuität der menschlichen Existenz. Gesammelte Aufsätze I*, 1967, 99–112: 109f.: 'It is natural for our relationship to history to apply a term from ancient christology as it were in an extended interpretation and say that in view of that centre we can only have an "anhypostatic" relationship to history. Just as according to that christological reflection human "nature" has no hypostasis of its own, no essence in itself, so we may say, history has no essence in itself.' But either Jesus was wholly man or we should honestly concede that the question of history serves only as an excuse and really does not count.

8. Emanuel Hirsch, 'Verkündigung und Zwiesprache', in Joachim Ringleben (ed.), *Christentumsgeschichte und Wahrheitsbewusstsein. Studien zur Theologie Emanuel Hirschs*, TBT 50, 1992, 247–54: 247.

9. Wolfhart Pannenberg, *Jesus – God and Man*, 1968, 98.

10. Ibid.

11. Wolfhart Pannenberg, *Systematische Theologie 2*, 1991, 404 n. 15.

12. Cf. Gunther Wenz, 'Ostern als Urdatum des Christentums. Zu Wolfhart Pannenbergs Theologie der Auferweckung Jesu', in Ingo Broer and Jürgen Werbick (eds.), *'Der Herr ist wahrhaft auferstanden' (Lk 24, 34). Biblische und systematische Beiträge zur Entstehung des Osterglaubens*, SBS 134, 1988, 133–57. However, one misses any criticism of Pannenberg in this interesting contribution. By contrast see Kendrick Grobel, 'Revelation and Resurrection', in James M. Robinson and John B. Cobb (eds.), *Theology as History*, Frontiers of Theology 3, 1966, and individual questions in William Lane Craig, 'Pannenbergs Beweis für die Auferstehung Jesu', *KuD* 34, 1988, 78–104. However, it is depressing to see how in North America Pannenberg's works on Easter are almost exclusively being taken up by fundamentalist theologians, of whom Craig is also one.

13. Wolfhart Pannenberg, *Jesus – God and Man*, 401 (from the postscript to the fifth German edition).

14. As a negative reaction cf e.g. Karl Martin Fischer, *Das Ostergeschehen* ²1980, 16–20.

15. Hans Kessler, *Sucht den Lebenden nicht bei den Toten. Die Auferstehung Jesu Christi in biblischer, fundamentaltheologischer und*

*systematischer Sicht,* ²1987 (subsequent references to this work are in the text).

16. For a critique of Kessler see the review by Hansjürgen Verweyen in *ZKT* 108, 1986, 70–4.

17. Karl Barth, *Church Dogmatics* II/2, 1960, 446. This statement is taken positively by Gerhard Friedrich, 'Die Auferweckung Jesu, eine Tat Gottes oder ein Interpretament der Jünger', 1971, in id., *Auf das Wort kommt es an. Gesammelte Aufsätze,* 1978, 319–53: 352.

18. Rudolf Bultmann, 'The Problem of Hermeneutics' (1950), in *Essays,* 1955, 234–62: 260.

19. Hans-Georg Geyer, 'The Resurrection of Jesus Christ: A Survey of the Debate in Present-Day Theology', in C. F. D. Moule (ed.), *The Significance of the Message of the Resurrection for Faith in Jesus Christ,* SBT II 8, 1968, 105–136: 119.

20. Cf. my *Texte und Träume,* BensH 71, 1992, 15–17 and passim.

21. Eugen Drewermann, *Das Markusevangelium* II, ³1990, 699f., cf. 700 n.6.

22. Cf. the memorable remark that Theodosius Harnack made to his son Adolf in a letter of 29 January 1886: 'Christianity stands and falls . . . with the fact of the resurrection' (cf. Agnes von Zahn-Harnack, *Adolf von Harnack,* ²1951, 105; it continues, 'for me the Trinity is also utterly certain', ibid.). The saying is quoted as a motto by Gerhard Kittel, 'Die Auferstehung Jesu', *DTh* 4, 1937, 133–68.

23. Maurice Goguel, *La foi à la résurrection de Jésus dans le christianisme primitif. Étude d'histoire et de psychologie religieuses,* 1933, 6. For the problem generally cf. Eduard Spranger, *Der Sinn der Voraussetzungslosigkeit in den Geisteswissenschaften,* SAB, phil.-hist Klasse, 1929, 2–30.

24. Cf. Hugh Anderson, *Jesus and Christian Origins: A Commentary on Modern Viewpoints,* 1964, 185–240; John E. Alsup, *The Post-Resurrection Appearance Stories of the Gospel Tradition,* CThM A.5, 1975, 19–55; Kessler, *Sucht den Lebenden* (n.15), 161–207; Hans Hübner, 'Kreuz und Auferstehung im Neuen Testament', *ThR* 54, 1989, 262–306; and also the works mentioned by Hüber: Pheme Perkins, *Resurrection: New Testament Witness and Contemporary Reflection,* 1984; William J. Lunny, *The Sociology of the Resurrection,* 1989, 17–39; and Otto Hermann Pesch, '"Wenn aber Christus nicht auferweckt worden ist, dann ist euer Glaube nutzlos . . .", *Börsenblatt für den Deutschen Buchhandel* 159, 1992, 34–42, who for all his fairness in describing different positions and despite a noteworthy synthesis (41f.) attempts to get round the concrete problems with formulas like this: 'A historical event towers into the transhistorical reality of God; the transcendent reality of God extends into the historical event' (41). Cf. also Paul de Surgy/Pierre Grelot/ Maurice Carrez/ Augustin George/Jean Delorme/Xavier Léon-Dufour, *La résurrection du Christ et l'exégèse moderne,* LeDiv 50, 1969.

25. Fischer, *Ostergeschehen* (n.14), 16.

# 188 Notes

26. Van A. Harvey, *The Historian and the Believer. The Morality of Historical Knowledge and Christian Belief*, 1969, xvi.

27. Gerhard Marcel Martin, *Werdet Vorübergehende. Das Thomas-Evangelium zwischen Alter Kirche und New Age*, 1988, 12.

28. Cf. Richard R. Niebuhr, *Resurrection and Historical Reason. A Study of Historical Method*, 1957, 18: 'As long as theologians hope to take seriously the historical origins of the church and its proclamation, understanding the resurrection narratives constitutes the first step in the study of the New Testament.' According to Niebuhr, 'The history of recent Protestant theology can be read as a series of attempts to halt the conflict between the insistent canons of historical criticism and the unquenchable resurrection tradition' (2). But his attractively written book does not go into exegetical and historical questions enough. In Niebuhr's view, 'The resurrection of Jesus Christ . . . offers no possibility of generalizing and projecting universal laws; it offers only itself as an analogy of what is to come, and we have no rules by which to determine what is to be negated and what affirmed in this analogy . . . But of course, the resurrection, despite its similarity to all historical events, is an event unlike any other' (176f.). For criticism cf. C. F. Evans, *Resurrection in the New Testament*, SBT II 12, 1970, 176f., who among other things points out that 'we have no criteria for judging an event which is strictly without parallel' (177).

29. Eugen Drewermann, *Tiefenpsychologie und Exegese* II, ²1991, 311f.

30. Cf. also G. Ebeling, *Theologie und Verkündigung*, HUTh 1, 1962, 120: 'It is difficult to banish theological interpretation from historical work altogether'(120). To go into the psychological interpretation of Klaus Berger (*Historische Psychologie des Neuen Testaments*, SBS 146/147, 1991) would take us too far here. Cf. my brief enquiry in *Texte und Träume* (n.20), 45 n.62.

31. Goguel, *La foi à la résurrection* (n.23), 8. Interestingly he refers (ibid.) to similar remarks by Eduard Meyer (*Ursprung und Geschichte der Mormonen*, 1912, 10–13) – an indication that thorough historical work was always also concerned with the psychological interior of the history it investigated and the persons acting in it.

32. For a first orientation see 'Allgemeine Psychologie', in Walter Rebell, *Psychologisches Grundwissen für Theologen*, 1988, 34–49, and *Die Psychologie des 20.Jahrhunderts* III, 1977, 716ff. (C. T. Frey-Wehrlin).

33. The term 'depth psychology' is to be understood as 'a blanket term for the science of investigating the unconscious part of the soul and its effect on the whole of human life' (Peter-Michael Pflüger, in id. [ed.], *Tiefenpsychologische Ansätze zur Theologie, Psychologisch gesehen* 22, 1975, 10 n.3).

34. But see the historical-critical solemnity with which Fischer (see n.14) rejects a psychological diagnosis of the conversion of Paul. Among other things he writes: 'What we need here is unconditional honesty . . . We know

too little about Paul before his conversion' (75). We shall see later whether Fischer's judgment here is correct; at this point I would already conjecture that Fischer really has no interest in psychological questions, although he recognizes his obligation to the legacy of the Enlightenment, honesty or truthfulness as the 'morality of thought' (cf. also the 'obligation to truthfulness' which he mentions in the context of remarks on preaching at Easter [105]).

35. Oscar Pfister, *Die Aufgabe der Wissenschaft vom christlichen Glauben in der Gegenwart*, 1923, 13. Cf. also the important article by Kurt Niederwimmer, 'Tiefenpsychologie und Exegese', in Richard Riess (ed.), *Perspektiven der Pastoralpsychologie*, 1974, 63–78.

36. Cf. also William Wrede, *The Messianic Secret* (1901), 1971, 6f., on the limits to, but also the *necessity* of, psychological questions.

37. Albert Schweitzer, *The Mysticism of Paul the Apostle*, 1931, ixf.

38. Karl Jaspers, *Der philosophische Glaube*, 1948, 61.

39. Emanuel Hirsch, *Christliche Rechenschaft. Erster Band*, 1989 (= 1978), 9.

40. See the closing sentences of a work from the old age of the classical philologist Wilhelm Nestle (*Die Krisis des Christentums. Ihre Ursachen, ihr Werden und ihre Bedeutung*, 1947 [= 1969]), which one could wish were widely disseminated today: 'But we know that historical "Christianity" is in a serious crisis from which we can only emerge if Christians again become *honest* people, reject all hypocrisy and all that is outdated in religion and honour only the truth. Only then will the word of the Johannine Christ be fulfilled in them: "The truth will make you free"' (558).

41. Hans Grass, *Ostergeschehen und Osterberichte*, ⁴1970, 13 (author's italics). Further references to this book are in brackets in the text. For what follows see also Evans, *Resurrection* (n.28), 170–83 (Appendix: 'The Resurrection: Theology and History').

42. Alsup, *Post-Resurrection Appearance Stories* (n.24), comments critically on Grass. He regrets that in Grass the question of historicity has so shaped consideration of the resurrection stories that these are not treated in their own right. In this context the question similarly arises what one then understands by a historical investigation (for the justification of such a question see 10ff. below). The snag in Alsup becomes clear at the latest in the following mitigating (? GL) remark: 'However, one should not mistakenly assume that we *doubt* the resurrection of Jesus itself. Rather, we have made a distinction between that way of questioning and our own . . .' (Alsup, 54). The last two sentences in the book (274) then even seem to assume the historicity of the resurrection of Jesus (cf. also the preface, 7). For criticism cf. Stanley B. Marrow, *CBQ* 40, 1978, 112.

43. Ulrich Wilckens ('Der Ursprung der Überlieferung der Erscheinungen des Auferstandenen. Zur traditionsgeschichtlichen Analyse von 1Kor 15,1–11' [1963], in Paul Hoffmann [ed.], *Zur neutestamentlichen Überlieferung von der Auferstehung Jesu*, WdF 522, 1988, 139–93)

endorses the historical thrust of the works of von Campenhausen (n.57) and Grass but makes the following point: 'Now in principle one cannot consider basically historical events by themselves in isolation from their context in history. And the context of the Easter events is on the one hand the history of Jesus and the history of the beginning of Christianity and on the other the history of religious ideas which forms the horrizon of the language of the Easter witnesses' (140). The distinction made here always needs to be observed (see also below), but does not change the necessary investigation of the facts in any way.

44. Cf. simply the attempts in the volume edited by Gary A. Phillips, *Poststructural Criticism and the Bible: Text/History/Discourse*, Semeia 51, 1990. Phillips thinks historical reconstruction with the aim of objectivity 'a modern survivalist gesture that must be recognized as such' (36), thus illustrating a mood which is widespread, and not just in North America.

45. David Friedrich Strauss, *Der alte und der neue Glaube. Ein Bekenntnis*, ⁴1873, 73. The sentence before the quotation above reads: 'Historically speaking, that is, combining the tremendous effects of this faith with its complete groundlessness, the history of the resurrection of Jesus can only be described as a humbug of world history' (72f.).

46. Samuel Eck, 'Ueber die Bedeutung der Auferstehung Jesu für die Urgemeinde und für uns', HCW 32, 188, 21. Cf. id., *David Friedrich Strauss*, 1899 (dedicated to Martin Rade), cf. further Erich Grässer, ZKG 102, 1991: Easter and not suffering and dying are the basic facts 'without which there would be no New Testament' (416). The author says this against Albert Schweitzer's theology, which, he claims, 'here has really come up against its limits' (ibid.).

47. Eck, 'Bedeutung', 27.

48. Cf. also Harenberg, *Jesus und die Kirchen* (n.1), 125–66.

49. For example, in a letter to the *Göttinger Tageblatt* of 30 June 1992, which was also circulated as a press release, thirteen Göttingen professors of theology state: 'The Christian church is called by the mission charge of *the risen Christ*, "You will be my witnesses in Jerusalem and throughout Judaea and Samaria and to the ends of the earth"' (Acts 1.8), to be the witness to all individuals and peoples . . .' (my italics). As if Acts 1.8 were not the basic plan of Acts which wholly goes back to Luke.

50. Kessler, *Sucht den Lebendigen* (n.15), 19.

51. Jürgen Moltmann, *Theology of Hope*, 1967, 165.

52. Hans Küng, *On Being a Christian*, 1977, 381. Cf. also Heinrich Ott, 'Ich werde nach dem Tode nicht nichts sein . . .', in F. Buri, J. M. Lochman and H. Ott, *Dogmatik im Dialog*, 1, 1973, 273, and the criticism of Moltmann and Küng by Karl Heinz Ohlig, *Fundamentalchristologie. Im Spannungsfeld von Christentum und Kultur*, 1986, 81f.

53. The following statements may confidently be applied also to wide areas of present-day (neo-orthodox) Protestant theology in Germany.

54. Ingo Broer, "Seid stets bereit, jedem Rede und Antwort zu stehen, der

nach der Hoffnung fragt, die euch erfüllt" (1Petr 3.15). Das leere Grab und die Erscheinungen Jesu im Lichte der historischen Kritik', in id. and Jürgen Werbick (ed.), *'Der Herr ist wahrhaft auferstanden' (Lk 24, 34). Biblische und systematische Beiträge zur Entstehung des Osterglaubens*, SBS 134, 1988, 29–61: 48.

55. Kessler, *Sucht den Lebendigen* (n.15), 275. Cf. also Marxsen, *Resurrection* (n.3): 'It is of the essence of the thing, that only those who believed told of seeing Jesus. In the same way it was only those who believed who could confess the resurrection of Jesus – only those who knew that *he* comes *today* because they had experienced it' (128). Cf. also Moltmann, *Theology of Hope* (n.51): 'To put the question of the resurrection in exclusively historical terms is to alienate the texts of the Easter narrative . . . These, however . . . alienate the historian from that context of experience of the world in which he seeks to read the texts. All real understanding begins with such alienations' (182).

56. Cf. Theodor Haering, 'Das "Wie" der "Auferstehung" Jesu', in *Theologische Festschrift für G.Nathanael Bonweth zu seinem siebzigsten Geburtstag*, 1918, 120–6; Haering refers to his article, 'Gehört die Auferstehung zum Glaubensgrund?', *ZTK* 7, 1897, 331–51, and to Max Reischle, 'Der Streit über die Begründung des Glaubens auf den "geschichtlichen" Jesus Christus', *ZTK* 7, 1897, 171–264; Theodor Haering and Max Reischle, 'Glaubensgrund und Auferstehung', *ZTK* 8, 1898, 129–33; and Max Reischle, 'Zur Frage der leiblichen Auferstehung Christi', *CW* 14, 1900, 3–10.

57. Hans von Campenhausen, *Der Ablauf der Osterereignisse und das leere Grab*, SAH, phil.-hist. Klasse, 1952, ⁴1977, 54 (= id., *Tradition und Leben, Kräfte der Kirchengeschichte*, 1960, 48–113: 111f.).

58. David Hume, *An Enquiry concerning Human Understanding* (1748), Section X, 'Of Miracles'.

59. Cf. the contribution by Friedrich Wilhelm Graf, 'Rettung der Persönlichkeit. Protestantische Theologie als Kulturwissenschaft des Christentums', in Rüdiger von Bruch, id., and Gangolf Hübinger (ed.), *Kultur und Kulturwissenschaften um 1900. Krise der Moderne und Glaube an die Wissenschaft*, 1989, 103–31: 117f., on the historicization of theology and its interpretation as a historical cultural science.

60. Cf. Ebeling, *Theologie* (n.30), 1–9.

61. Cf. Emanuel Hirsch, *Osterglaube. Die Auferstehungsgeschichten und der christliche Glaube* (ed. Hans Martin Müller), 1988, 23–26.

62. Cf. e.g. Paul Hoffmann, in id., *Überlieferung* (n.43), 2: 'The old questions of the historicity of the empty tomb or the quality of the Easter appearances have been dealt with in numerous publications with long-known arguments without leading to any progress in knowledge. So I have not documented them. That also applies to the primarily apologetic-systematic question of the facticity of the resurrection. Only the earliest Christian faith in the resurrection can be the object of historical investiga-

tion, not the resurrection itself.' Why does the author stress the latter so much? For apologetic reasons? And what do we grasp historically of Easter faith if we do not investigate its historical starting point?

63. Marxsen, *Resurrection* (n.3), 128.

64. Bernhard Bron, *Das Wunder. Das theologische Wunderverständnis im Horizont des neuzeitlichen Natur– und Geschichtsbegriffes*, GTA 2, 1976. References to this book will be given in the text. Cf. also Kittel, 'Auferstehung' (n.22), 164: 'that hardly any serious reason can be offered against the New Testament interpretation of the miracle from a historical-critical analysis of the sources . . . What is there now is the claim of the miracle . . . of the event which took place through God's action in space and time. In the face of this miracle there is only the decision of faith or not faith.' These theses correspond precisely to the claims of Kittel's pupil Gerhard Friedrich, 'Auferweckung' (n.17), though remarkably he does not mention Kittel's article.

65. But cf. Friedrich Schleiermacher, according to whom the creation is described perfectly as *creatio continua*: 'however far our consciousness extends, we find nothing the origin of which cannot be brought under the concept of preservation' (*The Christian Faith*, 1928, §38.1, p.146). See also the account by Martin Ohst, 'Jesu Wunder als Thema der Dogmatik Schleiermachers', in Günter Meckenstock (with Joachim Ringleben) (ed.), *Schleiermacher und die wissenschaftlifche Kultur des Christentums*, TBT 51, 1991, 229–45.

66. Hoffmann, in id., *Überlieferung* (n.43), 13.

67. In Origen, *Contra Celsum* II, 59f.: a half-crazy woman saw Jesus after his death (59): the explanation of this could be 'that someone dreamt in a certain state of mind or through wishful thinking had a hallucination due to some mistaken vision (an experience, he says, which has happened to thousands)' (60).

68. According to Porphyry Christians worship a dead person. He asks why the 'Risen One' did not appear to Pilate or Herod, the Jewish high priest or, best, to the Roman Senate and people (cf. Adolf Harnack, 'Kritik des Neuen Testaments von einem griechischen Philosophen des 3.Jahrhunderts', *TU* 37.4, 1911, 25; Wilhelm Nestle, 'Die Haupteinwände des antiken Denkens gegen das Christentum' [1941], in id., *Griechische Studien* 1968 [= 1948], 597–660: 614.

69. I am expressing this carefully, because in the future things could perhaps be different, to go by the reflections of Wolfgang Kraus, 'Ende der Metaphysik oder Rückkehr zur Metaphysik?', in Willi Oelmüller (ed.), *Metaphysik heute? Kolloquien zur Gegenwartsphilosophie* 10, 1987, 91–6: 95f. 'Metaphysics has . . . an important task before it, namely the clarification of the limits of rationality . . . It seems to me that the revival needs a modest metaphysic. That is where a consistently thought through *ratio* leads. Many approaches are known; I find one in the late Karl Popper and his "searchlight theory". We find only what our searchlight picks out of

the dark. Who has given us the searchlight? Who leads us to turn it round, to direct it here and there? Who leads us to believe that it makes sense to seek the truth? Without this credit of the creed we would have no searchlight, nor would we have any intention of indefatigably shining it into the dark. After a further turn of the spiral we are perhaps not so far from Augustine's *Crede ut intellegas*. But we have achieved very sharp and sensitive instruments which prevent us from falling victim to the illusion of any systems of knowledge.' In my view this also applies to the theological system of knowledge (scholasticism) and not wanting to know (= kerygma theology).

70. Cf. Emanuel Hirsch, *Geschichte der neuern evangelischen Theologie* V, [3]1964, 505, on the supernaturalist critics of Strauss; cf. also 490: the 'theology of the absolute presupposition' manoeuvres itself into a *cul de sac* if it shuts out honest research and simple humanity which has not been pre-formed by Christianity (cf. 507: 'The religious do-not-touch-me').

71. Cf. J. D. M. Derrett, *The Anastasis: The Resurrection of Jesus as an Historical Event*, 1982. For this strange book, which revives the pseudo-death hypothesis (after his real death Jesus was burnt by his disciples), cf. Hans Hübner, 'Kreuz und Auferstehung im Neuen Testament', *TR* 54, 1989, 262–306: 290f.

72. Ferdinand Christian Baur in a letter of 20 December 1835, reprinted in Ulrich Köpf, 'Ferdinand Christian Baur als Begründer einer konsequent historischen Theologie', *ZTK* 89, 1992, 440–61: 458.

73. von Campenhausen, *Ablauf* (n.57), 7.

74. David Friedrich Strauss, *Das Leben Jesu für das deutsche Volk. Erster Theil*, [9–11]1895, 365.

75. Hirsch, *Osterglaube* (n.61), 24.

76. But cf. Rudolf Bultmann's preface to the first edition of *The History of the Synoptic Tradition* (1921, not in the English translation) and the exchange of letters between Wilhelm Heitmüller and Bultmann on Bultmann's intention to dedicate his work to the memory of David Friedrich Strauss. Heitmüller writes in a letter of 30 April 1920 to Rudolf Bultmann: 'In substance the dedication (viz. of your *Synoptic Tradition*) to David Friedrich Strauss is only to be welcomed; I protest in my lectures against the scurrilous but universal assertion that Strauss is outmoded.' However, Heitmüller advised his pupil Bultmann against the dedication, since it would have been regarded as provocative. Bultmann took this advice. The second edition of the work (1931) was then, as we know, dedicated 'To the Memory of Wilhelm Heitmüller'.

77. For the nature of historical method cf. Lüdemann, *Earliest Christianity* (n.6), 20f., and Harvey, *Historian* (n.26), chs. I–IV; I have long been more indebted to this than is evident from the number of explicit references.

78. Hirsch, *Geschichte* (n.70), V, 518.

79. Cf. 3f. above and e.g. also Jacques Perret, *Ressuscité? Approche historique*, 1984, 16: 'To envisage a historical approach to the resurrection of Jesus is certainly not to try to bring it totally down to the level of this

world; like everything that concerns him and his public life, the resurrection has a transcendent dimension.' These statements almost already pre-programme the author essentially to regard the New Testament accounts as reliable and the discovery of the empty tomb as historical (36). So I have not made further use of the book by this respected classical philologist (and convinced Catholic [cf. 13f.]).

80. Cf. Walter Köhler, *Ernst Troeltsch*, 1941, 405. Cf. also the complaint by Wilhelm Herrmann about the Protestant systematic theology of his time. He writes: 'Even among Protestants this study has, as a rule, been employed, not to serve religion, but to secularize it. It weaves the broad cloak under which all may creep who either do not know the terrors of religion, or who want to avoid them, but would like to live in a religion of the human sort. That semblance of scientific character which systematic theology knows well how to assume is disappearing now that even in theology a scientific work is beginning which follows seriously those laws of investigation of the truth which have been reasoned out in other spheres. Even attempts to preserve that semblance of scientific character by using the most dignified termino-logy possible will make but little difference. But all the while the disposition prevalent in this wordly procedure has been blossoming into a giant flower within the Church itself' (*The Communion of the Christian with God. Described on the Basis of Luther's Statements* [⁴1903], 1971, 236f.).

81. Cf. Hans Grass, *Theologie und Kritik. Gesammelte Aufsätze und Vorträge*, 1969, 12f.: 'Nietzsche is filled with great scorn against profes-sional historians and their eunuchistic objectivity which with the usual means of rational and causal reflection scours the nomenclature of events in order to explain everything and thus dissolve it. Authentic history has to serve life. In intuitive artistic vision it has to understand the great historical figures and events in such a way that they become effective in history ... Only monumental history has the power to shape pioneering symbols. Kierkegaard shares with Nietzsche a contempt for historical scholarship ... For here there is a concern to have objective knowledge, to make dispassionate statements and in that way to avoid the questions which existence really raises ... Historical and existential attitudes exclude one another ...' However, it has to be noted that Nietzsche does not attack historical reflections, but primarily a rationalistic version which cannot describe history in a living way. And possibly Kierkegaard's absolute alternative of the decision between history *or* existence is to be challenged.

82. 'If Christ has not been raised, then our preaching is in vain and your faith is in vain' (I Cor.15.14). We shall return to this matter and its context on pp. 45–7 below.

83. Klaus Wengst (*Ostern – Ein wirkliches Gleichnis, eine wahre Geschichte. Zum neutestamentlichen Zeugnis von der Auferstehung Jesu*, KTB 97, 1991) refers by way of warning to the example of Hermann Samuel Reimarus (see below, n. 499) and writes: 'There is no escaping in this field, but only hopeless entanglement in irreconcilable contradictions. What is

told there (viz. in the Gospels) cannot have been historical. Reimarus concluded from this that the disciples stole the body and did not agree precisely enough what they were to say '(94). Wengst himself thinks that for a historical enquiry almost everything here remains in the dark. Moreover it does not do justice to the text. Does that make any difference to the need to ask behind the texts? What needs to be said has been said against the two objections on pp. 11–15 above.

84. Cf. the powerful book by Helmut Groos, *Christlicher Glaube und intellektuelles Gewissen. Christentumskritik am Ende des zweiten Jahrtausends*, 1987. Despite rejecting Christian faith he nevertheless insists that without the traditional doctrine of the resurrection of Jesus no Christian faith is possible. Similarly the philosopher Kurt Hübner (see n.691 below).

85. Von Campenhausen, *Ablauf* (n.57), 52. Evidently he is alluding to the Jewish thesis that the disciples had stolen the body of Jesus (Matt.28.15). For this text see below, 124f.

86. Cf. Wilhelm Knevels, *Der Kreuzestod Jesu und die Botschaft von der Auferstehung*, 1980, 25: 'In no way is the "empty tomb" a proof for the resurrection of Jesus.' A physical resurrection proved by the empty tomb could not be the foundation of Christian faith (23f.).

87. Cf. the admirable work of Adela Yarbro Collins, *The Beginnings of the Gospel. Probings of Mark in Context*, 1992, 126: the author also refers in this context to Dan.12.2f., where those who awaken are not reunited with their physical bodies.

88. Goguel, *Foi à la résurrection* (n.23), 9.

89. Hans Lietzmann, *The Beginnings of the Christian Church*, [2]1949, 61f.

90. Ibid.

91. Cf. generally the major article by Thomas Nipperdey, 'Neugier, Skepsis und Erbe. Vom Nutzen und Nachteil der Geschichte für das Leben', in id., *Nachdenken über deutsche Geschichte. Essays*, [2]1986, 7–20.

92. Cf. Theodor Mommsen on the appropriate attitude for the historian: it is 'a ruthlessly honest quest for truth which yields to no doubt, does not whitewash any gaps in the tradition or in its own knowledge, and always gives an account of itself and others' (in Gerd Lüdemann, 'Emanuel Hirsch als Erforscher des frühen Christentums', in Joachim Ringleben [ed.], *Christentumsgeschichte und Wahrheitsbewusstsein. Studien zur Theologie Emanuel Hirschs*, TBT 50, 1991, 15–36: 16).

93. Ohlig, *Fundamentalchristologie* (n.52), 77.

94. Cf. also Grass, *Ostergeschehen* (n.41): the Easter experience 'was only the decisive occasion for the kerygmatic dogmatics of Easter . . . the Easter witness was from the beginning not the account of an experience but a confession of the saving action of God in Christ' (261).

95. Cf. also Rudolf Bultmann, *The History of the Synoptic Tradition*, 1968, 284–90, as a critical summary and development of Martin Albertz, 'Zur Formengeschichte der Auferstehungsberichte' (1922), in Hoffmann, *Überlieferung* (n.43), 259–70, and Lyder Brun, *Die Auferstehung Christi in*

*der urchristlichen Ueberlieferung,* 1925. The important works on the form criticism of the resurrection texts which have been written since Bultmann are noted in connection with the relevant pericopes.

96. Joachim Jeremias, *New Testament Theology, I. The Proclamation of Jesus,* 1971, 300. Further references to this book are given in brackets in the text. It is amazing, and needs explanation, how Jeremias discusses the resurrection of Jesus in the part of his *New Testament Theology* which is devoted to the proclamation of Jesus. Nikolaus Walter ('"Historischer Jesus" und Osterglaube', *TLZ* 101, 1976, 321–38) speaks in his otherwise admirable article of a 'relativization of the Easter faith . . . in Jeremias' (col.323). But the last chapter of Jeremias's *New Testament Theology* tells against this.

97. Jeremias mentions no New Testament texts and makes a general reference to the Gnostic dialogue of the Risen Christ with his disciples. On p.302 he imagines the development as follows: originally the saying of the 'Risen Lord' was limited to the calling of a name like 'Saul' (Acts 9.4); 'Mary' (John 20.16); 'Simon son of John' (John 21.15,16,17) or to a greeting (Luke 24.34; John 20.19,26) combined with a brief question ('Why are you persecuting me?' [Acts 9.4]; 'Why are you weeping?' [John 20.15]; 'Whom are you seeking?' [John 20.15]; 'Do you love me?' [John 21.15, 16, 17]) and a brief instruction (Acts 9.6; John 20.17; John 21.15,16,17).

98. Brun, 'Auferstehung' (n.95), 8.

99. François Bovon, 'Le Privilège Pascal de Marie Madeleine', *NTS* 30, 1984, 50–62: 51: 'As primitive Christianity was not monolithic, each group found its *raison d'être* and its dignity as people of God in an appearance of the risen Jesus to its first leader'; unfortunately Bovon does not discuss the historical question of the traditio-historical relationship of the appearances to one another.

100. At any rate it would be more than misleading to say: 'The resurrection tradition exhibits the same concreteness and historicity as the crucifixion pericopes' (Niebuhr, *Resurrection* [n.28], 67).

101. Goguel, *Foi à la resurrection* (n.23), 14.

102. In that context Paul refers to the successful mission in Thessalonica and in vv.9–10 he reproduces traditional formulae of faith (which can be recognized by the un-Pauline vocabulary). The Thessalonians 'turned to God from idols, to serve a living and true God, and to wait for his Son from heaven, whom he raised from the dead, Jesus who delivers us from the wrath to come' (I Thess.1.9–10).

103. Jürgen Becker, 'Das Gottesbild Jesu und die älteste Auslegung von Ostern' (1975), in Hoffmann, *Überlieferung* (n.43), 203–27: 219–24. Subsequent references to this article are given in the text.

104. Günter Klein, 'Aspekte ewigen Lebens im Neuen Testament', *ZTK* 82, 1985, 48–70: 57.

105. Cf. Philipp Vielhauer, *Geschichte der urchristlichen Literatur,* 1975, 15.

106. Paul-Gerhard Klumbies ('"Ostern" als Gottesbekenntnis und der Wandel zur Christusverkündigung', *ZNW* 83, 1992, 157–65) even thinks that: 'For the group which confesses God as the one who raised Jesus, the death of Jesus does not confirm its previous view of God. It does not go on proclaiming the God of Jesus and does not offer a basis for a continuity with Jesus' picture of God' (164).

107. However, Friedrich, 'Auferweckung' (n.17), thinks it possible with a reference to II Macc.1.24–29 that the second benediction was not present in the original version of the Eighteen Benedictions (334).

108. For the text see S. Singer, *Authorized Daily Prayer Book*, ³1890. Cf. Friedrich Wilhelm Horn, *Das Angeld des Geistes. Studien zur paulinischen Pneumatologie*, FRLANT 154, 1992, 91–5.

109. Cf. Martin Dibelius, *From Tradition to Gospel* (1971), 18–22.

110. According to Joachim Jeremias, *Die Sprache des Lukasevangeliums*, KEK Sonderband 1980, 319, this is an 'old pre-Pauline cry of Easter jubilation'.

111. The subject of *anastas* (v.19) is to be derived from the preceding pericope and appears explicitly only in v.19. But the frequent use of participles (vv.9, 10, 11, 13, 15, 20), the regular *kai – de* interchange and the frequent use of *ekeinos* (vv.10, 20) or *kakeinos* (vv.11, 13) show that the pericope is a formal unity with coherent content.

112. Joachim Gnilka, *Das Evangelium nach Markus*, EKK II.2, 1979, 353.

113. Cf. Eduard Schweizer, *Good News according to Mark*, 1970, 374.

114. However, reference should be made to the possibility that the piece of tradition is independent of the present form of the New Testament texts mentioned and goes back to the pre-Lukan tradition.

115. Drinking poison without coming to harm does not occur in Acts. Cf. a story told by Papias of Herapolis about Justus Barsabbas (Acts 1.23) as reported by Eusebius, *Church History* III, 39.9: 'He (viz. Papias) reports a further miracle about Justus surnamed Barsabbas. Although he had drunk deadly poison, through the grace of the Lord he felt no evil consequences.'

116. Cf. Rudolf Pesch, *Das Markusevangelum* II, HTK II.2, ⁴1991, 550.

117. Arnold Meyer, *Die Auferstehung Christi. Die Berichte über Auferstehung, Himmelfahrt und Pfingsten, ihre Entstehung, ihr geschichtlicher Hintergrund und ihre religiöse Begründung*, Lebensfragen, 1905, 63f.

118. C.H.Dodd, 'Die Erscheinungen des auferstandenen Christus' (1957), in Hoffmann, *Überlieferung* (n.43), 297–330: 299–305. References to the article are given in brackets in the text.

119. Dodd reckons that this group represents 'a freer and more individual treatment of the still "unformed" tradition' (314).

120. Cf. Helmut Koester, 'Überlieferung und Geschichte der frühchristlichen Evangelienliteratur', *ANRW* II 25.2, 1984, 1463–1542: 1508, and Luise Schottroff, 'Maria Magdalena und die Frauen am Grabe

Jesu' (1982), in id., *Befreiungserfahrungen. Studien zur Sozialgeschichte des Neuen Testaments*, ThB 82, 1990, 134–59: 149f.

121. Brun, *Auferstehung* (n.95), 31.

122. Cf. the commentary by Hirsch, *Osterglaube* (n.61), 51f.

123. Cf. still the attitude of Fischer, *Ostergeschehen* (n.14), to the back-dated Easter stories. He writes: 'These are texts in which one can still trace that they fit only with difficulty into the framework of a presentation of the activity of Jesus and still give some intimation of the veil which lies over the earlier view of the Easter stories' (37 – too subjective a criterion?).

124. Nikolaus Walter, 'Eine vormatthäische Schilderung der Auferstehung Jesu', *NTS* 19, 1972/73, 415–29.

125. Benjamin Allen Johnson, *Empty Tomb Tradition in the Gospel of Peter*, DissHarvard 1965.

126. 'There appeared a certain man named Jesus of about thirty years of age, who chose *us* . . .' (Fragment 4, Epiphanius, *Haer.* 30.13.2, in W.Schneemelcher [ed.], *New Testament Apocrypha* I, ²1991, 170 [P.Vielhauer and G.Strecker]; cf. the fragment from the Kerygma Petri cited at 100 below).

127. Cf. Schneemelcher, *New Testament Apocrypha* I, 228–31; Pheme Perkins, *The Gnostic Dialogue. The Early Church and the Crisis of Gnosticism*, 1980.

128. David Friedrich Strauss, *The Life of Jesus* (1836), 1973, 740. Moreover Strauss also made this point against Schleiermacher's 'second life of Jesus', i.e. against his hypothesis of a pseudo-death. For according to I Cor.15 it was not a revived human being but a heavenly being who appeared to Paul. Cf. David Friedrich Strauss, *Der Christus des Glaubens und der Jesus der Geschichte. Eine Kritik des Schleiermacher'schen Lebens Jesu*, 1865, 198f.

129. Craig, *Beweis* (n.12) differs: 'What is of interest is not how the appearances took place but who appeared' (99). But Craig speaks dogmatically of historical matters, avoids concrete investigations and finally postulates the corporeality of the *soma pneumatikon* in Paul, to be taken literally, and not opposed to the corporeality of the risen Christ in the Gospels (95–102).

130. It is another question whether I Cor.15.5 is the summary of an originally detailed narrative of the first appearance to Peter or whether there was only individual information behind it. Wilckens, 'Ursprung' (n.43), 171f., is restrained at this point.

131. This not for *a priori* reasons but from observations on the text – on Pierre Benoit, 'Die Himmelfahrt', *RB* 56, 1949, 161–203 = id., *Exegese und Theologie, Gesammelte Aufsätze*, KBANT, Düsseldorf 1965, 182–218.

132. Cf. the defence of the originality of the Galilean tradition by Fischer, *Ostergeschehen* (n.14), 45–55, and the differing thesis of Bernd Steinseifer, 'Der Ort der Erscheinungen des Auferstandenen. Zur Frage alter galiläischer Ostertraditionen', *ZNW* 62, 1971, 232–65; for criticism of Steinseifer cf.

Notes                                   199

Thorwald Lorenzen, 'Ist der Auferstandene in Galiläa erschienen?', *ZNW* 64, 1973, 209–21.

133. von Campenhausen, *Ablauf* (n.57), 37, 48f.

134. Barn.21.2–9 belongs to the secondary framework of the letter.

135. Rudolf Bultmann, 'Karl Barth, *The Resurrection of the Dead*' (1926), in id., *Faith and Understanding* (1933), 1969, 66–94: 83. However, Gerhard Sellin, *Der Streit um die Auferstehung der Toten. Eine religionsgeschichtliche und exegetische Untersuchung von I Korinther 15*, FRLANT 138, 1986, 254, differs: 'I Cor.15.1–11 is not about providing historical credibility but about the soteriological function of the kergyma.' This alternative is wrong. Hans-Heinrich Schade, *Apokalyptische Christologie bei Paulus. Studien zum Zusammenhang von Christologie und Eschatologie in den Paulusbriefen*, GTA 18, 1981, 199f., passes a more appropriate judgment – because it is historical.

136. Wolfgang Schrage, 'I Korinther 15,1–11', in Lorenzo de Lorenzi (ed.), *Résurrection du Christ et des Chrétiens (1Co 15)*, 1985, 21–45: 48.

137. E.g. Philip E. Devenish, 'The So-Called Resurrection of Jesus and Explicit Christian Faith: Wittgenstein's Philosophy amd Marxsen's Exegesis as Linguistic Therapy', *JAAR* 51, 1983, 7–90: 177, has described how Paul uses the appearances of the Risen Christ for the purposes of his own argument.

138. However, that is vigorously disputed by the extremely learned work of Margaret M. Mitchell, *Paul and the Rhetoric of Reconciliation* HUTh 28, 1991, 243–50. The author writes that the only possible accusation against Paul which could underlie I Cor.9 is the Pauline refusal to accept support, and that such an accusation is historically implausible (246). But accusation is one thing and reference is something else. Paul's opponents doubted his status as an apostle by referring to his refusal to accept support, since the right to support is the characteristic of an apostle. It should be noted that in religious controversy (and not only there) any kind of argument will do for attacking the adversary. Unfortunately the author has not assessed the cross-connections between I Cor.9 and the rest of the Corinthian correspondence. Here I keep to my reconstruction in *Opposition to Paul in Jewish Christianity* (1983), 1989, 65–72. A rhetorical analysis of whatever kind would do well to take note of *historical* observations.

139. 'If' (*ei*) here has an almost causal significance, as in I Thess.4.14.

140. Sellin, *Streit* (n.135), without any real justification sees in them 'the theological spokesmen of the whole community' (15) and on p.37 can therefore already understand them as 'the Corinthians'; finally this alleged identity serves him as a criterion for source division: 'In the same I Cor. in which Paul concerns himself in detail with the fact that the (sic!) Corinthians categorically rejected talk of a resurrection of the dead, he argues at another point in a completely open way in this respect, talking of the resurrection of dead Christians, namely in 6.14. But how can Paul cite anything as a reason

that is not accepted by his conversation partners – as according to I Cor.15 he ought to have known? The only possible answer is that I Cor.6.14 and ch.15 did not stand in the same letter' (49).

141. Gerhard Barth ('Zur Frage nach der in I Korinther bekämpften Auferstehungsleugnung', *ZNW* 83, 1992, 187–201) distinguishes four reconstructions of the Corinthian denial of the resurrection in previous scholarship: 1. Everything ends at death (but the vicarious baptism for the dead in I Cor.15.29 tells against this). 2. Only those have anything to hope for who are alive at the return of Christ (but I Cor.15.29 can be advanced against this, and the polemic of I Cor.15.19, 30–32 would then be incomprehensible). 3. The Greek view of the immortality of the soul is irreconcilable with the 'Jewish' doctrine of the resurrection of the body. (But in this case the polemic of I Cor.15.18,30–32 is unclear.) 4. The Corinthians were spiritual enthusiasts, who were already then participating in the perfect heavenly life. 'Their teaching did not exclude the future, but simply brought it more massively into the present' (192).

142. Cf. Wilckens, 'Ursprung' (as n.43), 145f.: 'But among these Gentile Christians, as I Cor. shows throughout, an overall understanding of the tradition was in vogue, the notional framework of which is not – as in Paul himself – the primitive Christian eschatology of the early Jewish tradition but a manifestly Hellenistic notion of epiphany. Thus all religious experience and thought is so orientated on the present experience of the Spirit as the manifest presentation of the exalted Kyrios, that the contents of the eschatologically orientated tradition are included in this overall aspect. "Resurrection of the dead" – such an un-Hellenistic notion, and essentially understandable only in the context of early Jewish tradition – here so to speak fell out of the framework, and had to be regarded as a completely new doctrine which was only required as an addition to the gospel. As such, it has been rejected by a group within the community, whereas in Paul's thought the resurrection of Jesus and the future resurrection of Christians essentially belong together in the same complex of final events, as is shown by the whole of the subsequent polemical discussion in I Cor.15.12ff.' However, the Corinthians also might have understood the 'resurrection' of Jesus differently from Paul, had they been asked.

143. Karl Heinrich Rengstorf, *Die Auferstehung Jesu. Form, Art und Sinn der urchristlichen Osterbotschaft*, ⁵1967, 84.

144. For this reason a warning should be issued against any too precise reconstruction of the position of some Corinthians (I Cor.15.12), which similarly is accessible to us only in its interpretation by Paul.

145. Cf. I Thess.4.16f., and my remarks in *Paul: Apostle to the Gentiles: Studies in Chronology* (1980), 1984, 221–32. However, Barth, 'Frage' (n.141), emphasizes that 'at the time of Paul there were wide circles in which the resurrection faith . . . had not become established' (199) and refers to Mark 12.18–27 as an example of the discussion of the early Christian community with their Jewish neighbours on this point (197). Cf. also

Wilckens, 'Ursprung' (n.4), 16: 'In early-Jewish/Pharisaic Judaism the notion of the resurrection of the dead included the corporeality of the dead person – although usually there was no reflection or emphasis on this. Paul also understood it in this way: as raising from the tomb. That is particularly clear – apart from I Cor.15.12ff., a section which is understandable only on this presupposition – from passages like I Cor.6.14 and Rom.8.11; 8.29, from which it emerges that Paul thought of the future resurrection of dead Christians as being similar to the resurrection of Christ which had taken place. The mention of the burial of Jesus in the first missionary tradition (I Cor.15.4a) thus served as an explication of the *ek nekron* in the subsequent statement about the resurrection.'

146. It was again argued for by Wilhelm Pratscher, *Der Herrenbruder Jakobus und die Jakobustradition*, FRLANT 139, 1987, 29–32, reporting and critically discussing different theses.

147. Formula of the death: Rom.5.8; 14.15; I Cor.8.11; Gal.2.21; I Thess.5.10. Formula of the resurrection: Rom.4.24; 10.9; I Thess.1.10. Cf. Vielhauer, *Geschichte* (n.105), 15–18.

148. This does not put in doubt a unity of formula which goes back a very long way (see below, 38).

149. Cf. rightly Evans, *Resurrection*, 75 (and literature).

150. For the question which passage(s) of scripture possibly underlie(s) this, see n.163.

151. The perfect form is striking in comparison with the other three verbs in the aorist. Perhaps this is deliberate emphasis on the significance of the resurrection for the present (cf. similarly the frequent perfect 'crucified' [*estauromenos*] in Paul).

152. Cf. e.g. Dibelius, *Tradition* (n.109), 18f. n.2.

153. Joachim Jeremias, *The Eucharistic Words of Jesus*, 1966, 101–5.

154. Eduard Lohse, *Märtyrer und Gottesknecht*, FRLANT 64, ²1963, 113.

155. Jeremias, *Eucharistic Words*, 103. Cf. also the careful account of the controversy in Karl Lehmann, *Auferweckt am dritten Tage nach der Schrift*, QD 38, 1968, 87–115.

156. The possibility cannot be excluded that 'then' (*eita*) referring to the further appearances which he wanted to add was inserted by Paul instead of an original 'and' (*kai*, cf. Alfred Seeberg, *Der Katechismus der Urchristenheit*, 1903, 57). But even then an individual appearance to Cephas remains probable.

157. But see Pratscher, *Herrenbruder Jakobus* (n.146), who regards v.5 only as a 'non-formal element of tradition'. I will not argue over this subtlety ('non-formal element of tradition' instead of 'independent element of tradition'), but it does not change the situation. With regard to the whole of Pratscher's book, attention should be drawn to his tendency to harmonize the early period of the history of the earliest Jerusalem community. Thus he does not understand *dokountes* in Gal.2 ironically (67), and while the

agitation in Gal.2.4 is indeed anti-Pauline, the intervention of James's emissaries in Gal.2.11f. (83f.) is not. James did not have the leading position (68f.).

158. Cf. also the question touched on in the previous note as to whether v.5 is a non-formal or an independent element of tradition.

159. For this term cf. the reflections by Lehmann, *Auferweckt* (n.155), 60–7.

160. Rudolf Pesch, 'Zur Entstehung des Glaubens an die Auferstehung Jesu. Ein Vorschlag zur Diskussion', *ThQ* 15, 1973, 201–28: 214f. (It should be emphasized that I am in agreement with the thrust of this article, which is an urgent plea to academic theologians to give an answer to the question of the origin of the Easter faith.) In the meantime Pesch has withdrawn his thesis, in 'Zur Entstehung des Glaubens an die Auferstehung Jesu. Ein neuer Versuch' (1983), in Hoffmann, *Überlieferung* (n.43), 228–55: 243.

161. For the further question cf. Lüdemann, *Opposition* (n.138), 72–4.

162. They had already been in part combined at the level of the tradition (see above, 35, on I Cor.15.3–5), but this does not alter the need to investigate the original significance of individual elements.

163. Cf. the reflections of Burton L. Mack, *A Myth of Innocence: Mark and Christian Origins*, 1988, 106f., who in connection with Sam K. Williams, *Jesus' Death as a Saving Event. The Background and Origin of a Concept*, HDR 2, 1975, emphasizes the Antiochene origin of the formula. Earlier scholarship (cf. Lohse, *Märtyrer* [n.154], 114f.) stressed Isa.53 and connected the earliest community with it. But the remark on 35 above also applies to this question.

164. If Isa.53 underlies the saying in (a), the same could also be true of (b) (cf. Isa.53.9; 'And they made his grave with the wicked'). Could, say, the pre-Markan tradition that someone who was not a disciple, Joseph of Arimathea, buried Jesus, be connected with this?

165. However, according to Sellin, *Streit* (n.135), the formula in I Cor.15.3–5 need not be much earlier than the foundation of the Corinthian community (251). But the parallel I Cor.1.23 prompts reflection, and if the first mission in Corinth was around 41 CE (cf. Lüdemann, *Paul*, n.145), then the existence of the formula in the thirties would be certain.

166. Cf. Martin Hengel, 'Christology and Chronology' (1972), in *Christology and New Testament Chronology*, 1983, 30–47, and my chronology (n.145), based on quite different presuppositions, which comes to similar results to those of Hengel in respect of the date of the christophany to Paul.

167. Cf. von Campenhausen, *Ablauf* (n.57), 10: 'Even with the greatest scepticism which rightly leaves out of account a "purely historical" interest of those concerned, it is almost inconceivable that the basic events which the normative personalities themselves experienced and to which they referred in their preaching should nevertheless never have been discussed among

them. So Paul was also at the same time informed at first hand of what he is handing down. Furthermore Paul, who was no scatterbrain, lays emphasis on the reliability of these accounts; he does not merely mention them in passing or incidentally in connection with quite different questions, but emphasizes quite firmly with a solemn stress that they are completely certain and indubitable. Finally, here it is not a matter of some complicated things, theological interpretations and selected texts in which some small shifts and nuances could have arbitarily arisen, but of quite simple, important, definite and well-known facts.'

168. Cf. Wilckens, *Ursprung* (n.43), 149 n.14: 'The origin of the tradition of a narrative of the appearance of the risen Christ to more than 500 brethren might be most convincingly explained by the fact that it was the foundation legend of the post-Easter community. Those involved in this understandably also remained known by name afterwards.'

169. It is impossible here to go into the difficult problem of the relationship between event and development of tradition. The possible objection that event and tradition are identified in the text does not affect the comments above for the reasons mentioned. Cf. Albert Eichhorn, *Das Abendmahl im Neuen Testament*, HCW 36, 1898, 7, and the commentary by Henning Paulsen, 'Traditionsgeschichtliche Methode und religionsgeschichtliche Schule', *ZTK* 756, 1978, 20–55: 30f. Eichhorn's criticism is directed against a one-sided literary criticism that thinks that when it has reconstructed the earliest stratum of a source it has also already found the real historical derivation. Accordingly, in the quest of the historical Jesus scholars thought that with the earliest Gospel, Mark, they had also already found a sketch of the real life of Jesus. That this was not the case was demonstrated by Eichhorn's pupil William Wrede, *Messianic Secret* (n.36).

170. It is worth mentioning that representatives of rationalism and even Friedrich Schleiermacher himself put forward the hypothesis of a pseudo-death (see also above n.71 and Hirsch, *Geschichte* V [n.70], 37f.), which in more recent times has again been warmed up by Franz Alt (*Jesus – der erste neue Mann*, 1989, 56). Nor should we forget the popular sensationalized debate over the Turin shroud, in the course of which defenders of its great antiquity have similarly put forward the pseudo-death hypothesis.

171. Bultmann, *Tradition* (n.95), 274.

172. Cf. Heinz-Wolfgang Kuhn, 'Die Kreuzesstrafe während der frühen Kaiserzeit. Ihr Wirklichkeit und Wertung in der Umwelt des Christentums', *ANRW* II, 25.1, 1982, 648–793: 751f. (on the duration of hanging on the cross). Cf. Josephus, *Vita*, 420f.:'On the return (viz. from Tekoa to Jerusalem), I saw many prisoners who had been crucified, and recognized three of my acquaintances among them. I was cut to the heart and came and told Titus with tears what I had seen. He gave orders immediately that they should be taken down and receive the most careful treatment. Two of them died in the physicians' hands; the third survived.' Scholars have often

assumed a 'traumatic shock' or 'severe loss of blood' (in the scourging) to explain the relative brevity of Jesus' last torment (less than six hours, cf. Mark 15.25,33).

173. Cf. Johannes Schreiber, 'Die Bestattung Jesu. Redaktionsgeschichtliche Beobachtungen zu Mk 15.42–47 par', *ZNW* 72, 1981, 141–77: 141–3.

174. Cf. Raymond E. Brown, 'The Burial of Jesus (Mark 15.42–47)', *CBQ* 50, 1988, 233–45: 239; id., *The Death of the Messiah. From Gethsemane to the Grave* (2 vols), 1994, 1199–1313 (the book appeared too late to be used here).

175. Against Schreiber, 'Bestattung', 143, according to whom the mention of the kingdom of God 'explains why he helped in the murder of Jesus'. For criticism cf. also Brown, 'Burial', 239 n.22.

176. Cf. the change of terminology: v.45 says that Pilate had the corpse (*ptoma*) of Jesus given to Joseph. In v.43 Joseph had asked for the body (*soma*) of Jesus.

177. Cf. Robert Mahoney, *Two Disciples at the Tomb. The Background and Message of John 20.1–10*, TW 6, 1974, 115.

178. Cf. David Daube, *The New Testament and Rabbinic Judaism*, 1973 (= 1956), 312. The following remarks about the dishonourable burial of Jesus are made in close connection with Daube (301–24).

179. 'One does all that is needed for the corpse, one anoints and washes it . . .'

180. 'The addition of Nicodemus to Joseph commended itself, because he too was a counsellor, and above all because he was a secret disciple like Joseph. Mark's very general remark that Joseph was waiting for the kingdom of God is given concrete form by the Johannine introduction of Nicodemus in connection with what John 3 says of him. Matthew with his brief, unqualified remark that Joseph had also been a disciple of Jesus really already says more than John, according to whom the relationship of the two counsellors to Jesus remains in a strange twilight. This restraint of the last evangelist indicates that the earlier tradition knew nothing of Joseph and Nicodemus belonging to the Christian community' (Grass, *Ostergeschehen* [n.41], 177f. n.4). Josef Blinzler, 'Die Grablegung Jesu in historischer Sicht', in E.Dhanis (ed.), *Resurrexit*, 1974, 56–102: 77, differs: 'If one can already infer from the synoptic account that Joseph was not alone in laying the body in the tomb, then there is really nothing decisive against the presence and collaboration of a second person of class.' However, the question is: what is in favour of it? The completely legendary character of the Johannine account is also evident from John 19.39b. Cf also the narrative of the burial of Adam in VitAd 48: 'And again the Lord spoke to Michael and Uriel, the angels: bring me three byssus linens [precious, soft silk weave, GL] and spread these over Adam and other (!) linens over Abel his son.' Just as Adam here is buried at enormous expense in keeping with his religious significance, so the New Testament tradition also tends towards the description of an honourable burial of Jesus.

181. Gospel of Peter 2.3 describes Joseph as a 'friend of the Lord'. A later

stage of the tradition seems to me to be visible here, but that does not exclude the possibility that other passages in the Gospel of Peter may be earlier. How far this is removed from the oldest tradition becomes all the clearer when in the same passage Joseph is similarly called a 'friend of Pilate', implying an exculpation of Pilate (cf. similarly 1.1; 11.46); this is developed further in the late Acts of Pilate (cf. W.Schneemelcher [ed.], *New Testament Apocrypha I*, ²1991, 501–36 [Felix Scheidweiler]).

182. Joseph 'took the Lord, washed him, wrapped him in linen and brought him into his own sepulchre, called Joseph's Garden'.

183. Origen (*Contra Celsum* II, 69) explains it like this: 'Thus, just as his birth was purer than all other births in that he was born not of sexual intercourse but of a virgin, so also his burial had the purity which was symbolically shown by the fact that his body was put away in a newly-made tomb . . .'

184. Stanley E. Porter, 'Joseph of Arimathea', *The Anchor Bible Dictionary* II, 1992, 971f., who does not note the traditio-historical tendency and harmonizes the texts.

185. For this text, in addition to the commentaries see the analyses by Mahoney, *Two Disciples*, 122–4, and Ingo Broer, *Die Urgemeinde und das Grab Jesu. Eine Analyse der Grablegungsgeschichte im Neuen Testament*, StANT 31, 1972, 205–29. Broer (like Maloney) does not regard John 19.31 as an old fragment of tradition but says that the verse is 'the necessary introduction to the crurifragium story which comes from a relatively late tradition' (229). But the view of v.31 as redactional introduction to what follows (the crurifragium story [the breaking of the legs] is manifestly really of a later date) does not exclude the possibility that there is an earlier underlying tradition. Cf. also Jean-Pierre Lémonon, *Pilate et le Gouvernement de la Judée*, 1981, 196–8, whom the above account follows.

186. 'Since Jesus was to be the Passover lamb of whom no bone was broken; since he was to be the one like God who was pierced; since in blood and water he was to show the gift of the Spirit springing from his death; the evangelist with the help of his inexact knowledge of the Roman means of execution created the narrative which slips through our hands' (Theodor Keim, *Geschichte Jesu von Nazara III, Das jerusalemische Todesostern*, 1872, 512).

187. 'We cannot get round the impossibility of reconciling the two accounts; they cannot have originally stood side by side . . . However, there is a possibility that the conclusion of the first has been cut off for the second to be attached; for even the most great-hearted redactor cannot cope with having someone buried twice' (Julius Wellhausen, *Das Evangelium Johannis*, 1908, 90).

188. Cf. Broer, *Urgemeinde* (n.185), 250–63 (Acts 13.27–29 is completely created by Luke [263]).

189. William Lane Craig, *Assessing the New Testament Evidence for the Historicity of the Resurrection of Jesus*, 1989, 195, differs; however, he does

not analyse the text and, totally fixated on the thesis of the empty tomb, challenges the existence of this tradition.

190. 'It is quite credible that Acts 13:29 is as precise a historical report of the burial of Jesus as can be reconstructed. The Joseph story may be an apologetic legend; at least it seems to grow into one, as is evident from a comparison of the four canonical Gospels' (Collins, *Beginning* [n.87], 128).

191. Grass, *Ostergeschehen* (n.41), 180, claims that the tradition developed as follows: 'If the corpse of Jesus had really been removed by his enemies, the tradition would have grown like this. Jesus was laid in a common grave, like anyone who had been executed. Soon people found this intolerable, but knew that none of his followers had shown him, or could have shown him, the least service of love. A stranger did, and preserved his body from the ultimate shame. Now this could not have been an insignificant stranger, but had to be someone who could dare to go to the court authorities; he had to be a counsellor. The name was to be found in the Gospel tradition, like any other name, and gradually – this last phase is reflected in the Gospels themselves – the pious stranger became a secret . . . or even an open . . . disciple of Jesus, someone who did not approve of the counsel and action of the Sanhedrin . . . someone who was a friend not only of Jesus but also of Pilate (Gospel of Peter 3). So the story of Joseph of Arimathea is not completely impossible to invent.'

192. Cf. Blinzler, 'Grablegung' (n.180), 85–7, on the treatment of those executed in Roman legal practice. As an illustration see the story of the widow of Ephesus contained in Petronius, *Satyricon*, 111f.: a virtuous woman who had lost her husband remained in his tomb for many days in deep mourning. Nearby, a soldier was guarding three crosses, to prevent the relatives from taking down the bodies hanging on them and burying them. With the widow's maid as a go-between, the soldier became intimate with the virtuous widow, and while he was absent, relatives of one of the crucified men took down his body from the cross and gave him the last rite of burial. In order to protect the soldier, the widow told him to take the corpse of her husband from the coffin and nail it to the empty cross (Loeb Classical Library, 1916, ed. W. H. D. Rouse, 229–35).

193. Cf. Philo, *In Flaccum* 83: 'I have known instances before now of men who had been crucified when this festival and holiday was at hand, being taken down and given up to their relations, in order to receive the honours of sepulture, and to enjoy such observances as are due to the dead; for it used to be considered, that even the dead ought to derive some enjoyment from the natal festival of a good emperor, and also that the sacred character of the festival ought to be regarded.'

194. Cf. Samuel Krauss, *Talmudische Archäologie* II, 1911, 73 and 487. He refers to MSanhedrin VI 7 as evidence for tombs for those executed. The text, which is really in Mishnah Sanhedrin VI 5, runs: 'The court established two burial places: one for those executed by the sword and strangled and one for those stoned and burned.' There is no mention of *Roman* justice.

195. But cf. Brown, 'Burial' (n.174), 243 n.31. Brown refers to the most recent excavations, according to which the traditional tomb of Jesus was surrounded by a quarry and Golgatha was a rock-free mound of earth which had presumably been caused by an earthquake. Joseph of Arimathea – if one follows Mark's account – will have put the corpse of Jesus in one of the caves of this quarry, which served as a burial place for those executed.

196. For details cf. Kuhn, 'Kreuzesstrafe' (n.172), 711–17. In the ossuary of the crucified person, who was between twenty-four and twenty-eight years of age, there were also the bones of a three- to four-year-old child who bore the same name.

197. Thus Peter Stuhlmacher, 'Kritischer müssten mir die Historisch-Kritischen sein!', *TQ* 153, 1973, 244–51: 245f.

198. Cf. here generally Eric Meyers, *Jewish Ossuaries: Reburial and Rebirth*, BibOr 24, 1971, and for the present state of knowledge of ancient Jewish burial customs Rachel Hachlili, 'Ancient Jewish Burials', *The Anchor Bible Dictionary* I, 1992, 789–94 (with bibliography).

199. That kinsfolk and friends of the executed person did this is presupposed in the brief Talmud tractate Semachot, cf. Sem.II 10: 'We do not withhold mourning rites from those executed by the government. When do we begin to count the days of mourning for them? From the time that the relatives despaired in their appeal for the body to be delivered to them for burial but had not given up the hope of stealing it' (Soncino Talmud, *Minor Tractates* I, 1965, 333).

200. I rule out as a historical possibility for the Judaism of the time that Jesus was buried by women disciples – a man by women! – not to mention the lack of any attestation to this in the sources.

201. Cf. MSanhedrin VI 6: 'When the flesh had wasted away they gathered together the bones and buried them in their own place. The kinsmen came and greeted the judges and the witnesses as if to say, "We have naught against you in our hearts, for you have judged the judgment of truth." And they used not to make lamentation but they went mourning, for mourning has a place in the heart alone.'

202. The instruction reads: if a kinsman has been crucified in a city, one should leave this city until the flesh has wasted away.

203. Martin Hengel, 'Ist der Osterglaube noch zu retten?', *TQ* 153, 1973, 252–69: 263.

204. Cf. Lüdemann, 'Texte' (n.20), 255f., following Bultmann, *History* (n.95), 290.

205. John Dominic Crossan, *The Historical Jesus. The Life of a Mediterranean Jewish Peasant*, 191, 294. Crossan also thinks that 'Joseph of Arimathea' is unhistorical (393), but this is probably going too far. In my view his reconstruction of a 'Cross Gospel' at another point (*The Cross that Spoke. The Origins of the Passion Narrative*, 1988) on the basis of the Gospel of Peter needs to be treated with caution. (I shall return to this elsewhere.)

208 *Notes*

206. Joachim Jeremias, *Heiligengräber in Jesu Umwelt (Mt 23, 29; Luke 11, 47). Eine Untersuchung zur Volksreligion der Zeit Jesu*, 1958.

207. Cf. Jeremias, *Heiligengräber*, 145: 'This world of sacred tombs was a real element of the environment in which the earliest community lived. It is inconceivable that, living in this world, it could have allowed the tomb of Jesus to be forgotten. That is all the more the case since for it the one who had lain in the tomb was more than one of those just men, martyrs and prophets . . .' Cf. also Wolfgang Nauck, 'Die Bedeutung des leeren Grabes für den Glauben an den Auferstandenen', ZNW 47, 1956, 243–67: 261f. (veneration of the tomb of Jesus).

208. I am grateful to Byron McCane of Duke University for his scholarly advice on the question of the burial of Jesus.

209. Paul Althaus, *Die Wahrheit des kirchliche Osterglaubens. Einspruch gegen Emanuel Hirsch*, BFCT 42.2, ²1941, 35. Cf. similarly Kittel, 'Auferstehung' (n.22), 154, and at the present day Craig, *Evidence* (n.149), 35, who surpasses all his predecessors in diligence and finally declares, 'Paul did believe in the empty tomb' (360). Cf. by contrast the more subtle position of Lorenz Oberlinner, 'Die Verkündigung der Auferweckung Jesu im geöffneten und leeren Grab. Zu einem vernachlässigten Aspekt in der Diskussion um das Grab Jesu', ZNW 73, 1982, 169–82: 163–8 (bibliography).

210. Heinrich Julius Holtzmann, 'Das leere Grab und die gegenwärtigen Verhandlungen über die Auferstehung Jesu', ThR 9, 1906, 79–86, 119–32: 128f. Friedrich Loofs' polemic aainst this (*Die Auferstehungsberichte und ihr Wert*, HCW 33, 1908, 15 n.*) is not convincing.

211. Marxsen, *Resurrection* (n.3), 70.

212. Johannes Weiss, *Der erste Korintherbrief*, KEK 5, ⁹1910 (= 1970), 349.

213. Cf also R. E. Brown, *The Virginal Conception and Bodily Resurrection of Jesus*, 1973, 83f.: he thinks that to read a reference to the empty tomb into I Cor.15.4a goes beyond the limits of the probable.

214. Collins, *Beginning of the Gospel* (n.87), differs. She connects Paul's notion with Jub.23.31 (see above, 18). She writes: 'Paul's understanding of the resurrection of Jesus does not involve the revival of his corpse' (124). This thought may be too modern.

215. Cf. Lüdemann, *Paul* (n.145), 236 and n.141.

216. In his all too systematic book, Gerhard Koch, *Die Auferstehung Jesu Christi*, BHTh 27, 1959, is taking a methodological short cut when he states: 'The significance of the fact of the empty tomb for the kerygma is that the kerygmatic statement about the third day has been derived from it.'

217. Cf. Harvey K. McArthur, '"Am dritten Tag". 1Kor.15.4b und die rabbinische Interpretation von Hosea 6.2' (1971/2), in Hoffmann, *Überlieferung* (n.43), 194–202.

218. However, one could just as well infer from the fact that it is not mentioned in the New Testament 'that its use had been early, and had left its

mark on the tradition at a level deeper than explicit quotation' (Evans, *Resurrection* [n.28], 49).

219. Cf. McArthur, '"Am dritten Tag"', 201f.

220. Cf. Fischer, *Ostergeschehen* (n.14), 72; Lehmann, *Auferweckt*, 221–30.

221. For what follows cf. Anton Vögtle, in id. and Rudolf Pesch, *Wie kam es zum Osterglauben?*, 1975, 38f.

222. Cf., rightly, Evans, *Resurrection* (n.28), 64.

223. Cf. Vögtle, *Wie kam es zum Osterglauben?* (n.221), 39.

224. Cf. Paul Hoffmann, 'Auferstehung Jesu Christi II.1', *TRE* 4, 1979, 478–513.

225. Cf. Ingo Broer, '"Der Herr ist dem Simon erschienen" (Lk 24.34). Zur Entstehung des Osterglaubens', *SNTU* 13, 1988, 81–100: 90f.; id., '"Der Herr ist wahrhaft auferstanden" (Lk 24, 34). Auferstehung Jesu und historisch-kritische Methode. Erwägungen zur Entstehung des Osterglaubens', in Lorenz Oberlinner (ed.), *Auferstehung Jesu – Auferstehung der Christen. Deutungen des Osterglaubens*, QD 105, 1986, 39–62: 57f.

226. Rudolf Pesch, in Vögtle and Pesch, *Wie kam es zum Osterglauben?* (n.221), 154. Pesch also rightly stresses: 'At least Peter and the Twelve had already been called and sent by the earthly Jesus (Mark 1.16–20; 3.13–19; 6.7–13). So in their case one could at most speak of a further calling; but this would be a different phenomenon from the first calling of Paul, the persecutor of the Christians.'

227. Marxsen, *Resurrection* (n.3). Further references to this work are given in the text.

228. What follows is in implicit dialogue with a verdict of Evans, *Resurrection* (n.28), which is to my mind too sceptical, namely that 'Paul nowhere in his letters elaborates on what he means by "seeing the Lord" (it is not clear that Gal.1.16 refers to this at all; the meaning may be "to reveal his Son through me to the Gentiles"), and the argument of I Cor.15 is not sufficiently precise, nor the two parts of it sufficiently closely linked, to be able to deduce from the exposition of the spiritual body of Christians how Paul thought of the risen body of Christ or of the nature of his appearance. Thus the Pauline evidence hardly provides a fixed point from which the rest of the resurrection tradition may be assessed' (56, cf. 66).

229. Cf. Gerhard Delling, 'The Significance of the Resurrection of Jesus for Faith in Jesus Christ', in C. F. D. Moule (ed.), *The Significance of the Message of the Resurrection for Faith in Jesus Christ*, SBT II 8, 1968, 77–104: 85.

230. Hans-Willi Winden, 'Wie kam und wie kommt es zum Osterglauben?', *DiTh* 12, 1982. Further references to this book are given in the text.

231. That does not alter the fact that at other points, too (Rom.2.5; 8.18, 19; 16.25; I Cor.1.7; 3.13; Gal.3.23), which do not relate to the 'Damascus

event', Paul speaks of revelation/reveal. Beverly Roberts Gaventa, *From Darkness to Light. Aspects of Conversion in the New Testament*, 1986, 23, differs: 'Paul's use of *apocalypsis* . . . and the related verb *apocalyptein* . . . elsewhere makes it even less certain that he has reference here to a vision or a miraculous encounter.'

232. Kessler, 'Sucht den Lebenden' (n.15), 232. Kessler thinks that it is impossible to imagine how the Easter experiences came about (230). This remark is just one example of the alliance of a historical scepticism with an apologetic theology.

233. Hoffmann, *Auferstehung* (n.224), 494.

234. Marxsen, *Resurrection* (n.3), 105.

235. Cf. F. Stanley Jones, *'Freiheit' in den Briefen des Apostels Paulus*, GTA 34, 1987, 25f.

236. Cf. Num.23.3 (of Balaam): 'I will go away, perhaps Yahweh will encounter me: the Word that he lets me see I will make known to you' (my translation).

237. On Wilhelm Michaelis, *Die Erscheinungen des Auferstandenen*, 1944, 100–3. Cf. also Seyoon Kim, *The Origin of Paul's Gospel*, WUNT II/4, ²1984, 55 n.1.

238. Cf. Günter Klein, 'Antipaulinismus in Philippi: Eine Problem-skizze', in Dietrich Alex Koch, Gerhard Sellin and Andreas Lindemann (eds.), *Jesu Rede von Gott und ihre Nachgeschichte im frühen Christentum (FS Willi Marxsen)*, 1989, 297–313.

239. Cf. e.g. Dieter Lührmann, *Das Offenbarungsverständnis bei Paulus und in paulinische Gemeinden*, WMANT 16, 1965, 74.

240. 'But the possibility cannot be excluded that Paul is referring in general to the divine activity in the new creation of Christians' (Werner Georg Kümmel, *Römer 7 und das Bild des Menschen im Neuen Testament. Zwei Studien*, ThB 53, 1974, 147, though he also regards the interpretation in terms of the conversion as more probable).

241. Cf. Peter Stuhlmacher, '"Das Ende des Gesetzes". Über Ursprung und Ansatz der paulinischen Theologie', ZTK 67, 1970, 14–39: 27 n.29 (and bibliography). Cf. also Paul Volz, *Die Eschatologie der jüdischen Gemeinde im neutestamentlichen Zeitalter*, 1934 (= 1966), 364f., on salvation and blessedness under the image of light.

242. Cf. Dieter Wyss, *Psychologie und Religion. Untersuchungen zur Ursprunglichkeit religiösen Erlebens*, 1991, 93 (following Eugen Biser).

243. Cf. Friedrich Pfister, 'Ekstase', RAC IV, 1959, 944–87; Wolfgang Speyer, *Frühes Christentum im antiken Strahlungsfeld*, WUNT 50, 1989, s.v. 'Ekstase' – with a happy evaluation of parallels ancient and modern (Nietzsche!).

244. Cf. the definition of vision in Johannes Lindblom, *Gesichte und Offenbarungen. Vorstellungen von göttlichen Weisungen und übernatürlichen Erscheinungen im ältesten Christentum*, 1968, 32: 'By "visions" one generally understands visual appearances of figures, things or

events or perceptions of voices and sounds which have no sensual or objective reality but in the view of the persons who see and hear them come from another, invisible world.'

245. Hans Kessler, *Sucht den Lebenden nicht bei den Toten. Die Auferstehung Jesu Christ in biblischer, fundamentaltheologischer und systematischer Sicht,*[2] 1987. Further references to this book are given in brackets in the text.

246. The same could also be said of the closed Roman Catholic outline by Franz Mussner, *Die Auferstehung Jesu,* Biblische Handbibliothek, VII, 1969; he understands the 'Easter event' as an 'eschatological event in which God has acted in us and announced himself to us . . . Therefore this event is not bound to a particular picture of the world but transcends any picture of the world from the human past, present and future' (138). What contribution can a historical work make in the face of such dogmatism?

247. A brief collection from the present: Josh McDowell, *Die Tatsache der Auferstehung. Bestätigen die historischen Fakten die Auferstehung Jesu Christi?,* [3]1987: Murray J. Harris, *Raised Immortal. Resurrection and Immortality in the New Testament,* 1983; id., *From Grave to Glory. Resurrection in the New Testament. Including a Response to Norman L. Geisler,* 1990; Norman L. Geisler, *The Battle for the Resurrection,* 1992. Cf. also the review articles of Francis J. Beckwith, Gary R. Habermas, Scot McKnight, in *JETS* 33, 1990, 369–82; Gary R. Habermas, 'Resurrection Claims in Non-Christian Religions', *Religious Studies* 25, 1989, 17–77; Gary R. Habermas and Antony G. N. Flew, *Did Jesus Rise from the Dead? The Resurrection Debate,* 1989.

248. 'Einige die Individualität des Apostels betreffende Züge', in *Paulus, der Apostel Jesu Christi,* 1845, 651–70.

249. Ferdinand Christian Baur, *Das Christenthum und die christliche Kirche der drei ersten Jahrhunderte,* [2]1860, 45 (= F.C.Baur, *Ausgewählte Werke in Einzelausgaben,* ed.Klaus Scholder, Vol.3 [with an introduction by Ulrich Wickert], 1966).

250. This remark was not made at Baur's grave, as C. Holsten (*Das Evangelium des Paulus* II, 1898, xv) thought, but in the Aula of the university on 7 February 1861 (M. A. Landerer, *Zur Dogmatik. Zwei akademische Reden, beigegebene Gedächtnisrede auf F. C. Baur,* Tübingen 1879, 76f.). – Cf. Werner Georg Kümmel, *The New Testament. The History of the Investigation of its Problems,* 1973, 429 n.200.

251. For him cf. Paul Mehlhorn, 'Holsten, Karl Christian Johann', *PRE*[8] VIII (1900), 281–6. Born in 1825, until 1867 he taught in a Gymnasium in Rostock and then was Ordinarius Professor of New Testament, from 1869 in Bern and from 1876 in Heidelberg (as the successor to Heinrich Julius Holtzmann).

252. Carl Holsten, *Zum Evangelium des Paulus und des Petrus,* 1868, 3. The book is dedicated to F. C. Baur, 'who though dead has not died, the Protestant scholar with an unerring awareness of the truth, with an

indefatigable striving for truth.' Further references to this work are given in brackets in the text.

253. Carl Holsten, *Das Evangelium des Paulus* I, 1880, ix.

254. Cf. the view of Ingo Broer, "Der Herr"' (n.225), 54 n.28: 'The issue is that of looking at the genesis of belief in the resurrection on presuppositions valid today. If Jesus Christ is the revelation of God for all times, then even on today's presuppositions an approach to them and to it must be possible . . . So rational explanation seeks to aid the appropriation of faith.'

255. The first person to put this forward was presumably Christoph Hermann Weisse, *Die evangelische Geschichte kritisch und philosophisch bearbeitet* II, 1838, 305–438 (cf. Hirsch, *Geschichte* V [n.70], 510, 550f.; Hoffmann, in Hoffmann, *Überlieferung* [n.43], 31ff.). It appears in Keim, *Geschichte Jesu von Nazara* (n.186), in the formula of the 'telegram from heaven', and in the present still in Grass, *Ostergeschehen* (n.41), 233–49. Reference should be made to Johannes Müller, *Über die phantastischen Gesichtserscheinungen. Eingeleitet und herausgegeben von Dr Martin Müller*, Klassiker der Medizin, 1927 [= 1826], in whose work there is a criticism of the 'objective vision' even before the appearance of Weisse's book. He writes: 'Physiology regards all appearances in the form of a vision which can be seen only by the visionary as subjective expressions of the inner sense. For the objective vision, or the vision which has an objective basis, coincides with ordinary seeing, and an appearance of this kind must be visible to anyone and not merely to the visionary. So if there is anything miraculous about an objective vision, that does not lie in the vision in itself, but in what the vision can stimulate by affecting the organ of seeing. This miraculous element that lies in the object is not the concern of physiology. But the subjective vision which has objectivity only for the visionary, invisible to anyone else, belongs only before the tribune of physiology' (61).

256. Rolf Schäfer, *Jesus und der Gottesglaube*, ²1962, 92.

257. Cf. Johannes Rathje, *Die Welt des freien Protestantismus*, 1952, 129f.

258. Cf. merely William Wrede, 'Paulus', *RGV* I, 5–6, 104, 9 n.10: 'Some theologians have spoken of "objective visions", but that is not a scientific concept'; Johannes Weiss, *Earliest Christianity* (1917), 1959, I, 26–31.

259. Cf. also the remarks by the practical theologian Otto Baumgarten, 'Die Osterthatsache und die Osterpredigt', *Zeitschrift für Praktische Theologie* 23, 1901, 123–7: 124: historical criticism 'challenges . . . the objectivity of all the christophanies; the impossibility of imagining them and the way in which they break through all historical life in space and time, is an offence to anyone who with F. A. Lange esteems consistency, maintaining the categories of historical judgment as the "morality of thought"'. The magnum opus of Friedrich Albert Lange is *Geschichte des Materialismus und Kritik seiner Bedeutung in der Gegenwart*, 1866 (¹⁰1921).

260. The following comments are made in close conjunction with my

book, *Earliest Christianity according to the Traditions in Acts*, 1989, 106ff., tightening up and making more specific what is said there.

261. Cf. Deut.4.12: 'Then the Lord spoke to you out of the midst of the fire; you heard the sound of words, but saw no form; there was only a voice.'

262. That is not to say that the events concerned are unhistorical.

263. Grass refers to the story of Heliodorus (II Macc.3), who at the command of the Syrian king Seleucus was to hand over the treasure in the Jerusalem temple, but was then forcibly prevented by God, 'the ruler over the spirits and every power' (II Macc.3.24).

264. Grass, *Ostergeschehen* (n.41), 129f.

265. This is rightly stressed by James M.Robinson, 'Jesus – From Easter to Valentinus (or to the Apostles' Creed)', *JBL* 101, 1982, 5–37: 7.

266. Lindblom, *Gesichte*, 48. There is exaggerated scepticism in Jürgen Becker, *Paulus. Der Apostel der Völker*, 1989: 'Acts does not help us to understand the calling of the apostle historically . . . Its nucleus of historical truth (i.e. that of the legend) consists in the local tradition of Damascus, in the information about the persecution as such and in the fact of the change in Paul' (64f.). Cf. 80: 'It is striking that in contrast to Acts the apostle nowhere even hints at an audition. He describes his visionary experince . . . That raises the question whether Paul could not have inferred everything else solely from the appearance of the Lord, so that in this case he did not need any words.'

267. Acts 9.15a: *bastazein to onoma enopion . . .* does not mean 'bear the name to (someone)' (= the idea of mission') but 'bear the name before (someone)', which touches on the theme of suffering. However, in that Paul will bear the name before Gentiles and Jews (Acts 9.15b), there is an anticipation of the notion of the mission which will be carried out in the course of Acts.

268. For the above cf. Lindblom, *Gesichte* (n.244), 49f.

269. Paul Tillich, *Systematic Theology* I, 1952, 59–65.

270. Friedrich Schleiermacher, *The Christian Faith*, 1928, §§3–5 (5–26).

271. Cf. also Schalom Ben-Chorin, *Paulus. Der Völkerapostel in jüdischer Sicht*, ²1983: 'I tend towards leaving the Damascus experience of Paul as it stands in the Acts of the Apostles. However, it is clear that here we have a legendary embellishment, which must make it questionable whether those around Paul saw and heard more than a babbling man falling to the ground who then, after this shock, got up blinded, surrounded by darkness in the brightness of midday. What happened before Damascus ultimately remains the mystery of Paul's soul. Revelations of such a kind are a dialogical event which excludes the world' (33).

272. The basically theological criticism of such an understanding of vision by Winden, 'Osterglauben' (n.230), 118f. ('If one attributes to God a qualitatively new act of revelation after the death of Jesus, the Easter appearances . . . immediately acquire a special status' [119]), can be left aside here (for criticism see above, 54–6). Instead, reference should be

made to the differentiations in Peter Simon, *Zur Phänomenologie der religiösen Imaginationen. Eine medizinisch-psychologische Studie*, medical dissertation, Göttingen 1979.

273. Cf. the major book by Gustav Hölscher, *Die Propheten. Untersuchungen zur Religionsgeschichte Israels*, 1914; also Friedrich Horst, 'Die Visionsschilderungen der alttestamentlichen Propheten' (1960), in Peter H. A. Neumann (ed.), *Das Prophetenverständnis in der deutschsprachigen Forschung seit Heinrich Ewald*, WdF 307, 1979, 438–54. Cf. especially the following texts: Job 4.12–16; Isa.6; Dan.10.4–21; Ezek.1.1–3.15; Amos 7.1–9.10 (and Walter Beyerlin, *Bleilot, Brecheisen oder was sonst? Revision einer Amos-Vision*, OBO 81, 1988). He rightly remarks: 'It is regrettable that far too little attention is paid to the special features of Old Testament accounts of visions' [31]).

274. Cf. only I Enoch 14: IV Ezra 3.1–9, 25 (with the explanations by Hermann Gunkel, in Emil Kautzsch [ed.], *Die Apokryphen und Pseudepigraphen des Alten Testaments* II, [2] 1962 [= 1900], 341f.).

275. Cf. Friedrich Pfister, 'Epiphanie', *PRE.S* IV, 1924, 277–323; E.Pax, 'Epiphanie', *RAC* V, 1962, 832–909; Klaus Berger, 'Visionsberichte. Formgeschichtliche Bemerkungen über pagane hellenistische Texte und ihre frühchristlichen Analogien', in id., François Vouga, Michael Wolter and Dieter Zeller, *Studien und Texte zur Formgeschichte*, TANZ 7, 1992, 177–255 (numerous examples in German translation – distinguishing between visions and accounts of epiphanies).

276. Robinson, 'Jesus' (n.265), 210, refers to Rev.1.13–16 as the only detailed resurrection appearance in the New Testament and also to Acts 7.55f. The character of light in the appearances has remained in later Gnosticism, whereas 'orthodoxy', diverging from the primary experience, emphasized the fleshly nature of the Risen Christ. 'Orthodoxy defended the bodilinessness by replacing luminousness with fleshliness, heresy exploited the luminousness by replacing bodiliness with spiritualness' [17]. Cf. also Elaine H.Pagels, 'Visions, Appearances and Apostolic Authority: Gnostic and Orthodox Tradition', in Barbara Aland (ed.), *Gnosis* (FS H. Jonas), 1978, 415–30.

277. Cf. Ernst Benz, *Paulus als Visionär. Eine vergleichende Untersuchung der Visionsberichte des Paulus in der Apostelgeschichte und in den paulinischen Briefen*, AAWLM.G 1952, no.2, 112 (36): 'The proclamation of the apostle was more strongly permeated with visionary experiences than most of his present-day exegetes are willing to accept. But this fact was known to the communities which he founded and to which he preached, and when he was speaking to them he could refer to it. His present-day readers and hearers must learn to hear the visionary tones of his message again in all their resonance and to understand his theology as the experiential theology of a visionary.' Cf. also Ernst Benz, *Die Vision*, 1969, 279: 'The apostle Paul's consciousness of mission rests on the experience of his personal call to be an apostle by the risen Lord in the vision of light before Damascus . . . He

Notes    215

does not have the slightest doubt about the divine nature of the guidance which makes itself known in his numerous visions from Damascus on.'

278. Eduard Meyer, *Ursprung und Anfänge des Christentums III, Die Apostelgeschichte und die Anfänge des Christentums*, 1923, 238. However, according to Friedrich Wilehlm Horn, *Das Angeld des Geistes. Studien zur paulinischen Pneumatologie*, FRLANT 154, 1992, the very mention of the date 'fourteen years before' shows that 'it is extremely improbable that Paul is here extracting an experience "from a comprehensive collection of experiences"' (255). For criticism see 77f. below.

279. Wilhelm Michaelis, *Die Erscheinungen der Auferstandenen*, 1944, 98.

280. Lührmann, *Offenbarungsverständnis* (n.239), 58 n.2.

281. Cf. also John G. Gager ('Some Notes on Paul's Conversion', NTS 27, 1981, 697–704: 697) and Alan F. Segal (*Paul the Convert. The Apostolate and Apostasy of Saul the Pharisee*, 1990, 69 and passim), who refreshingly again recall the experiential character of Paul's theology and rightly root it in the 'Damascus event'.

282. Gerhard Lohfink, 'Der Ablauf der Osterereignisse und die Anfänge der Urgemeinde', ThQ 160, 1980, 162–76: 167. Cf. also the explicit reference to the significance of the works of Ernst Benz for the exegesis of Paul by Rudolf Pesch, in Vögtle and Pesch, *Wie kam es zum Osterglauben?* (n.221), 146.

283. Benz, *Paulus* (n.277), 81 (5).

284. 'This hardly means a lack of rhetorical training, but, as the context suggests, a failure to speak powerfully under the influence of the Spirit' (Vielhauer, *Geschichte* [n.105], 147).

286. This is often translated 'appearances', but that unnecessarily leaves open the question whether this was a 'seeing', which is certainly the case, since the basis is the verb *horan* (= see). So in what follows the terms 'seeing' and 'vision' are used without distinction.

286. Cf. e.g. Josef Zmijewski, *Der Stil der paulinischen 'Narrenrede'. Analyse der Sprachgestaltung in 2Kor 11, 1 – 12,10 als Beitrag zur Methodik von Stiluntersuchungen neutestamentlicher Texte*, BBB 52, 1978: the visions and revelations of the opponents are pneumatic ecstasies, a direct vision of the Lord, combined with eschatological revelations of the word. By contrast, Paul's experience is 'one *caused* by Christ, which has grown out of personal communion with him, and is not to be confused with the eschatological vision of the Lord' (345). Historically, that cannot be demonstrated from the text, since in the case of Paul and his 'opponents' we have visions of one and the same Lord. It is also impossible to discover how Paul can have two different visions of the same Lord – one in personal communion with him and another at the end of time.

287. Cf. Hans Windisch, *Der Zweite Korintherbrief*, 1970 (= 1924), 368.

288. Cf. Adolf Schlatter, *Paulus, der Bote Jesu, Eine Deutung seiner Briefe an die Korinther*, 1934, 658, 662f. Against this, W.G.Kümmel refers to

Hans Lietzmann, *An die Korinther I/II*, HNT 9, 1949, 212: 'On the contrary, it is significant that there is no mention of an object which is seen in this rapture: the content of what Paul experienced is not only *arrheton* but also inessential for his apostolate' (but that is the question).

289. Cf. e.g. Victor Paul Furnish, *II Corinthians*, Anchor Bible 32A, 1984, 524 ('granted by the Lord').

290. E.g. the saying I Thess.4.16, which depicts the descent of the Lord from heaven, has been given to Paul by the Lord (I Thess.4.15, 'word of the Lord').

291. For the third person see the utterly convincing remarks by Lindblom, *Gesichte* (n.244), 45f. From the Old Testament he refers to Isa.21.6: 'Go, set a watchman, let him announce what he sees' (cf. also Bernhard Duhm, *Das Buch Jesaia*, ⁴1922, 52f.). 'This objectification of the I probably in part relates to a feeling of humility and unworthiness. But that is not the whole explanation. A tendency to a duplication of the I lies in the ecstatic experience itself . . .' (Lindblom, 46). But that this is in fact a vision of Isaiah only becomes clear in the following verse. What does remain unclear is whether Isaiah *sees* only the watchman who calls (or does he only *hear* him?), or whether he *is* himself the watchman, so that he has seen the baggage train in v.9. Paul is equally unclear in II Cor.12.2.

292. Cf. also I Enoch 70.2f. and in addition the remarks by Segal, *Paul* (n.281); I Enoch 37–71 have not been found in Qumran; whatever the original date of I Enoch 70–71 may be, I Enoch 14 precedes Paul's heavenly journey and may have influenced his ideas about heavenly journeys (47f.).

293. Cf. also Windisch, *2Kor*, 370. Lührmann, *Offenbarungsverständnis* (n.239), 58, differs: 'That Paul is speaking here of himself in the third person is not "modest style" but indicates that for him ecstasy is not an experience of revelation and therefore is not the foundation of preaching either.' But v.5a clearly tells against this. According to Lührmann (ibid.), the rapture or heavenly journey has the quality of revelation in the later interpretation of II Cor.12 by the Apocalypse of Paul, contrary to the intention of the apostle (as with Paul's opponents in II Cor). For this Apocalypse of Paul cf. Wilhelm Schneemelcher (ed.), *New Testament Apocrypha* II, ²1992, 712–47 (H. Duensing and A. de Santos Otero); for the Coptic Apocalypse of Paul from Nag Hammadi, which is to be distinguished from the long-known apocalypse of the same name, cf. ibid., 695–9 (Wolf-Peter Funk) and the thorough analysis by Hans-Josef Klauck, *Die Himmmelfahrt des Paulus (2Kor 12.2, 4) in der koptischen Paulusapokalypse aus Nag Hammadi* (NHC V.2), SNTU A/10, 1985, 151–90.

294. The suggestion might already be made here that the detail 'fourteen years' is closely connected with the context. Paul had previously (II Cor.11.32f.) reported his flight from Damascus. The event depicted in II Cor.12 took place only a few years after this flight.

295. Thus most scholars; cf. most recently Furnish, *II Corinthians* (n.289), 542 (bibliography).

296. 'It seems certain to me that in II Cor 12.2, 4 Paul is describing two different stages of his ascent to God. Otherwise Paul would have been expressing himself in an intolerably broad way' (Wilhelm Bousset, *Die Himmelsreise der Seele* [1901], Libelli 71, nd, 12 n.3).

297. James D. Tabor, *'Things Unutterable.' Paul's Ascent to Paradise in its Greco-Roman, Judaic, and Early Christian Context*, 1986, 115, thinks of a 'two-stage journey'. First he was translated to the third heaven, and then into paradise. For an analogy, reference is made to Lucian, *Icaromenippus* 22. According to Tabor (118f.), paradise denotes the throne of God in the highest (seventh) heaven. He describes the train of thought as follows: first of all Paul stresses that he has had revelations of heavenly mysteries in the same way as his opponents (the term 'third heaven' is said to be a phrase used by his opponents). In the second section of his account he distances himself from this kind by depicting his transportation into paradise (120). Criticism: why are the two reports told as they are, in parallel?

298. For the third heaven: Slavonic Enoch 18: 'And they led me round in the third heaven and placed me in the midst of paradise'; Apocalypse of Moses 37.6: God's command to the archangel Michael runs: 'Raise him (viz. Adam) to the third heaven, into paradise, and leave him there until the great fearful day which I have still to give to the world.'

299. Cf. Bousset, *Himmelsreise* (n.296); Tabor, *'Things Unutterable'* (n.297). On 69–97 he distinguishes the following types of 'heavenly ascents': 1. Ascent as an invasion of heaven (cf. e.g Isa.24.14–20; Lucian, *Icaromenippus*); 2. Ascent to receive revelation (e.g. I Enoch 14.18–25; TestLevi 2.7–3.3; 4.1–5.3; VitAd 25.1–3); 3. Ascent to heavenly immortality (cf. Dan.12.3; Acts 1.9–11; Scipio's dream in Cicero; Orphic gold plates; Aristophanes, *Peace* [831]); 4. Ascent as a foretaste of the heavenly world (cf. I Enoch 29; 70f.; Ascension of Isaiah 7: Apuleius, Poimandres, Mithras liturgy). Cf. also Alan F. Segal, 'Heavenly Ascent in Hellenistic Judaism, Early Christianity and their Environment', *ANRW* II 23.2, 1980, 1333–94.

300. By contrast, Hans Dieter Betz, *Der Apostel Paulus und die sokratische Tradition*, BHTh 45, 172) argues: 'Paul parodies the typical and identifies himself with it only in an ironic way. Here it can neither be proved nor disputed that there is an allusion to real events in the life of Paul and if so to which' (89). I do not believe that the reference to a rhetorical form ('fool's talk', see below, 75) and irony in II Cor.10–13 can fully explain away the *real* character of II Cor.12.1–10.

301. Cf. the contrast between heavenly journey and rapture in Gerhard Lohfink, *Die Himmelfahrt Jesu*, StANT 26, 1971, 37–41.

302. Gershom Scholem, *Die jüdische Mystik in ihren Hauptströmungen*, ³1988. References to this work are given above in the text.

303. For criticism cf. Peter Schäfer, 'New Testament and Hekhalot Literature: The Journey into Heaven in Paul and Merkavah Mysticism', *JJS* 35, 1984, 19–35. However, this criticism of Scholem goes too far. It says

very little about Paul and formally explains history away because the real historical question of what happened is rarely, if ever, put.

304. Cf. also already Bousset, *Himmelsreise* (n.296), 14–17, with important consequences for the pre-Christian Paul: 'What one is inclined to regard as Paul's most personal property, the experiences that he reports in II Cor.12, is according to the external form of the ecstatic experiences utterly a characteristic of the school . . . and is taken over by Paul from his rabbinic past into his new life' (16f.).

305. However, Tabor, '*Things Unutterable*', 118, does not refer 'paradise' to the future time of bliss.

306. Lindblom, *Gesichte* (n.244), 45.

307. Benz, *Vision* (n.277), 220.

308. Cf. below 104f.

309. Bousset, *Himmelsreise* (n.296), links II Cor.12 with I Cor.2.6–16: 'The "wisdom" of which Paul boasts here has been granted to him as a result of that ecstatic elevation to Paradise' (13).

310. Windisch, *2Kor*, 377.

311. For understanding II Cor 12.4, Hans Bietenhard, *Die himmlische Welt im Urchristentum und Spätjudentum*, WUNT 2, 95, 1 167), refers to Slavonic Enoch A17.1, which reads: 'In the midst of heaven I saw armed hosts who constantly sang praises to the Lord with drums and symbols. I delighted in them.' Schäfer, 'New Testament' (n.303), thinks that Paul heard the praises of the angels. But in his view, in II Cor.12.4 Paul would hardly have spoken of 'words' had he meant 'songs'. Therefore he regards the parallels adduced by Bietenhard for the interpretation of II Cor.4 as misleading and emphasizes that Paul did not say that he 'saw' something (23). By contrast, see above in the text, and also Benz, *Vision* (n.277), 418–40 ('the heavenly music').

312. Benz, *Vision* (n.277), 415.

313. It is not to be concluded from this that there is no historical basis to II Cor.12.1–10, as Betz, *Apostel* (n.300), evidently thinks possible. By contrast, in 'Eine Christus-Aretalogie bei Paulus (2Kor 12,7–10)', *ZTK* 66, 1969, 288–305, he had still rightly spoken of the 'experience of an ecstatic rapture in 2Kor.12.1–4' (289).

314. For the construction with *hyper ho*, cf.I Cor.4.7.

315. Cf. Lietzmann, *I/II Kor*, 155: 'His authority is not to rest on uncontrollable small talk of mystery but on what the Corinthians can see and hear – and that is the weakness. He reserves the right to boast of revelations because they are in fact true expressly for himself.'

316. The deletion of *dio* would make things far too easy, cf. Lietzmann, *I/II Kor*, 155: 'The solution is too easy to be right.'

317. The interpretation of the angel of Satan in terms of opponents of Paul (cf. II Cor.11.13–15), which was first advanced by the church fathers and has been put forward in different ways in modern times, can be left on one side; for this cf. the learned article by Ulrich Heckel, 'Der Dorn im Fleisch.

Die Krankheit des Paulus in 2Kor 12,7 und Gal 4, 13f.', *ZNW* 84, 1993, 65–92: 76–8 (bibliography). However, one would hesitate to follow Heckel in making the beginning of the sickness or the beginning of the suffering coincide precisely with the event described in II Cor.12 (75, 77 n.38, referring to the ingressive aorist *edothe* [v.7]). Paul is writing in a general way (cf. simply his reference to the threefold prayer to the Lord).

318. Cf. Benz, *Vision* (n.277), 15–34 ('Vision and Sickness'). However, Benz also wants to show that in many cases the vision does not lead to sickness but to healing (in contrast to the 'seer of Prevorst', Frau Hauffe, as described by J. Kerner).

319. Cf. also the ironic question in II Cor.1.7: 'Did I commit a sin in abasing myself so that you might be exalted, because I preached Christ's gospel without cost to you?'

320. Betz, 'Christus-Aretalogie' (n.313), here esp. 300. It should be stressed that I do not see Betz's form-critical investigation at this point as opposed to my own historical reconstruction.

321. Cf. the analogies given by Betz, 'Christus-Aretalogie', 295f., e.g. Lucian, *Alexander*, 28: 'Spare yourself the trouble of looking for a remedy for this sickness, for your fate is near and you cannot possibly escape it.'

322. Grass, *Ostergeschehen* (n.41), 190.

323. Rudolf Bultmann, *Der zweite Brief an die Korinther*, KEK Sonderband, 1976, 227.

324. Cf. for a first survey Vielhauer, *Geschichte* (n.105), 485–94.

325. Cf. already the conjecture by Windisch, *2Kor*, 386: 'However, we cannot completely exclude the possibility that he in fact had to pay for his visions and revelations with constantly new outbreaks of his illness.' Paul interpreted the two by saying that the sickness further intensified the vision and thus became the expression of the all-surpassing power of Christ.

326. Hirsch, *Osterglaube* (as n.61), 190.

327. Schlatter's objection (*Paulus* [n.288]) misses the point: 'A psychologist may say that it is impossible to understand in a clear form the distinction which Paul maintains between the vision of the Risen Christ and visionary converse with Christ. But we may be quite certain in asserting that Paul made this distinction and called neither the events during the Easter period nor his own experience a vision' (400).

328. Windisch, *2Kor* (n.287), 380.

329. Ibid.

330. Heckel, *Der Dorn im Fleisch* (n.317), 87–92.

331. Cf. ibid. 86 (bibliography). This hypothesis can also easily be connected wth Gal.4.13 and Gal.6.11. However, I would not attach any importance to this. According to Guido Kluxen, 'Sehstörungen des Apostel Paulus', *Deutsches Ärtzeblatt* 90, 28/29, 19 July 1993, B 1457–9), Paul was 'presumably suffering only from exhaustion as a result of heat and sun after a long journey' (B 1458).

332. Cf. Martin Hengel, *The Pre-Christian Paul*, 1991. This book will

long remain the basis for any concern with the pre-Christian Paul. Cf. also Hans Hüber, 'Paulusforschung seit 1945. Ein kritischer Literaturbericht', *ANRW* II 25.4, 1987, 2649–840: 2658–67.

333. In Philemon 9 Paul calls himself an 'older man' (*presbytes*), which according to the understanding of Hippocrates denotes someone up to the age of fifty–six. (At any rate *presbyteros* always refers to the last stage of life.) The letter to Philemon was written around 55; Paul's conversion took place around 32.

334. Cf. in general Ulrich Luz, in Rudolf Smend and id., *Gesetz*, 64–9 (64–7: Love as an answer to the kingdom of God; 67–9: The love of the kingdom of God and the Old Testament).

335. The other possibility, that 'us' in Gal.1.23 refers to Christians in Jerusalem, probably comes to grief on Gal.1.22. It is not otherwise significant for the question discussed here.

336. Werner Georg Kümmel, 'Römer 7 und die Bekehrung des Paulus', 1929 = id., *Römer und das Bild des Menschen im Neuen Testament. Zwei Studien*, ThB 53, 1974, 1–160.

337. See n.332 above. Further references to this work are in the text.

338. Cf. his major book, *The Johannine Question*, 1989.

339. Even Hengel is making a psychological statement when he says that no one who (formerly) has been visited by depressions can (later) describe (or remember or feel) himself as a clearly confessing character. What psychological theory underlies this statement? What understanding of psychology (and theology and history) underlies the satisfaction that – supposedly – no psychological statement can be made about a historical matter? In his most recent publication Hengel conjures up the works of the 'great' fathers and grandfathers of modern exegesis – and it is good that he does – but he does not note that this period of historicism also saw the birth of psychoanalysis, which present-day theology and the church can no longer simply ignore.

340. Gerd Theissen, *Psychological Aspects of Pauline Theology*, 1987, 1–39. Further references to this book are given in the text.

341. Cf. further Dieter Wyss, *Die tiefenpsychologischen Schulen von den Anfängen bis zur Gegenwart. Entwicklung, Probleme, Krisen*, ⁶1991; id., *Psychologie* (n.242), 149–58; Eckart Wiesenhütter, *Die Begegnung zwischen Philosophie und Tiefenpsychologie*, 1979.

342. In addition he also distinguishes between the theoretical approach, which describes religion as experience and behaviour which is learned socially (14–20), and the cognitive approach, which understands religion as a tendency to build up an interpreted world (38–49).

343. Carl Gustav Jung, 'Psychology and Religion', in id., *Collected Works* 11, 1958, 3–106: 50.

344. There is an unqualified acceptance of Jung's theory in Rolf Kaufmann, *Die Krise des Tüchtigen. Paulus und wir im Verständnis der Tiefenpsychologie*, 1983; a criticism of Jung can be found in Margaret E.

Thrall, 'Resurrection Traditions and Christian Apologetic', *The Thomist*, 1979, 197–216 (in my mind she resorts too quickly to 'some transcendent reality' [216]).

345. However, not all fanaticism is defensive. Cf. Kümmel, 'Röm.7' (n.336), 157: 'There can spring from an authoritative faith without any second thoughts the consciousness that a rejected religious view attacks the honour of God, of the church, etc., or that it destroys the divinely willed purity of a religious community and therefore must be eradicated.' However, this, as Theissen, *Aspects* [n.340], 239 n.37, points out, is only another psychological interpretation of Paul's activity as a persecutor.

346. In my view the key passage is Romans 7, for the understanding of which see Theissen, *Aspects*, 177–249. Cf. also my article 'Psychologische Exegese', in Friedrich Wilhelm Horn (ed.), *Bilanz und Perspektiven des Neuen Testaments*, BZNW, 1994.

347. C. G. Jung, 'The Psychological Foundations of Belief in Spirits' (1928), in id., *Collected Works 8*, 1960, 301–18. Further references to this work are given in the text.

348. 'Romans 7 is the result of a long retrospective bringing to consciousness of a conflict which had once been unconscious' (Theissen, *Aspects* [n.340], 242).

349. Oskar Pfister, 'Die Entwicklung des Apostels Paulus', *Imag* 6, 1920, 243–90. Further references to this work are given in the text.

350. 'Hallucination' nowadays has negative connotations, in the sense of illusion. I follow Simon in also regarding hallucination as vision. 'Visions are optical appearances of persons, things or scenes which have no objective reality . . . Visions or auditions do not reach their recipients . . . by the sense organs as defined anatomically but are the products of imagination and the power of ideas' (16f.). Cf. n.244 for Lindblom's definition.

351. Cf. Theissen, *Aspects*, 229 and n.18.

352. Cf. Lüdemann, *Opposition to Paul* (n.138), 47 n.55.

353. Adolf von Harnack, 'Die Verklärungsgeschichte Jesu, der Bericht des Paulus (1 Kor 15,3ff.) und die beiden Christusvisionen des Petrus' (1922), in Hoffmann, *Überlieferung* (n.43), 89–117. Further references to this article are given in brackets in the text.

354. Another possible explanation for this evidence is a purely literary mediation through I Cor.15 or through other New Testament witnesses, but this is improbable (see below, 148f.).

355. Cf. Rudolf Bultmann, *Die Geschichte der synoptischen Tradition, Ergänzungsheft*, ed.Gerd Theissen and Philipp Vielhauer, ⁴1971, 83 (with bibliography).

356. Brun, *Auferstehung* (n.95), 52; cf. Grass, *Ostergeschehen* (n.41), 82f.

357. François Bovon, *Das Evangelium nach Lukas (Lk 1,1–9,50)*, EKK III/1, 189. His view is: 'Mark 1.16–20 and Luke 5.1–11 are closer to the tradition than John. The saying about being "fishers" of men is anchored in a

revelation scene, not in an Easter apperance. The Johannine redaction had to push the whole scene to the time after Easter because John 21 could be put only as a postscript and not as an interpretation at the beginning of the Gospel' (234). Cf. also Bultmann, *History* (n.95), 230: 'I think it likely that the story of the miraculous draught of fishes in Luke 5.1–11 had its origin in the saying of Jesus about "Fishers of Men", in the same way that this saying may also have led to the stories of the calling of the disciples in Mark 1.16–20.'

358. Günter Klein, 'Die Berufung des Petrus' (1967), in id., *Rekonstruktion und Interpretation*, BEvTh 50, 1969, 11–48: 28. The quotation continues: 'If for anyone, for Peter his mission coincides with his Easter experience' (ibid.).

359. Hirsch, *Osterglaube* (n.61), 50. On the other hand Bultmann opposes this most resolutely, but without giving any reason (*The Gospel of John*, 1971, 705 n.2), referring to Dibelius, *Tradition* [n.109], 113.

360. Hirsch, *Osterglaube* (n.61), 50.

361. Grass, *Ostergeschehen* (n.41), 80f. R. E. Brown, *The Gospel according to John XIII–XX*, Anchor Bible 29A, 1970, also thinks it possible that Luke 5.8–10 can be understood as a scene of repentance, forgiveness and reconciliation (1111).

362. Cf. generally Wolfgang Dietrich, *Das Petrusbild der lukanischen Schriften*, BWANT 94, 1972, 49f. Joachim Jeremias (*Die Sprache des Lukasevangeliums*, KEK Sonderband, 1980) shows that in v.8 *idon de* and *aner* are redactional, in v.9 *thambos, pantas, tous syn auto, hon synelabon*, and in v.10, *de kai, pros* (+ accusative), *ese zogron* (134–6).

363. For *kyrios* as an element of tradition cf. Jeremias, *Sprache*, 135f.

364. Bultmann, *History* (n.95). Further references to this work are given in the text.

365. Cf. Georg Strecker, *Der Weg der Gerechtigkeit. Untersuchung zur Theologie des Matthäus*, FRLANT 82, ³1971, 206.

366. Ulrich Luz, *Das Evangelium nach Matthäus (Mt 8–17)*, EKK 1/2, 1990. Further references to this work are given in the text.

367. Cf. Lüdemann, *Opposition to Paul* (n.138), 40–65.

368. Against Marxsen (n.3), 96: 'To the question of what can be established by historical investigation, we can only answer – the faith of Simon as constitutive of the church, and the *assertion* of the early church that this faith was grounded on the seeing of Jesus.'

369. On the other hand it is true, as William Wrede points out, that we can 'often get nearer to the truth only by inferences and hypotheses. In fact the scientific conjecture, the hypothesis, plays quite a major role in this sphere. Wherever that is the case, there is also the possibility of error. That is what people are so ready to hold against free theological research: it works so much with hypotheses, and so many hypotheses prove untenable. But only the ignorant can be deterred by this. The hypothesis is a quite necessary means of progressing gradually towards better

knowledge in dark areas. Only those deserve censure who construct frivolous hypotheses and do not know how to distinguish between hypothesis and assured result. Moreover sometimes one even has to have the courage to make mistakes. For mistakes can be fruitful; they can contain elements of truth and help to mark out a path. Science itself sees that they do no damage, because it incessantly corrects them itself' (William ‍Wrede, *Die Entstehung der Schriften des Neuen Testaments*, Lebensfragen 18, 1907, 5). Adolf Harnack observed in a letter to Gustav Krüger of 3 February 1905: 'As if science made progress other than by constructing hypotheses. Nine may be wrong, the tenth is correct. There are no trees all of whose blossom bears fruit' (Agnes von Zahn-Harnack, *Adolf von Harnack*, 1936, 365f.).

370. The interlocked pericope has in each case been put in square brackets.

371. However, Gnilka's view, *Mk* II, 290, that the balanced narrative structure tells in favour of the originality of the tripartite division is not convincing. Cf. also the view of Dietfried Gewalt, 'Die Verleugnung des Petrus', *LingB* 44, 1979, 113–44: 136: the thesis that Mark 14.54, 66–72 has to be divided by literary criticism and possibly reduced to a single act of denial cannot be maintained, as the structure of the text resists such an attempt.

372. *oute oida oute epistamai* is a hendiadys.

373. The third denial is told in such a way that the situation becomes transparent to the reader, who like Peter is faced with the decision between confession and denial (cf. Mark 13.9–13). That is true independently of the question, which can hardly be decided in the absence of an object for 'curse', whether Peter is cursing himself or Jesus. Perhaps the verse reflects a situation in which Christians escape punishment if they curse Jesus (cf. Justin Apology I, 31.6 [for the time of Bar Kokhba]).

374. Eta Linnemann, *Studien zur Passionsgeschichte*, FRLANT 102, 1970. Further references to this work are given in the text.

375. Cf. by way of anticipation the view of Julius Schniewind: 'In truth the saying in Luke says the same thing as Mark 14.30 ... It is quite inconceivable that the community should have spun out a legend about its recognized leader which humiliated him so deeply if something of the kind had not in fact happened. And what is told us of the character of Peter in Mark 8.29,32f. and Gal.2.11f. corresponds to this account' (*Das Evangelium des Markus*, 1968, 196).

376. Bultmann, *History* (n.95), 267. Further references to this work are given in the text.

377. Jack Finegan, *Die Überlieferung de Leidens– und Auferstehungsgeschichte Jesu*, BZNW 15, 1934, 15 n.1.

378. However, Linnemann, *Passionsgeschichte* (n.374), questions the traditional reference of Luke 22.31f to the passion of Jesus. In her view 'this is an ... early Christian prophetic saying which was spoken in the name of

the exalted Lord and was to prepare the community to withstand a particular tribulation' (76); cf. Rev.2.10 and 1 Peter 5.6,8.

379. Günter Klein, 'Die Verleugnung des Petrus', (1961), in id., *Rekonstruktion und Interpretation*, BEvTh 50, 1969, 49–60 (supplement, 90–8): 74.

380. Ulrich Wilckens, *Auferstehung*, Themen der Theologie 4, 1970, 148. However, Wilckens thinks historical what I reckon to be tradition. Cf. the view of Schniewind (above, n.375).

381. Klein, 'Verleugnung' (n.379), 74–90.

382. In my view Klein exaggerates correct insights into the general early Christian tendency to suppress Peter as the first witness to the resurrection (above, 85).

383. Dibelius, *Tradition* (n.109), 315. Linnemann, *Passionsgeschichte* (374), 82, however, objects that in that case I Cor.15.5 would have had to read: 'And he was seen by Peter, who denied him.' That is not convincing, because I Cor.15.5 is part of a creed composed of different elements and so no longer represents any personal tradition (with a statement of denial).

384. Mack, *Myth of Innocence* (n.163), makes the question of Peter's denial too easy for himself. He writes: 'Some story had to be told to bring the discipleship theme to a conclusion' (305). 'There is nothing in the story that reflects historical reminiscence' (306). Maurice Goguel ('Did Peter Deny His Lord? A Conjecture', *HTR* 25, 1932, 1–27) challenges the historicity of the denial, but assumes that the historical Jesus had prophesied such a denial (27). That is to put the cart before the horse.

385. The historicity of the 'flight of the disciples' is certain, even if Mark 14.50 agrees with Zech.13.7 (Mark 14.27) and the Mark account emphasizes the *pantes* theme (14.27, 31, 50; cf. v.53). On historical considerations it follows that the disciples of Jesus must have left him – otherwise they themselves would have been crucified. E.g. Ernst Fuchs, *Glaube und Erfahrung. Zum christologischen Problem im Neuen Testament*, 1965, 18, differs: 'The "flight of the disciples" is a literary motif just like the "betrayer" . . . What could they have done when the police came? Two swords are already too many!' Fuchs makes the historical questions too easy for himself, though his hermeneutical efforts deserve recognition.

386. Cf. Erich Dinkler, 'Petrusbekenntnis und Satanswort. Zum Problem der Messianität Jesus' (1964), in id., *Signum Crucis. Aufsätze zum Neuen Testament und zur christlichen Archäologie*, 1967, 283–312: 288f. The criticism of Hans Conzelmann ('Historie und Theologie in den synoptischen Passionsberichten' [1967], in id., *Theologie als Schriftauslegung*, BEvTh 65, 1974, 74–90: 79 n.13) is just an oracle.

387. For the conceptuality 'original-dependent revelation' cf. Paul Tillich, *Auf der Grenze*, 1965, 67; cf. *Systematic Theology* I, 1953, 140–2.

388. Tillich, *Grenze*, 67f., writes somewhat imprecisely: 'Whereas Peter encountered the man Jesus, whom he called the Christ, in the original ecstasy of revelation, subsequent generations met the Jesus who had already been

Notes 225

accepted by Peter and the apostles as the Christ. Thus ever new revelation took place in the course of church history, but as dependent revelation.' Unfortunately Tillich leaves open the relationship between the revelations in the circle of disciples.

389. Cf. rightly Hans Dieter Betz, *Galatians*, Hermeneia 1979, 117. Like most books, unfortunately the admirable study by Andreas Wechsler (*Geschichtsbild und Apostelstreit. Eine forschungsgeschichtliche und exegetische Studie über den antiochenischen Zwischenfall [Gal.2.11–4]*, BZNW 62, 1991, especially 296–395) says nothing about this.

390. Cf. Norbert Brox, *Der erste Petrusbrief*, EKK XVI, 1979, 47–51 (on the Paulinism of I Peter).

391. Thus e.g. Vielhauer, *Geschichte* (n.105), 584.

392. Cf. the saying, 'Speak to me, so that I can see you', and further comments on it in David Chichester, *Word and Light. Seeing, Hearing, and Religious Discourse*, 1992.

393. Yorick Spiegel, *Der Prozess des Trauerns. Analyse und Beratung*, KT 60, ⁷1989. Further references to this work are given in the text (unfortunately these passages do not appear in the much abbreviated English translation, *The Grief Process*, 1978).

394. Aniela Jaffé, *Geistererscheinung und Vorzeichen. Eine psychologische Deutung*, with a preface by C. G. Jung, 1958, 67f.

395. Again I follow Spiegel and give references to his book in the text. In terms of method Spiegel is indebted to the psychoanalyis of Freud.

396. Cf. Samuel Vollenweider, 'Ostern – der denkwürdige Ausgang einer Krisenerfahrung', *ThZ* 49, 1993, 34–53: 41.

397. Cf. Igor Caruso, *Die Trennung der Liebenden. Eine Phänomenologie des Todes, Geist und Psyche*, 1974, 113.

398. Colin Murray Parkes and Robert S. Weiss, *Recovery from Bereavement*, 1983.

399. For what follows see Carol Leet Kerr, *Dreams and Visions of Those who Grieve. A Psychological and Theological Approach*, D.Min, Newton Center MA, 1987.

400. Presupposing that the prophecies of Jesus' passion (Mark 8.31; 9.31; 10.32–34) are not historical and/or were not taken seriously by the disciples.

401. Clement of Alexandria, *Stromateis*, VI,6,48 in W. Schneemelcher (ed.), *New Testament Apocrypha II: Writings relating to the Apostles, Apocalypses and Other Related Subjects*, ²1992, 39 (W. Scheemelcher).

402. Cf. Vielhauer, *Geschichte* (n.106), 680–92.

403. Among earlier scholars C. Hermann Weisse, *Evangelische Geschichte* (n.255), 416–20, claimed this, and more recently it has been suggested by Jeremias, *Theology* (n.96), 307. Cf. also the survey in S. MacLean Gilmour, 'Die Christophanie vor mehr als fünfhundert Brüdern' (1961), in Hoffmann, *Überlieferung* (n.43), 133–8; id., 'Easter and Pentecost', *JBL* 81, 1962, 62–6; id., 'The Evidence for Easter', *Andover Newton Quarterly* NS 5, 4, March 1965, 7–23; id., 'The Theology and Psychology of

the Easter Faith', ibid., 24–40. For criticism cf. C. Freeman Sleeper, 'Pentecost and Resurrection', *JBL* 84, 1965, 389–9: he argues that this thesis is improbable because of "insufficient evidence' (399).

404. The Jewish pentecost, which took place on the fiftieth day after passover, is the Old Testament feast of weeks (Ex.34.22) and in the first century CE, as in the Old Testament, had assumed the character of a harvest festival. Cf. Eduard Lohse, *'pentekoste'*, *TDNT* VI, 1968, 44–53.

405. Horn, *Angeld des Geistes* (n.108), thinks that this statement of Paul's is rhetorically motivated, and thus unhistorical (255f.), but that must be ruled out. By the same 'logic' one could for example also dismiss a statement like I Cor.15.10 (Paul did more missionary work than all the other apostles) as rhetorical – without any historical basis, which is impossible given Paul's powerful missionary work.

406. The picture of 'quenching' expresses the almost archaic activity of the Spirit as fire (cf. Acts 2.3, tongues as of fire). Here I am presupposing that an inference from a metaphor to historical reality is possible. Cf. also I Thess.1.5 with Rom.15.19.

407. Horn, *Angeld des Geistes* (n.108), 129, takes quite a different view: 'We have no reason to assume that glossolalia was one of the manifestations of the Spirit in Thessalonica.' His remarks seek to dispute the theory of a pneumatic enthusiasm in the Hellenistic communities – with reference to early Pauline (!) theology (157 and passim). We cannot enter into a detailed discussion here, but first, the question of n.422 whether this is not perhaps basically a nominalistic exegesis needs to be raised here, and secondly, reference must be made to the complex of Paul's action which Horn does not discuss (cf. also I Cor.5.3–5 [the remote pneumatic influence of Paul's spirit]), which would also have included a survey of the miracle tradition of Acts associated with Paul. In that case the totally unpneumatic picture of the 'early' Paul would not have been so easily possible.

408. For details cf. Gerhard Dautzenberg, 'Glossolalie', *RAC* XI, 1981, 225–46.

409. The expression 'ecstasy' does not occur here or anywhere in I Cor.14, but this is the underlying phenomenon. But cf. II Cor.5.13.

410. As in I Cor.14.14, the prophet (or glossolalist) caught up in ecstasy is under the impression of being delivered over to the power of the Spirit which has him or her in its grasp.

411. For the translation of *diakrinein* as 'interpret' (instead of 'discern') cf. Gerhard Dautzenberg, *'diakrino'*, *EWNT* I, 1890, 732–8, here 737.

412. The terminology here as compared with I Cor.14 is *dialektos* instead of *glosse* (48.3; 49.2; 50.1; 52.7) and *semeiosis* instead of *hermeneia* (51.3f.). The objects of the discourse are the *megaleia* and not the *mysteria* (51.3). We find esctatic (48.2; 49,1; 50.1) speech or singing (48.3; 49.3; 51.4) comparable to glossolalia in various angelic tongues. Cf. Gerhard Dautzenberg, 'Glossa', *EWNT* I, 1980, 604–14: 611; Horn, *Angeld des Geistes* (n.108), 212f.

413. Cf. Pieter W. van der Horst, *Essays on the Jewish World of Early Christianity*, NTOA 14, 1990, 104–10; Berndt Schaller, 'Das Testament Hiobs', *JSHRZ* III.3, 1979, 303–87: 305f.; id., 'Zur Komposition und Konzeption des Testaments Hiobs', *Studies on the Testament of Job*, MSSNTS 66, 1989, 46–92 (a basic work).

414. Cf. Lohse, '*pentekoste*' (n.404), 51: 'The most that one can say is that very probably Luke utilized a tradition concerning the first outbreak of inspired mass ecstasy in Jerusalem'.

415. 'It is certainly quite possible that this event did in fact take place on the occasion of the first Pentecost after the crucifixion, when many pilgrims were in Jerusalem' (Lohse, ibid.).

416. Lohse, '*pentekoste*' (n.404), 51f.n.51, is restrained here. But if the dating of the mass ecstasy to the first Pentecost after the death of Jesus, which he favours, should be right, then does not the identification of the appearance to the 'more than 500' with the tradition behind Acts 2 gain more plausibility?

417. This is also suggested by the number 500. For according to Acts 2.41 the event there involves around 3000 people; according to Acts 1.15 in the time after Easter around 120 brethren were assembled for the choice of Matthias to fill the circle of Twelve. Although the increase from 120 to 3000 certainly derives from Luke's tendency to illustrate the magnitude of the success of the mission, behind it there may at the same time be knowledge of a smaller but by no means tiny group of Christians in the early period, which he multiplied. Paul seems to have knowledge of the life of the 'more than 500', as the subordinate clause in I Cor.15.6 attests.

418. Reference should be made to the fifty sons of the prophets who fell into rapture near Elijah (II Kings 2.7), the 100 whom Elisha the man of God fed (II Kings 4.43), and the 400 who prophesied to Ahab (I Kings 22.6).

419. Cf. the word statistics and Henry J. Cadbury, 'Lexical Notes on Luke-Acts III. Luke's Interest in Lodging', *JBL* 45, 1926, 305–22; remarkably, Acts 2.2 has escaped him.

420. Lüdemann, *Earliest Christianity* (n.60), 43.

421. Hans Conzelmann, *Acts* ([2]1972), Hermeneia 1987, 16. Similarly, Grass, *Ostergeschehen* (n.41), thinks it impossible 'to transfer the enthusiastic features of this story (viz. Acts 2) without further ado into the christophany (viz. I Cor.15.6) mentioned by Paul' (101).

422. At this point there are signs of an unhistorical *nominalistic* exegesis which brackets out history. Such 'exegesis' evidently regards as real only what stands directly in the text, without recognizing that texts are merely a *extract* from this history. In what has been said, clearly there is no dispute that a *reason* must be given why the phenomenon of the Spirit is contained in early Christian resurrection texts from the beginning.

423. Cf. Weisse, *Geschichte*, 419: 'The apostle Paul evidently knows no second event relating to his own person after the appearance of the Lord to

him which equipped him with the gifts of the Holy Spirit; the latter was as it were given to him with the former.'

424. Cf. Ingo Hermann, *Kyrios und Pneuma. Studien zur Christologie der paulinische Hauptbriefe*, StANT 2, 1961. The learned work by Horn, *Angeld des Geistes* (n.108), excludes the early Paul (including I Thess.) from this thesis. He claims that in I Thess. the Spirit is the present gift of God, while the Kyrios is exclusively the parousia Christ (159). But in the event underlying II Cor.12, which takes us to the beginning of the 40s, the Exalted One to whom Paul prays (v.8) is effectively present.

425. Benz, *Paulus* (n.277), 120. Cf. also Hermann Gunkel, *Die Wirkungen des heiligen Geistes nach den populären Anschauungen der apostolischen Zeit und der Lehre des Apostels Paulus*, 1888; Heinrich Weinel, *Die Wirkungen des Geistes und der Geister im nachapostolischen Zeitalter bis auf Irenäus*, 1899. Despite the imaginative work of Horn, *Angeld des Geistes* (n.108), neither book is superseded. Cf. my assessment, 'Das Wissenschaftsverständnis der Religionsgeschichtliche Schule im Rahmen des Kulturprotestantismus', in Hans Martin Müller (ed.), *Kulturprotestantismus. Beiträge zu einer Gestalt des modernen Christentums*, 1992, 78–102: 88–94.

426. Cf. Horn, *Angeld des Geistes* (n.108), 338.

427. According to Horn, ibid., 339, however, the apostle had the outline presented in I Cor.15 at the time of I Thess., and not already at the time of the Damascus event. But the reference made in ibid. to the 'realistic description of the parousia of the Lord and the rapture of those who are raised with the living in I Thess.4.13–18' is not a viable argument, as the notion of transformation in I Thess.4 is not a theme, though it is not excluded either (cf. my comment in *Paul* [n.145], 236 and n.141).

428. Ernst von Dobschütz, *Ostern und Pfingsten. Eine Studie zu 1Korinther 15*, 1903. Further references to this work are given in the text.

429. Cf. also Rudolf Otto, *The Idea of the Holy*, 1958, 222–9 (on resurrection experience as spiritual).

430. Jacob Kremer, *Pfingstbericht und Pfingstgeschehen*, SBS 63/64, 1973, 236.

431. Kremer's other arguments against the above identification (the uniqueness of the Easter appearance in comparison with later visions and experiences of the Spirit [ibid., 235]) have already been noted in the text above.

432. Gustav Le Bon, *Psychologie der Massen* (1911), with an introduction by Peter R. Hofstätter, [15]1982. Further references to this work are given in the text. It should be emphasized that Le Bon is making these remarks to discredit all religion in the traditional sense. Here are some examples from his book: 'The great driving force behind the development of peoples was never truth, but error' (78). 'The great men of conviction, who had raised the soul of the masses, like Peter of Amiens, Luther, Savonarola ... first enthused when they themselves had been enthused by a faith. Then,

however, they could produce in souls that fearful power which is called faith, and which makes men the complete slaves of its dream. To arouse faith, whether this be religious, political or social faith, or faith in a person or an idea, is the special role of the great leader . . . It is not the scholars and philosophers, and above all not the sceptics, who have created the great religions which have dominated the world and the tremendous empires which have stretched from one hemisphere to the other' (84). 'The crazy nonsense of the myth of a God who takes vengeance on his Son by fearful torture for the disobedience of one of his creatures was not noted for many centuries . . .' (104). 'The only true tyrants of humanity have always been the shadows or the dead, or the imaginations that it has created for itself' (105). But why should the author not have some sound insights at decisive points, despite this anti-religious attitude? In what follows I am acting in accordance with Paul's motto in I Thess.5.21.

433. Ernst Renan (*The Apostles*, 1869), describes it as follows: 'It is the characteristic of those states of mind in which ecstasy and apparitions are commonly generated, to be contagious. The history of all the great religious crises proves that these kinds of visions are catching; in an assembly of persons entertaining the same beliefs, it is enough for one member of the society to affirm that he sees or hears something supernatural, and the others will also see and hear it . . . In cases of this kind, the most excited are those who make the law and who regulate the degree of the common atmospheric heat. The exaltation of individuals is transmitted to all the members; no one will be behind or confess that he is less favoured than the others . . .' (51f.).

434. Paul Wilhelm Schmiedel, *Die Briefe an die Thessalonicher und an die Korinther*, HCNT 2, 1893, 188f.; id., 'Resurrection and Ascension Narratives', *Encyclopaedia Biblica* IV, 1903, 4039–87: 4083.

435. Cf. Hermann Reuter, *Geschichte Alexanders des Dritten und der Kirche seiner Zeit* IV, 1864, 105–26, 722–4. A new investigation is urgently needed.

436. Cf. Karl von Hase, *Heilige und Propheten, 2.Abteilung. Neue Propheten*, ³1893, 107–92: 171f.

437. Renan, *Apostles* (n.433), depicts the process from a perspective critical of Christianity as follows: 'These first days were thus like a period of intense fever, in which the faithful, mutually inebriated, and impressing upon each other their own fancies, passed their days in constant excitement, and were lifted up with the most exalted notions. The visions multiplied without ceasing. Their evening assemblies were the usual periods for their production. When the doors were closed and all were possessed with their besetting idea, the first who fancied that he heard the sweet word *shalom* . . . gave the signal. All then listened, and very soon heard the same thing . . . In a few days a complete cycle of stories, widely differing in their details, but inspired by the same spirit of love and absolute faith, was formed and disseminated. It is the greatest of errors to suppose

that legendary lore requires much time to mature; sometimes a legend is the product of a single day' (57f.).

438. The question whether all the 'more than 500' belonged to the community before the appearance is impossible to answer. Probably outsiders, too, were caught up in the vortex which produced increasingly large waves from the group of disciples of Jesus around Peter.

439. This Gospel is presumably to be dated to the first half of the second century. 'The title describes the book as the Gospel of Greek-speaking Jewish-Christian circles – and in contrast to the Gospel of other Gentile Christian groups existing nearby; for a distinction from the Gospels "according to Matthew" or "according to John" can hardly be intended (by the users) with such a title' (Vielhauer, *Geschichte* [n.105], 661).

440. 'Jerome did not compose his outline of the history of literature out of love of the subject, but with the intention of using it to attack the presumptions of the educated pagans. By describing more than a hundred writers he seemed to have shown that in intellectual matters Christians were not the obscurantists that they were made out to be. That also explains his striking adaptation to the kind of description given by Tranquillus Suetonius, to whose biographies of scholars, orators and poets, entitled *De viris inlustribus*, Jerome's tractate virtually claims to be the Christian counterpart. How little he was actually interested in the works of these writers is confirmed from the other side by the observation that Jerome read hardly any of these books before reporting on them in his catalogue. Of eighteen samplings of literature reported, we have only a section from the Gospel of the Hebrews, with which he was already familiar from elsewhere. Moreover he did not always apply the knowledge that he had' (Carl Albrecht Bernouilli, *Hieronymus und Gennadius, De viris inlustribus*, 1896 [= 1968], xif.).

441. The translation follows Schneemelcher, *New Testament Apocrypha* I, 178 (P. Vielhauer and G. Strecker).

442. However, the legend of the guard over the tomb is presupposed. (The Lord gave the linen cloth in which his own body had been wrapped to the servant of the high priest.) Here as in the New Testament Gospels we are to see an anti-docetic motive.

443. Pratscher, *Herrenbruder* (n.146), 47.

444. Vielhauer, *Geschichte* (n.105), 659.

445. Perhaps the Gospel of Thomas contains a reaction to supporters of Cephas. Logion 12 runs: 'The disciples said to Jesus: We know that you will depart from us; who is it who will be great over us? Jesus said to them: Wherever you have come, you will go to James the Just, for whose sake heaven and earth came into being' (Schneemelcher, *New Testament Apocrypha* I [n.401], 119).

446. Ethelbert Stauffer, 'Zum Kalifat des Jacobus', *ZRGG* 4, 1952, 193–214; Lüdemann, *Opposition to Paul* (n.138), 251 n.119 (with bibliography).

447. Cf. the major work by Mary Ann Tolbert, *Sowing the Gospel. Mark's World in Literary-Historical Perspective*, 1989, 290.

448. Ludger Schenke, *Auferstehungsverkündigung und leeres Grab*, SBS 33, 1968, 20–30; Pesch, *Mk* II, 507f., differs.

449. However, Pesch, *Mk* II, 505–7, favours four women, though without sufficient text-critical reasons, since the article *he* before 'Joses' in Vaticanus is certainly secondary. For the problem cf. also Gerd Theissen, *Lokalkolorit und Zeitgeschichte*, NTOA 8, 1989, 188–90.

450. In John 12.3–8 this anonymous woman has become Mary (a sure sign of a later tradition). Similarly, in an extremely concrete way, in John 12.4f. Judas makes a comment on the costly waste which is made in Mark.14.4 indefinitely by 'some'.

451. Cf. Perrin, *The Resurrection according to Matthew, Mark and Luke*, 1977, 29.

452. According to Pesch, *Mk* II, 520, the note about the rising of the sun has a symbolic significance. Cf. also Ps.143.8; Lam.3.22f.

453. I can only regard the interpretation of the 'young man' in terms of the community of those who are reborn in the Risen Christ (John Dominic Crossan, 'Empty Tomb and Absent Lord [Mark 16.1–8]', in Werner H. Kelber, *The Passion in Mark. Studies on Mark 14–16*, 1976, 135–52: 147f.) as a curiosity. Crossan regards Mark 16.1–8 *in toto* as a Markan construction – on the basis of the form of Mark 6.45–51 (150). But as Crossan himself sees, Mark 16.7 has no parallel in Mark 6.45–51.

454. Cf. Edward Lynn Bode, *The First Easter Morning. The Gospel Accounts of the Women's Visit to the Tomb of Jesus*, AnB 45, 1970, 27.

455. Since Jesus is further called 'the Nazarene' (cf. 1.24; 10.47; 14.67), a continuity with the earthly Jesus is assured.

456. Andreas Lindemann, 'Die Osterbotschaft des Markus. Zur theologischen Interpretation von Mark 16.1–8', NTS 26, 1980, 298–317: 305.

457. Günther Kegel, *Auferstehung Jesu – Auferstehung der Toten. Eine traditionsgeschichtliche Untersuchung zum Neuen Testament*, 197, 21.

458. Cf. Wolfgang Schenk, *Evangelium – Evangelien – Evangeliologie. Ein 'hermeneutisches' Manifest*, TEH 216, 1983, 115f. n.130.

459. The phrase 'the disciples and Peter' recalls I Cor.15.5, and may be regarded as an offshoot of that primal tradition of an appearance to Cephas and the Twelve.

460. Certainly there is no explicit mention in Mark 14.28 of a seeing of Jesus, but it is presupposed, since 16.8 (go before and see) regards itself emphatically as a parallel to 14.28 (go before).

461. Henning Paulsen, 'Mk XVI 1–8' (1980), in Hoffmann, *Überlieferung* (n.43), 377–415; 415.

462. Monika Fander (*Die Stellung der Frau im Markusevangelium. Unter besonderer Berücksichtigung kultur- und religionsgeschichtlicher Hintergründe*, MThA, ²1990) works out the theme of the way in v.7 well:

'So 16.7 is the challenge to the disciples to follow Jesus. The motif of the way in the basic tradition is here combined with Markan terminology' (173). 'If they are to see Jesus in Galilee, then here we have appearance terminology, but the seeing can also be understood in the sense of Markan terminology as the correct understanding' (74).

463. Cf. Willi Marxsen, *Mark the Evangelist*, 1969, 115: with this verse Mark is inviting Christians to leave Jerusalem and go to Galilee, there to experience the parousia. For criticism cf. Lüdemann, *Opposition to Paul* (n.138), 239.

464. Evans, *Resurrection* (n.28), 81; cf. Perrin, *Resurrection* (n.451), 26.

465. Cf. Perrin, *Resurrection* (n.451), 30: 'In the Gospel of Mark the discipleship failure is total. The disciples forsake Jesus as a group and flee from the arrest; Peter denies him with oaths while he is on trial; the women, in the role of the disciples in this final three-part narrative, fail to deliver the message entrusted to them.'

466. Schottroff, 'Maria' (n.120), 153.

467. Brun, *Auferstehung* (n.95), 11.

468. From a text-critical perspective cf. Kurt Aland, 'Der Schluss des Markusevangelliums' (1974), in id., *Neutestamentliche Entwürfe*, ThB 63, 1979, 246–83.

469. Lindemann, 'Osterbotschaft' (n.456), 314. 'Since it is said that the women "said nothing to anyone", the reader receives the Easter message as it were directly from the mouth of the *neaniskos*; i.e. in this way Mark makes it clear that all men and women are called to the faith in the same word and are not pointed towards a derived tradition' (315).

470. In Gospel of Peter 12.50–13.57 there is a narrative about the women at the tomb which recalls Mark 16.1–8 and which does not contain a command corresponding to Mark 16.7 and the silence of the women (v.8b). On occasion this has been understood to indicate that at this point the Gospel of Peter is independent of the account in Mark (cf. e.g. Benjamin Arlen Johnson, *Empty Tomb Tradition in the Gospel of Peter*, ThD Harvard University 1965, 120, etc.). However, the Gospel of Peter may have *changed* the text of Mark. Cf. Frans Neirynck, *Evangelica* II, BETL XCIX, 1991, 715–72 ('The Apocryphal Gospels and the Gospel of Mark'): 735–40.

471. Cf. Susanne Heine, 'Eine Person von Rang und Name. Historische Konturen der Magdalenerin', in Gerhard Sellin, Dietrich-Alex Koch and Andreas Lindemann (eds.), *Jesu Rede von Gott und ihre Nachgeschichte in frühen Christentum (FS Willi Marxsen)*, 1989, 179–94: 185.

472. The asterisk * indicates that here the pre-Marcan tradition underlying these verses is meant.

473. Cf. simply Dieter Lührmann, *Das Markusevangelium*, HNT 2, 1987, 10.

474. Cf. Frans Neirynck, *Evangelica*, BETL LX, 1982, 365–400 ('John and the Synoptics').

475. Paulsen, 'Mk XVI 1–8' (n.461), 396f.

476. Bultmann, *History* (n.95). Further references to this work are given in the text.

477. Wilhelm Bousset, *Kyrios Christos, Geschichte des Christusglaubens von den Anfängen des Christentums bis Irenaeus,* FRLANT 21, 1913, 79. However, Martin Hengel ('Maria Magdalena und die Frauen als Zeugen', in Otto Betz, id., and Peter Schmidt, *Abraham unser Vater [FS O.Michel],* AGJU 5, 1963, 243–56) thinks 'that in such a late construction the disciples would have been made the ones who discover the tomb rather than the suspect women, who are incapable of bearing witness' (254 n.1). Cf. further below, 117f.

478. Paulsen, 'Mk XVI 1–8' (n.461), 398.

479. Collins, *Beginning of the Gospel* (n.87), 127.

480. Cf. also the survey in Fander, *Stellung der Frau* (n.462), 154–70.

481. Ludger Schenke, *Auferstehungsverkündigung und leeres Grab. Eine traditionsgeschichtliche Untersuchung von Mk 16,1–8,* SBS 333, 1968, 88 (printed in italics in Schenke).

482. Hans Dieter Betz, 'Zum Problem der Auferstehung Jesu', in id., *Hellenismus und Urchristentum, Gesammelte Aufsätze* I, 1991, 230–61: 246f.

483. Martin Albertz, 'Zur Formengeschichte der Auferstehungsberichte' (1922), in Hoffmann, *Überlieferung* (n.43), 259–70: 265.

484. Elisabeth Schüssler Fiorenza, *In Memory of Her. A Feminist Theological Reconstruction of Christian Origins,* 1983, 139.

485. He was born not long before 480 BCE in Halicarnassus and died c.425. There is a selection of more recent research in W. Marg (ed.), *Herodot,* WdF 26, 1962. Recently Detlev Fehling (*Die Quellenangaben bei Herodot. Studien zur Erzählkunst Herodots,* Untersuchungen zur antiken Literatur und Geschichte 9, 1971) has wanted to qualify the historical value of Herodotus considerably. For criticism cf. Justus Cobet, in *Gnomon* 46, 1974, 737–46, who observes in his summary: 'Herodotus has long ceased to be measured so naively by the criterion of modern "historical science"' (745).

486. Translated by George Rawlinson, *The Histories* (1910), Everyman Library, 1992, 301.

487. However, Erwin Rohde (*Psyche. Seelencult und Unsterblichkeits- glaube der Griechen,* II ²1898 [= 1961]) assumes that Herodotus is inaccurate and prefers the account of Maximus of Tyre (second century CE), according to whom Aristeas was in ecstasy. 'When his soul . . . left his body, it appeared, as his other self, visibly in distant places' (92). E. R. Dodds (*The Greeks and the Irrational,* 1951) could then consistently understand Aristeas as a kind of shaman (77). For a survey of research on Aristeas cf. J. D. P. Bolton, *Aristeas of Proconnesus,* 1962, esp.119–73, who in 142ff. attacks the priority of the version of Maximus of Tyre preferred by Rohde and others to Herodotus.

488. Translation by Rawlinson, *The Histories* (n.486), 334f.

489. Gregory of Nazianzus, *Oratio* IV 59 (printed in Bolton, *Aristeas*, 213).

490. Elias Bickermann, 'Das leere Grab' (1924), in Hoffmann, *Überlieferung* (n.43), 271–84. Further references to this work are given in the text.

491. Cf. Evans, *Resurrection* (n.298), 132–43 and bibliography; Eduard Schweizer, *Lordship and Discipleship*, 1960; Georg Bertram, 'Erhöhung', *RAC* VI, 22–43: 37ff.

492. Cf. Georg Strecker, 'Entrückung', *RAC* V, 461–76, though he indicates certain exceptions (cf.462).

493. In the story of the tomb, 'the original idea of exaltation is modified already' (Bultmann, *History*, 290). It cannot even presuppose an immediate exaltation, as the motif of the stone rolled away indicates (ibid., 290 n.3).

494. We find a *modern* variation on such a conclusion in Hugh Montefiore, *The Womb and the Tomb. The Mystery of the Birth and Resurrection of Jesus*, 1992, 184, which is so sympathetic but does not get us much further: 'The miracle of the opening of the empty tomb . . . must not be confused with the miracle of Jesus being raised to life in such a way that the tomb was found to be empty. The two are connected but separate.' Cf. Koch, *Auferstehung* (n.216): 'The question in which way the tomb became empty proves to be the wrong one . . . The only legitimate question is why the tomb became empty' (171).

495. Ernst Lohmeyer, *Das Evangelium des Matthäus*, KEK Sonderband, ⁴1967, 411.

496. Dialogue 108.2: 'Yet you not only have not repented, after you learned that he rose from the dead, but . . . have sent chosen and ordained men throughout all the world to proclaim that a godless and lawless heresy had sprung from one Jesus, a Galilean deceiver, whom we crucified, but his disciples stole him by night from the tomb, where he was laid when taken down from the cross, and now deceive men by asserting that he has risen from the dead and ascended to heaven.' Cf. Eusebius, *Church History* IV, 187.

497. Thus argued most recently by Craig, *Evidence* (n.189): the Jewish polemic never disputed that the tomb was empty, but attempted to explain it away (222).

498. Thus Paul Hoffmann, 'Das Zeichen für Israel. Zu einem vernächlässigten Aspekt der matthäischen Ostergeschichte', in id., *Überlieferung* (n.43), 416–52: 418 n.11.

499. Hermann Samuel Reimarus, *Apologie oder Schutzschrift für die vernünftigen Verehrer Gottes II* (ed. Gerhard Alexander), 1972, 202. On 188–206 Reimarus offers a penetrating analysis of the story of the guards at the tomb and attributes it to Matthew (197). We still need an evaluation of the whole of Reimarus' apology, which of course lacked a religious sense.

There is a widespread bad habit of still citing this important work from the
*Fragments* edited by G. E. Lessing.
  500. Julius Wellhausen, *Das Evangelium Matthaei*, ²1914, 142.
  501. Hirsch, *Osterglaube* (n.61), 57.
  502. Vielhauer, *Geschichte* (n.105), 642.
  503. Cf. the description of the Son of God in the book of Elchasai
(beginning of the second century): 'A certain Alcibiades, who lived in
Apamea in Syria . . . came to Rome and brought with him a book. Of it he
said that Elchasai, a righteous man, had received it from Seres in Parthia and
had transmitted it to a certain Sobiai. It had been communicated by an angel,
whose height was 24 *schoinoi*, which is 96 miles, his breadth four *schoinoi*,
and from shoulder to shoulder six *schoinoi*, and the tracks of his feet in
length 1½ *schoinoi*, which is 14 miles, and in breadth 3½ *schoinoi*, and in
height half a *schoinos*. And with him there was also a female figure, whose
measurements Alcibiades says were commensurate with those mentioned;
and the male figure was the Son of God, but the female was called Holy
Spirit' (Schneemelcher [ed.], *New Testament Apocrypha* II, 687 [Johannes
Irmscher]).
  504. Schneemelcher, *New Testament Apocrypha* I, 225 (Christian
Maurer).
  505. Cf. Joachim Jeremias, *Abba. Studien zur neutestamentliche
Theologie und Zeitgeschichte*, 1966, 323–31; Helmut Köster, *Synoptische
Überlieferung bei den Apostolischen Vätern*, TU 65, 1957, 28–31.
  506. Cf. Jürgen Denker, *Die theologiegeschichtliche Stellung des
Petrusevangeliums. Ein Beitrag zur Frühgeschichte des Doketismus*, 1975,
93–6: 'As I Peter 3.19f. speaks of disobedient spirits, whether fallen angels
or human beings of the generation of the flood, this passage is not the point
of contact for the Gospel of Peter. I Peter 3.18ff. does not contain the
important terms "fallen asleep" and "descent", perhaps precisely because
the prison means the place of the angels who have fallen from heaven, cf.
Slavonic Enoch 7, so that I Peter 3.18ff. says nothing at all about a descent
and a preaching to those who have fallen asleep' (94).
  507. Cf. Helmut Koester, *Ancient Christian Gospels. Their History and
Development*, 1990, 233 n.2. Koester himself regards the basis thus
reconstructed (plus the next verse, Gospel of Peter 11.45: 'When those who
were of the centurion's company saw this, they hastened by night to Pilate,
abandoning the sepulchre which they were guarding, and reported everything that they had seen, being full of disquietude and saying, "In truth he
was the Son of God."') as an old epiphany story from which Mark 15.39
comes (234). He regards this verse in the Markan context as 'quite
unmotivated. There was no spectacular event that the centurion could have
witnessed' (234). With due respect, the verse is very easy to understand as a
*Markan* interpretation (cf. Mark 1.11; 9.7). Furthermore three fragments of
this epiphany story are said to be contained in Matt.: 27.62–66; 28.2–4 and
28.11–15 (234–7). This is not the place to pursue Koester's important

reflections: however, it seems to me that the Gospel of Peter presupposes the four canonical Gospels, and especially Matthew, but not yet the canon of the four Gospels. In addition it uses oral tradition, some of which is earlier than the Gospels, see above on Matt.28.2–4 and Raymond E. Brown, 'The Gospel of Peter and Canonical Gospel Priority', *NTS* 33, 1987, 321–43; id., *Death of the Messiah* (n. 174), 1317–49.

509. Grass, *Ostergeschehen* (n.41), 26. In ibid., n.1, he points out that Luther (*WA* 26, 328) still held the view that Jesus had risen from the closed tomb through the stone.

509. The work 'in its present form . . . is a Christian work, which was put together at the earliest in the second half of the 2nd century. It was intended to combat in the manner of an ancient apocalypse, certain contemporary evils, the lack of discipline and the divisions in the Church. One cannot however fail to recognize that the work takes up traditions already in existence and makes them serve its purpose' (Schneemelcher [ed.], *New Testament Apocrypha* II, 604 [C. Detlef G. Müller]).

510. Ibid., 608.

511. Hans Werner Bartsch, 'Der Ursprung des Osterglaubens', *ThZ* 31, 1975, 16–31; id., 'Inhalt und Funktion des urchristlichen Osterglaubens', *ANRW* II 25 1, 1982, 794–843.

512. Hans Werner Bartsch, *Das Auferstehungszeugnis. Sein historisches und sein theologisches Problem*, ThF, 1965, 12.

513. Cf. Nikolaus Walter, 'Eine vormatthäische Schilderung der Auferstehung Jesu', *NTS* 19, 1972/73, 415–29: 418.

514. Cf. also Jan Helderman, 'Die Engel bei der Auferstehung und das lebendige Kreuz Mk 16,3 in *k* einem Vergleich unterzogen', in *The Four Gospels 1992 (FS Frans Neirynck)*, BETL C, 1992, 2321–42, which has a wealth of material.

515. Philipp Seidensticker (*Zeitgenössische Texte zur Osterbotschaft der Evangelien*, SBS 27, ²1968) translates: 'When he (Jesus) rose in the splendour of light of the living God . . .' (64); Helderman, 'Engel' (n.514), 2326: 'and they came forth in the glory of the living Jesus . . .'

516. Translation based on Walter, 'Schilderung' (n.513), 422.

517. Translation based on Seidensticker, *Texte* (n.515), 65.

518. Hirsch, *Osterglaube* (n.61), 57.

519. Matthew uses the verb 'worship' (*proskynein*) in 8.2; 9.18; 14.33; 15.25; 20.20 in contrast to Mark and thus indicates that the earthly Jesus already possesses the authority of the risen Christ. (Consequently he does not take over the mocking worship in Mark 15.19.)

520. E.g. Frans Neirynck, *Evangelica* BETL LX, 1982, 273–96 ('Les femmes au tombeau, Etude de la Rédaction matthéenne [Matt.XXVIII.1–1–10]'): 281–9, argues for redaction. Among others, Gnilka, *Mk* II, 493, argues in favour of a tradition which goes with John 20.14–18.

521. For the question of the relationship between Matt.28.10 and John 20.17 cf. below, 155.

# Notes

522. Elaine Mary Wainwright, *Towards a Feminist Critical Reading of the Gospel According to Matthew*, BZNW 60, 1991, 312.

523. Grass, *Ostergeschehen* (n.41), 27.

524. In general it is illuminating that in the face of questions from outsiders and because of their own reflection, the story of the tomb and the accounts of apperances had constantly to be brought closer together.

525. The use of John by Matthew is to be ruled out here; with Grass, *Ostergeschehen* (n.41), 27; cf. also the further remarks below. See also Walter, 'Schilderung' (n.513), 416: 'If this narrative (viz. Matt.28.9f.) had probably originally developed out of the need to let those who according to the earlier passion tradition (and still according to Mark and Matthew) had been the only ones to be faithful under the cross, the women, have their own share in the Easter event, without this share coming into conflict with the tradition of the real Easter experiences (I.Cor.XV.5–7), there was now a tendency to let the women share in a real Easter encounter – a tendency which has developed further in John XX, albeit limited to one woman (John XX.1 and 11–18).'

526. According to Grass, *Ostergeschehen*, 28, the late legendary character of the scene in Matt.28.9–10 is also shown by its realism. To this Heine, 'Person' (n.471), objects: 'But this conclusion is not convincing, for the nature of the mode of imagining is more dependent on the theological context and level of reflection than on the chronology' (186). That is right. But it does not heighten the historical value of Matt.28.9, as is sometimes evidently assumed.

527. Evans, *Resurrection* (n.28) differs from Dodd in regarding the pericope as a Matthaean construction (59). But the structure makes one think.

528. So Matt.28.9–10 hardly disturbs the flow of the narrative (thus Reginald Fuller, *The Formation of the Resurrection Narratives*, 1972, 78, who regards this as the criterion for the pre-Matthaean character of v.9).

529. For the Matthaean redaction in this section, in addition to the commentaries see Strecker, *Weg* (n.465), 208f.; Joachim Lange, *Das Erscheinen des Auferstandenen im Evangelium nach Mattäus. Eine traditions– und redaktionsgeschichtliche Untersuchung zu Mt 28.16–20*, 1973.

530. Vielhauer, *Geschichte* (n.105), 685.

531. Schneemelcher (ed.), *New Testament Apocrypha* I, 256 (C. Detlef G. Müller). For the structure of EpAp 9–12 see the admirable work by Julian Hills, 'Tradition and Composition in the Epistula Apostolorum', HDR 24, 1989, 67–95. According to Hills, EpAp 3–5 and 9–11 are 'prefaces to the revelatory dialogues in 13–51' (66). Hills sees merely New Testament writings and perhaps the Gospel of Peter reflected in EpAp 9–12.

532. This sounds like a seroius lack; however, it should not be, but is meant as a historical description.

533. Cf. Lange, *Erscheinen* (n.529), 270f.; Strecker, *Weg* (n.365), 116ff., differs.

534. The scene Matt.28.16,20 'covers over even more completely the whole living murmur of the recollection of the first Christian decades – and that is certainly the intention of the churchmen who stand behind this Gospel' (Hirsch, *Osterglaube* [n.69], 46f.).

535. Cf. Günther Bornkamm, Gerhard Barth and Heinz Joachim Held, *Tradition and Interpretation in Matthew*, ²1982, 125–30, 302.

536. Hans Dieter Betz, 'Zum Problem der Auferstehung Jesu im Lichte der griechischen magischen Papyri', in id., *Hellenismus und Urchristentum*, Gesammelte Aufsätze I, 1990, 230–61: 250f.

537. Cf. Benjamin Hubbard, *The Matthean Redaction of a Primitive Apostolic Commissioning: An Exegesis of Matthew 28:16–20*, SBLDS 19, 1974, 144.

538. 'What one would expect would be: proclaim the gospel! But this indicates the specific nature of the Matthaean text. The charge is directed towards the building of the church, the creation of communities. Confrontation with the word of the gospel alone is not enough' (Joachim Gnilka, *Das Matthäusevangelium*, II.Teil, HThK I.2, 1988, 509).

539. But the combination of God, Jesus and Spirit is already prepared for in Paul: II Cor.1.21f.; II Cor.13.13; I Cor.12.4–6.

540. But according to Vielhauer, *Geschichte* (n.105), 727, the words in Did.7.1 are to be deleted. Kurt Niederwimmer, *Die Didache*, KAV 1, 1989, 159 and n.2, differs.

541. Cf. the survey in Lange, *Erscheinen* (n.529), 171f.

542. Cf. Bornkamm, Barth and Held, *Tradition and Interpretation in Matthew* (n.535), 301–27.

543. Matthew speaks explicitly only of the eleven disciples (Matt.28.16), as do some codices at I Cor.15.5. That is a rationalization which has removed the figure of Judas from the Twelve. Originally the tradition reported an appearance to the Twelve.

544. Paul Schubert, 'Struktur und Bedeutung von Lk 24' (1954), in Hoffmann, *Überlieferung* (n.43), 331–59: 346.

545. Eduard Lohse, *Die Auferstehung Jesu Christi im Zeugnis des Lukasevangeliums*, BSt 31, 1961, 15.

546. Grass, *Ostergeschehen* (n.41), 35.

547. Here Luke smoothes over the style, as in Mark's account women had already been mentioned immediately beforehand (Mark 15.47), some of whom are identical with those in Mark 16.1. By speaking only generally of women in Luke 23.55 (and Luke 23.49), and mentioning them by name in Luke 24.10, he avoids the rough transition at Mark 16.1.

548. Bickermann, 'Das leere Grab' (n.490), rightly points out that a phrase like 'he was not found' constantly appears in rapture stories (180). Cf. 119 above.

549. Literally, 'the body of the Lord Jesus'. Some witnesses read only 'the body'. But this reading with outwardly weak attestation probably

came about through assimilation to Luke 23.55 and Luke 24.23. For 'the Lord Jesus', cf. Acts 1.21; 4.33; 8.16.

550. For the scene with angels in Luke 24.4–9 and Acts 1.10–12, which correspond in terminology and sequence, cf. Lohfink, *Himmelfahrt* (n.301), 196ff. He conclusively demonstrates that Acts 1.10–12 does not go back to earlier tradition. 'Rather, the scene with angels is a composition of Luke's, who here is using his own version of the story of the tomb as a model' (197f.).

551. The last clause is not contained in important manuscripts. For the question of the originality of this reading see on v.12 below.

552. Cf. 'into the hands of sinful men' (v.7).

553. Similarly Mark 14.28f. is *not* taken over by Luke.

554. Thus the role of the women as those who proclaim the Easter kerygma is hardly played down, as Elisabeth Schüssler Fiorenza thinks ('Word, Spirit and Power: Women in Early Christian Communities', in R. Ruether and E. McLaughlin [ed.], *Women of Spirit. Female Leadership in the Jewish and Christian Traditions*, 1979, 29–70: 52). In contrast to the report in Mark the women are in fact portrayed in a *positive* way, and the apostles (v.10f.) (and not the women) do not believe.

555. Cf. Anton Dauer, 'Lk 24,12 – ein Produkt lukanischer Redaktion?', in *The Four Gospels (FS F.Neirynck)*, BETL C, 1992, 1697–1716: 1698–1703.

556. Cf. Frans Neirynck, *Evangelica*, BETL LX, 1982, 313–28 ('Lc.XXIV 12. Les Témoins du texte occidental').

557. Cf. Joachim Jeremias, *Die Sprache des Lukasevangeliums*, KEK Sonderband, 1980, 312 on Luke 24.12.

558. Ibid., 130f.

559. Cf. e.g. Robert Mahoney, *Two Disciples at the Tomb. The Background and Message of John 20.1–10*, TW 6, 1974, 63.

560. Thus Neirynck, *Evangelica* (n.520), 331.

561. Thus with good reasons Dauer, 'Lk' (n.555), 1703–13.

562. Christian Dietzfelbinger, *Johanneischer Osterglaube*, ThSt 138, 1992, differs: 'Our starting point is that there is an older tradition in Luke 24.12 which was not included in Mark but which has been preserved in John 20.3,10' (10). However, the author cannot explain why Mark passed over this older tradition. The 'original tomb story' reconstructed by Dietzfelbinger can therefore be left aside.

563. Pierre Benoit, 'Maria Magdalena und die Jünger am Grabe nach Joh 20,1–18' (1960), in Hoffmann, *Überlieferung* (n.43), 360–76, has claimed that Luke 24.12 rests on a borrowing from John 20.3–10 which comes from the final redaction of the Johannine tradition (363). But in my view it is equally possible to imagine things the other way round (cf. 370). All that is certain is that because of the striking linguistic agreement there is a genetic relationship between the two texts. It must also be added that Mary Magdalene and the women have nothing to do with this tradition. Against Benoit, who lumps the two together and then even claims: 'In the light of this

original account which underlies Luke and John, the narrative of Mark 16.1–8 par. gives the impression of being a further theological development' (371).

564. Brun, *Auferstehung* (n.95), 53. Cf. also the view of Dodd, 'Erscheinungen' (n.118), 303f.: the Emmaus story is a 'carefully composed account which in the framework of a narrative with a marked dramatic interest contains most of what has to be said (from the standpoint of this evangelist) about the resurrection of Christ. However, it is remarkable that this story, like others, begins with the disciples missing their Lord . . .'

565. Joachim Wanke, '". . . wie sie ihn beim Brotbrechen erkannten". Zur Auslegung der Emmauserzählung Lk 24,13–35', *BZ* 18, 1974, 180–192: 189.

566. Hans Conzelmann, *The Theology of St Luke*, 1960, 149–54.

567. Wanke, 'Brotbrechen' (n.565), 190.

568. Lohfink, *Himmelfahrt* (n.301), 239.

569. Cf. the great theme in Luke-Acts (Wilhelm Ott, *Gebet und Heil. Die Bedeutung der Gebetsparänese in der lukanischen Theologie*, StANT XII, 1965; for first information Horst Balz, *EWNT* III, 407f.).

570. 'What is formally meant on their lips as an invitation imperceptibly becomes – in the reader's judgment – a prayer to the Kyrios Jesus, "Stay with us, for it is towards evening and the day is now far spent." This subtle irony is theologically quite appropriate: it matches the conduct of the risen Jesus. The traveller accedes to the disciples' request and goes with them into the house, "to stay with them", as it is said, not without further connotations' (Hans Dieter Betz, 'Ursprung und Wesen christlichen Glaubens nach der Emmauslegende [Lk 24,13–32]', *ZThK* 66, 1979, 7–21: 12 = id., *Synoptische Studien. Gesammelte Aufsätze* II, 1992, 35–49: 40).

571. Here one can see a motif from the ancient romance. 'Such an inexplicable quickening of the soul or heart in meeting a beloved person who has long been away but is not yet recognized is described in almost all the romances' (Roland Kany, 'Der lukanische Bericht von Tod und Auferstehung aus der Sicht eines hellenistischen Romanlesers', *NT* 18, 1986, 75–90: 89). The author refers (ibid.) for a close parallel to Heliodorus IX 1, 14–19 and IX 24, 56–60. Kany shows how far the rest of the Gospel of Luke is from the ancient romances. In particular the absence of the sensational from the resurrection stories tells against any proximity: 'Luke does not relate the events from Good Friday to Easter as an adventure; he does not pretend that he is omniscient, like the authors of the romances, and throughout shows no interest in psychology' (89f.).

572. Why is he so terse at this point and does he tell no story of the first appearance? As an attempt at an answer: the first appearance took place in Galilee and Luke had no room for it because of his Jerusalem perspective. Moreover, presumably with Luke 5.1–11 he had already transferred the first appearance to Peter into the life of Jesus (see above, 86f.).

573. Elisabeth Schüssler Fiorenza, *In Memory of Her. A Feminist Theological Reconstruction of Christian Origins*, 1983. Further references to this work are given in the text.

574. The German translation differs here (*Zu ihrem Gedächtnis . . . Eine feministisch-theologische Rekonstruktion der christlichen Ursprünge*, 1988, 85).

575. For these three texts see below, 159ff.

576. Again the German text differs, ibid., 187.

577. Hermann Gunkel, *Zum religionsgeschichtlichen Verständnis des Neuen Testaments*, FRLANT 1, 1903, 71. Cf. id., *Genesis*, ⁴1917, 193f. In connection with his exegesis of Gen.18.1–15, Gunkel comments: 'The feature that the deity appears to human beings unknown, in simple, human form, and only reveals himself to them afterwards, also occurs in Judg.6.13; Tobit 5 and elsewhere. In particular the theme that the deity unrecognized asks for hospitality and offers a splendid reward is also frequent: in the Old Testament in Gen.19; among the Greeks there must have been a series of similar sagas: "For the gods do take on all sorts of transformations, appearing as strangers from elsewhere, and thus they range at large through the cities, watching to see which men keep the laws, and which are violent" (*Odyssey* XVII, 485ff.). One might think of Philemon and Baucis (Ovid, *Metamorphoses* 8, 616ff.) and of the fable of Phaedrus (appendix 3), according to which Mercury is the guest of two women; also of Demeter's reception in the house of Celeus in Eleusis (*Homeric Hymns* V, 96f.), and the arrival of Jupiter with Lycaon (Ovid, *Metamorphoses* 1, 211ff.). Among the Germans, too, the gods wander through the world and return in the evening.'

578. Betz, 'Ursprung' (n.570), 9 n.8 thinks: 'We must distinguish between a deity who appears in the form of a human being . . . and the appearance of a human being after his death.' (But in this case do not these amount to the same thing?)

579. For the analysis of the tradition see Betz, 'Ursprung'; he regards the Emmaus story as a cult legend, not with missionary intent, but growing out of internal Christian reflection. As the first stage he sees an skilful combination of a description of the appearance of Jesus and a dialogue between the two disciples and Jesus. From this he distinguishes the passage vv.21b–24 as as secondary (pre-Lukan) extension. In keeping with the legend, the risen Jesus institutes the Lord's Supper as a Christian cult meal and initiates the disciples into the rite. For the Emmaus legend, 'the present of the crucified Jesus is the ground of possibility for Christian faith. Accordingly, Christian faith is fundamentally to be understood as faith in the risen Jesus of Nazareth' (14). 'The idea of the resurrection of Jesus has its significance primarily in the removal of all limits from the presence of Jesus; the limits which the historical existence of Jesus brought with it have been transcended' (15). According to the legend, the relationship of Christians to Jesus of Nazareth is fundamentally different from the relationship of a

disciple of the time to the earthly Jesus. The presence of the risen Jesus is
'limited to the "event of the Word" . . . Jesus is present where questions are
asked of him, where there is reflection on him, where there is discussion of
him and his significance' (15). Jesus of Nazareth is present in the exegesis of
scripture. 'The inter-personal event of a shared meal is emphasized to the
point where in principle it is thought of as being the place at which the Risen
Lord manifests himself as the one who acts' (16).

580. Clopas is simply the Jewish pronunciation of Cleopas, cf. Theodor
Zahn, *Forschungen zur Geschichte des neutestamentlichen Kanons und der
altkirchlichen Literatur* VI, 1890, 343f. n.3.

581. IV 22.4 is a quotation from Hegesippus, but III 11 is a paraphrase by
Eusebius, cf. my analysis, *Opposition to Paul* (n.138), 160f.

582. Cf. Zahn, *Forschungen* (n.580), 350–2, who regards Clopas and
Symeon as the two travellers (Brun, *Auferstehung* [n.95], 43 differs). Thus
already a glossator in the margin of Codex S (= 949 CE) on Luke 24.18
(Bruce M. Metzger, *A Textual Commentary on the Greek New Testament*,
1975, 185).

583. Lohse, *Auferstehung* (n.545), 24f. Cf. also *EWNT* 1, 1980, 1082f.
(Joachim Wanke).

584. Aristotle, *On the Art of Poetry*, ed. Ingram Bywater, 1909, 27.

585. Lohfink, *Himmelfahrt* (n.301), 148.

586. Specifically, no ghost. Luke is also combating magical and demonic
conclusions, cf. also below, 148.

587. Betz, 'Auferstehung' (n.482), 249f.

588. For the text and its relationship to Luke 24.36–43(49), see 162 below.

589. Helmut Köster, *Synoptische Überlierung bei den Apostolischen
Vätern*, TU 65, 1957. Further references to this work are given in the text.

590. Conzelmann, *Theology* (n.566), 94, still assumed that because of the
place name 'Bethany', Luke 24.50–53 was not part of the original Gospel of
Luke.

591. Michaelis, *Erscheinungen* (n.237), 24.

592. Cf. Lohfink, *Himmelfahrt* (n.301), 24.

593. Ibid., 151.

594. 'The Johannine Easter stories are . . . a mosaic of pericopes of a kind
that we do not find elsewhere in John. Nevertheless the discrepancies are not
disturbing. In ch.20 we feel a rich variation and a certain heightening' (Hans
Windisch, 'Der Johanneische Erzählungsstil', in *Eucharisterion, Festschrift
für Hermann Gunkel*, 2, FRLANT 36, 1923, 174–213: 206). There follows:
'If the message to Magdalene once formed the conclusion to the Gospel, the
confession of Thomas is a much more effective ending, since it leads back to
the lofty opening sentence of the prologue. By contrast, the end of the
appearance inserted in ch.21 with its over-subtle exegetical gloss marks a
great decline' (ibid.).

595. Grass, *Ostergeschehen* (n.41), 54.

596. Windisch, 'Erzählungsstil' (n.594), 206.

597. Thorwald Lorenzen, *Der Lieblingsjünger im Johannesevangelium. Eine redaktionsgeschichtliche Studie*, SBS 55, 1971, 25f.

598. It is sometimes doubted whether John 18.15f. is a reference to the Beloved Disciple (cf. e.g. Vielhauer, *Geschichte*, 454f.: the Beloved Disciple is elsewhere described as the other disciple [with the definite article] and is only so described after being previously mentioned). But cf. Frans Neirynck, *Evangelica*, BETL LX, 1982, 335–64 ('The Other Disciple in John 18.15– 16') and Kevin Quast, *Peter and the Beloved Disciple. Figures for a Community in Crisis*, JSNT.S 32, 71–89. Cf. also the suggestion by Ernst Haenchen (*John* II, Hermeneia, 1984), 'Perhaps the characterization of the "other disciple" as the "beloved disciple" is omitted here because this designation comports poorly with the position of someone known to the high priest' (167). Similarly Hengel, *Johannine Question* (n.338), 125.

599. Grass, *Ostergeschehen*, 56, remarkably succumbs to the view that both the Beloved Disciple and Peter had believed, although this is not said by Peter. However, Rudolf Bultmann, *The Gospel of John*, 1971, 684, who otherwise would have expected an explicit statement, remarks that 'Peter did not believe'. But at least here the question of Peter's faith remains open (cf. Quast, *Peter* [n.598], 120).

600. Cf. Haenchen, *John* 2, 208, 'The lack of knowledge of the scripture makes both points comprehensible: one disciple becomes a believer, the other doesn't.'

601. Cf. Rudolf Schnackenburg, *The Gospel according to St John* 3, 1982, 312: 'The fact that the narrative is so concerned about this careful inspection of the tomb by Peter confirms its apologetic intention. The "empty tomb", which cannot be any direct evidence for Jesus' resurrection, but is open to the suspicion that the body was somehow removed, now does become a convincing piece of evidence in view of the discovery of the cloths in which Jesus' body had been wrapped.'

602. Bultmann, *John* (n.599), 681.

603. Cf. Gospel of Peter 12.52: Mary Magdalene and her women friends speak at the tomb of Jesus: 'Although we could not weep and lament on that day when he was crucified, yet let us do so now at this sepulchre'; 14.59: 'But we, the twelve disciples of the Lord, wept and mourned, and each one, very grieved at what had come to pass, went to his own home.'

604. Bultmann, *John*, sees rivalry here and writes: 'the episode of the angels is original in the narrative of Mary; it corresponds to the type seen in Mark 15.5–7' (682).

605. Thus von Campenhausen, *Ablauf* (n.57), 32ff.

606. See an ancient Egyptian proverb, 'He whose name is spoken, lives' (Manfred Lurker, *Wörterbuch der Symbolik*, ⁴1988, 500).

607. Bultmann, *John*, 686.

608. Cf. Eduard Lohse, '*rabbi, rabbouni*', TDNT VI, 1968, 961–5: 964.

609. Lindblom, *Gesichte* (n.244), 98.

610. Ibid., 99.

611. Bultmann, *John*, 688.

612. 'In the history of the tradition the appearance of the Risen Christ to Mary Magdalene must be separated completely from the discovery of the empty tomb' (Hengel, 'Maria' [n.477], 255).

613. Others think that the visit to the empty tomb was already associated with an appearance to Mary Magdalene at the level of tradition. Thus Haenchen, *John* 2, constructs the following tradition: 'Mary Magdalene went alone to the tomb and found it empty. Jesus, whom she takes for the gardener, asks the weeping woman whom she seeks. She asks him to turn the body over to her, if he has taken it away. But instead of a corpse, she sees the living Jesus. Jesu speaks only a single, Aramaic word to her: her name, "Miriam". She likewise answers with a single, Aramaic word: "Rabboni". She is then given the task of telling the disciples that Jesus now goes to his and their Father and God' (216). This does not make much difference to the history of the tradition.

614. Dodd, 'Erscheinungen' (n.118), 311.

615. C. H. Dodd, *Historical Tradition in the Fourth Gospel*, 1965, 147.

616. For the brothers (and relations) of Jesus as *desposynoi* cf. also Lüdemann, *Opposition to Paul* (n.138), 158–68.

617. Luise Schottroff, 'Frauen in der Nachfolge Jesu in neutestamentlicher Zeit' (1980), in ead., *Befreiungserfahrungen. Studien zur Sozialgeschichte des Neuen Testaments*, ThB 82, 1990, 96–133: 117.

618. Heine, 'Person' (n.471), 185.

619. Schottroff, 'Frauen', 119. On p.117 she argues that a dispute over the 'chronological priority of the commissioning of the women by an angel epiphany as compared with the appearance of Jesus to Peter' is not really worthwhile. 'Whether the epiphany which brought the call of the women was the appearance of an angel or an appearance of Jesus may have been a subsidiary matter for the consciousness of those concerned' (ibid.). But this mitigating (historicizing) remark is not an answer to the traditio-historical problem.

620. In later tradition (since Gregory the Great) Mary Magdalene is identified with Mary of Bethany (Luke 10.38–42; John.11.2f.; 12.3) and the woman who was a sinner in Luke 7.36–50, demon possession here being connected with her former life of vice. I find this an attractive identification, but it is unfortunately only a possibility, and further note cannot be taken of it here.

621. Grass, *Ostergeschehen* (n.41), 111.

622. Cf. Hengel, 'Maria' (n.477), 246 and n.5 (bibliography).

623. Schneemelcher, *New Testament Apocrypha* I, 194 (Hans-Martin Schenke).

624. Kurt Rudolph, *Gnosis*, 1984, 245.

625. Schneemelcher, *New Testament Apocrypha* I, 337.

626. For first information cf. Vielhauer, *Geschichte* (n.105), 434f.: 'The misunderstandings are more than literary technique. They are an expression

of the Johannine understanding of revelation. The natural person must misunderstand Jesus; only those who have received the Spirit and are taught by the Spirit can receive him (2.22; 7.39; 14.26)' (435).

627. Wilhelm Pratscher, *Der Herrenbruder Jakobus und die Jakobustradition*, FRLANT 139, 1987, 169.

628. Schneemelcher, *New Testament Apocrypha* I, 192 (H.-M. Schenke). Cf. also Hans-Josef Klauck, 'Die dreifache Maria. Zur Rezeption von Joh 18, 25 in EvPhil 32', in *The Four Gospels (FS Frans Neirynck)*, BETL C, 1992, 2343–58 (bibliography). The author shows carefully, among other things, 'that Gospel of Philip 32 is part of the history of the Gnostic reception of John 19.25' (2358), and 'that sister, mother and consort denote one and the same person at a deeper level of understanding' (2357). The slightly divergent possibilities of translating Gospel of Philip 32 can be left on one side here.

629. Justin, Apology I, 26.3: 'A woman, Helena, who went about with him at that time, and had formerly been a prostitute, they say is the first idea (*ennoia*) generated by him.' Cf. also my article 'The Acts of the Apostles and the beginnings of Simonian Gnosis', NTS 33, 1987, 420–6 (bibliography).

630. Schneemelcher, *New Testament Apocrypha* I, 362 (id.).

631. Text and translation: *Die gnostischen Schriften des koptischen Papyrus Berolinensis 8502*, edited and translated by Walter C. Till, second edition by Hans-Martin Schenke, TU 60, 1972, 62–79. The brief work (eighteen pages), of which only half has been preserved, consists of two parts which a redactor has brought together. The first is a dialogue of Jesus with his disciples which after Jesus has gone away ends with the disciples' desperate question: 'How shall we go to the Gentiles and preach the Gospel of the kingdom of the Son of Man? If not even he has been spared, how shall we be preserved?' (9.7–12). The first part ends with the (successful) comforting of the disciples by Mary Magdalene and the second part is introduced by the report to them of a vision by Mary Magdalene (10.10–17.7 [11–14 have not been preserved]. Andrew does not believe Mary [17.11–15] and Peter exclaims: 'Did he then speak secretly with a woman before us and not openly? Are we to return and all listen to her? Has he preferred her before us?' (17.8–22). But Mary Magdalene's answer and Levi's retort to Peter's address support the authority of Mary Magdalene: 'Peter, you are always complaining. Now I see how you are attacking the woman as though she were the adversary. But if the Redeemer has made her worthy, who are you to reject her? Certainly the Redeemer knows her very well. Therefore he has loved her more than us . . .' (8.7–14). As the final sentences of the work have been preserved in Greek (Rylands Papyrus no.463 [beginning of the third century]), it is certain that the original was in Greek. The age of the papyrus indicates that the work was probably composed in the second century, when the significance of Mary Magdalene as a special bearer of revelation was recognized in Christian Gnosticism. But it should be stressed that New Testament writings give the ingredients for the

Gospel of Mary too, along with Gnostic Hermetic doctrines which are contained in the vision of Mary Magdalene about the rise of the soul (10.10–17.7). Cf. also R. McL.Wilson, 'The New Testament in the Gnostic Gospel of Mary', *NTS* 3, 1956/57, 236–43, and for first information Schneemelcher, *New Testament Apocrypha* I, 391–4 (Beate Blatz).

632. 'Simon Peter said to them: Let Mariham go out from among us, for women are not worthy of the life. Jesus said: Look, I will lead her that I may make her male, in order that she too may become a living spirit resembling you males. For every woman who makes herself male will enter into the kingdom of heaven' (Schneemelcher, *New Testament Apocrypha* I, 129 [B. Blatz]).

633. For a translation see *Koptisch-gnostische Schriften*, ed. Carl Schmidt, fourth edition ed. Hans-Martin Schenke, 1981, 1–254. The extensive Gnostic work Pistis Sophia consists of four parts and goes back to two underlying documents, the Greek originals of which date from the third century. In them the disciples and above all Mary Magdalene (and Mary the mother of Jesus, Martha and Salome) put questions to the risen Jesus and are given extensive instruction. Mary Magdalene has tremendous significance here and carries on the dialogue with Jesus almost alone, but this the basis is exclusively the New Testament plus Gnostic Valentinian doctrines. In addition, the critical remarks of Peter about Mary Magdalene are striking: 'My Lord, we cannot bear this woman, as she robs us of the opportunity and does not allow any of us to talk, but speaks often' (ch.36); (Mary Magdalene) 'I am afraid of Peter because he threatens me and hates our sex' (ch.72). But according to Jesus Mary Magdalene remains the one 'whose heart is directed towards the kingdom of heaven more than all your brothers' (ch.17). We still await a thorough analysis of the Pistis Sophia and the reconstruction of Christianity behind this interesting document. For first information see Schneemelcher, *New Testament Apocrypha* I, 361–70 (Beate Blatz).

634. Heine, 'Person' (n.471), 188.

635. Heine, 'Person', 184. The continuation of the sentence quoted runs: 'There is a tragic side in the fact that witness is borne to this by Gnosticism in particular, which beyond doubt did not remain true to the beginnings of the kerygma' (ibid.). This statement is wrong if it is not immediately supplemented by the statement that the mainstream church, too, did not remain faithful to the beginings of the kerygma (cf. Robinson, 'Jesus' [n.265]).

636. 'Fear of the Jews' is a general motif in the Gospel of Peter; cf. 12.51, Mary Magdalene and her friends 'are afraid that the Jews will see them'; 12.50, Mary Magdalene 'for fear of the Jews, since (they) were inflamed with wrath . . . had not done at the sepulchre of the Lord what women are wont to do for those beloved of them who die'. The motif appears in the later parts of the resurrection or tomb tradition, where there is already a clear distinction between 'Jews' and 'Christians'; the Jews are no longer seen

as a people but in general as a community hostile to Christians, and that is a further argument for the secondary or tertiary character of the Johannine account.

637. Therefore it is occasionally thought that originally doubt of the disciples was reported (cf. e.g. Brown, *John* [n.361], 1032).

638. Bultmann, *John*, 609.

639. Grass, *Ostergeschehen* (n.41), 67.

640. Anton Dauer, *Johannes und Lukas*, fzb 50, 1984, 235.

641. Ibid., 236.

642. Gen.2.7; Ezek.37.5–10, 14; Wisdom 15.1; more in Bultmann, *John*, 691 n.2.

643. Walter Bauer, Das *Johannesevangelium*, HNT 5, ³1933, 232.

644. The fact that only Matthew reports this authority of Peter to forgive sins and that John does not mention Peter in the present pericope, which is about authority to forgive sins, must not of course lead us astray into concluding that John is anti-Petrine (cf. rightly Quast, *Peter* [n.598], on theses to the contrary).

645. Cf. also Dauer, *Johannes* (n.640), who makes a detailed comparison of the nature and function of the ideas of spirit and ideas about the Spirit in the Paraclete sayings and in v.22 (237–41).

646. Cf. ibid., 288; he supposes that Luke 24.36–39 'had been abbreviated, reshaped and provided with new material at the stage of the pre-Johannine tradition' (ibid.).

647. For him cf. Eugen Ruckstuhl, *EWNT* II, 407–9.

648. Cf. Schneemelcher, *New Testament Apocrypha* I, 110–33 (Beate Blatz); alo Michael Fieger, *Das Thomasevangelium. Einleitung, Kommentar und Systematik*, NTA NF 22, 1991; Steven J.Patterson, *The Gospel of Thomas and Jesus*, 1992 (now basic).

649. Cf. Schneemelcher, *New Testament Apocrypha* I, 232–47 (H.-M. Schenke); also Hans-Martin Schenke, *Das Thomas Buch (Nag-Hammadi Codex II, 7)*, TU 138, 1989.

650. Cf. Schneemelcher, *New Testament Apocrypha* II, 322–411 (Han J. W. Drijvers)

651. Bultmann, *John*, 694.

652. In the Gospel of John as a form only elsewhere in 13.17.

653. The beatitude 'blessed are those who do not see and yet believe' (John 2.29) has an interesting parallel in the Letter of James from Nag Hammadi, Codex I: After the resurrection parallel of the ear of corn there follows a discourse of Jesus (to the twelve disciples): 'And as long as I am still with you, give heed to me and obey me! But when I go away from you, remember me! But remember me because I was with you, (and) you did not know me. Blessed will they be who have known me! Woe to those who have heard and have not believed! Blessed will they be who have not seen, (yet) have be[lieved]! . . .' (12.13–31, translation from Schneemelcher, *New Testament Apocrypha* I, 295 [Dankwart Kirchner]). It is quite possible that there

is a tradition in the beatitude at the end of the section quoted which is independent of John 20.29 (cf. Ron Cameron, *Sayings Traditions in the Apocryphon of James*, HTS 34, 1984, 53f.).

654. Bornkamm, Barth and Held, *Tradition and Interpretation* (n.535), 133.

655. Bultmann, *John*, 696.

656. Cf. similarly Finegan, *Überlieferung* (n.377), 95, and most recently Jacob Kremer, '"Nimm deine Hand und lege sie in meine Seite!" Exegetische, hermeneutische und bibeltheologische Überlegungen zu Joh 20, 24–29', *The Four Gospels 1992 (FS Frans Neirynck)*, BETL C, 1992, 2153–81: 2170 n.51. That the Roman Catholic theologian Kremer in his thorough article (cf.176) ignores questions about history can be left aside here. The criticism made in chs. I and II above applies here.

657. Grass, *Ostergeschehen* (n.41), 111, refers as an analogy to the narrative of the chafferers at the cross (Luke 23.39–43).

658. Nathanael or Thomas each time stand outside an event in the circle of disciples (John 1.45/20.24), are addressed (John 1.45/20.25), make an objection (John 1.46/20.25), are won over by Jesus (John 1.46/20.26f.) and express praise (John 1.49/20.28). Finally Jesus speaks once again and apportions blame (John 1.50f./20.29. Cf. the identical sentence structure: 'Because . . . you believe/have believed').

659. Cf. Dauer., *Johannes* (n.640), 253f.

660. Ibid., 253.

661. Haenchen, *John 2*, 229, mentions the following linguistic peculiarities in John 21 compared with 1–20: 1. causative *apo* (v.6), 2. partitive *apo* instead of *ek* (v.10); 3. *ischyo* instead of *dynamai* (v.6); 4. *extazo* instead of *erotao* (v.12); 5. *hypago* with infinitive (v.2).

662. Cf. Schnackenburg, *John III* (n.601), 352.

663. Ibid., 354.

664. Rudolf Pesch, *Der reiche Fischfang (Lk 5, 1–11; Jo 2, 1–14): Wundergeschichte – Berufungserzählung – Erscheinungsbericht*, 1969.

665. 'There do not seem to be real parallels to the story of the abundant catch of fish' (ibid., 125).

666. 'More than the others' in the first question (v.15) serves as a link with the previous unit in which the disciples have been spoken of.

667. Brun, *Auferstehung* (n.95), 52f.; similarly Grass, *Ostergeschehen* (as n.41), 82f.

668. Bultmann, *John*, 712.

669. Cf. Schnackenburg, *John III*, 347f.

670. For what follows cf. Bultmann, *John*, 716f.

671. Cf. John 18.28; 19.13; 13.1. According to the Synoptics the Friday is already the first day of the passover. But the first day of the passover as a date for an execution is extremely improbable.

672. Cf. David Friedrich Strauss, *Der alte und der neue Glaube. Ein Bekenntnis*, ⁴1873, 77: 'We are not even certain whether in the end he was

not wrong about himself and his cause', also Rudolf Bultmann, 'Das Verhältnis der urchristlichen Christusbotschaft zum historischen Jesus' (1960), in id., *Exegetica*, 1967, 445–69: 453: 'We must not disguise the possibility that he collapsed.'

673. Cf. Martin Hengel, 'Psalm 110 und die Erhöhung des Auferstandenen zur Rechten Gottes', in Villiers Breytenbach and Henning Paulsen (ed.), *Anfänge der Christologie (FS Ferdinand Hahn)*, 1991, 43–73: 67f.: 'Those "sent by the Messiah Jesus" were to announce . . . the crucified Messiah Jesus of Nazareth as the one who had been raised from the dead and exalted to God.'

674. There is polemic against this in Erich Fascher, 'Die Auferstehung Jesu und ihr Verhältnis zur urchristlichen Verkündigung', *ZNW* 26, 1927, 1-26: 5: 'Anyone who believes that at any rate according to the old tradition (viz.I Cor.15.3-8) this was a series of appearances is at liberty to think that Peter had an "infectious" effect here.' Here Fascher refrains from the task of translating traditions into history. But already previously, he had to say that he had given up on the task of saying what happened at Easter, 'the effects of which it is possible for the historian to note, even if he cannot grasp their cause' (4).

675. Hengel, 'Psalm' (n.673), 69.

676. Paul 'presumably knew well enough whose "cause" he was fighting when he persecuted the Hellenistic Jewish-Christian community, and without doubt he asked Peter about Jesus, even if he hardly states any real Jesus tradition in his letters' (Nikolaus Walter, '"Historischer Jesus" und Osterglaube', *TLZ* 101, 1976, 321-38: 331). 'Certainly Paul and Peter did not spend all the time "talking about the weather"' (C. H. Dodd, *The Apostolic Preaching and Its Development*, 1936, 256 [On Gal.1.18]).

677. Hengel, 'Psalm' (n.673), 73.

678. Cf. e.g. C. F. D. Moule and Don Cupitt, 'The Resurrection: A Disagreement', *Theology* 75, 1972, 507-19: 509. Moule thinks that in connection with the Easter events he must be concerned with 'something beyond history', 'something transcendent', and continues: 'The NT calls it the resurrection of Jesus.' But here he is presupposing a theory of the event which corresponds to a philosophical realism that has been untenable since Kant. Cf. the remarks by Don Cupitt in *Christ and the Hiddenness of God*, 1985, 138-53.

679. Cupitt thinks that the Easter faith precedes the Easter experiences: 'The arguments that led to the Easter faith are logically prior to the Easter appearances' (Cupitt, *Christ*, 8). But this thinking is too rationalistic. A vision is a primary experience and bears the religious truth completely in itself.

680. Cf. Friedrich, 'Auferweckung' (n.17), 335f.

681. What is correct in Friedrich's view above is that 'the Jewish future hope nowhere knows an appointment to messianic-eschatological dignity through resurrection' (Hengel, 'Psalm', 68). But as Hengel rightly states, the

claim to be Messiah – whether explicit or implicit – was made by Jesus himself. 'Without a messianic claim of Jesus the rise of christology would be completely inconceivable' (ibid). Cf. also Martin Hengel, *Studies in the Gospel of Mark*, 1985, 31-60: 45f.

682. For the terms eternity faith and end faith cf. Hirsch, *Osterglaube* (n.61), 74-80, 206-12.

683. In *Martin Luther's Basic Theological Writings*, ed. Timothy F. Lull, Minneapolis 1989, 471-96 (cf. Gerhard Ebeling, *Wort und Glaube* II, 1975, 33f.). 'Lutheran' does not automatically mean 'un-Pauline', as is thought in some places today.

684. Cf. Johannes Weiss, *Earliest Christianity* (1917), 1959, 27.

685. For the hermeneutical conflict cf. Gerd Theissen, *The Miracle Stories of the Earliest Christian Tradition*, 1983, 32-40.

686. 'Where historical criticism is taken seriously, so seriously that even the most critical possibilities are taken into account, i.e. in the case of the resurrection that it is impossible to demonstrate an empty tomb and appearances of the risen Christ in the "spatially physical world", but only visions of the disciples; and where on the other hand the belief cannot be surrendered that Christ lives as the exalted Lord, because without a living and exalted Lord the church would no longer have the right to exist, an attempt must be made to think of the two together. The objective vision hypothesis has made this attempt and done so in a theological way; for in contrast to the subjective vision hypothesis it is a theological and not a historical hypothesis, because it maintains the trans-subjective origin of the Easter vision and Easter faith and the transcendent reality of what is seen and believed in these visions' (Grass, *Ostergeschehen* [n.41], 248). The thesis of an 'objective vision' has rightly found no echo in more recent scholarship, but Grass does more in his excellent book than provide a basis for the objective vision hypothesis.

687. Theodor Keim, *Geschichte Jesu von Nazara III: Das Jerusalemische Todesostern*, 1872, 605; 'The sign that Jesus was alive, the telegram from heaven, was necessary after this unprecedented and convincing destruction in the childhood of humanity' (Keim gives an introduction to the vision hypothesis on 578-603 which is still worth reading).

688. Cf. Sigmund Freud, *New Introductory Lectures on Psychoanalysis*, Freud Penguin Library 2, 1962, 46; Paul Ricoeur, *Freud and Philosophy: An Essay on Interpretation*, 1962.

689. Paul Tillich, *Symbol und Wirklichkeit*, ²1966. Further references to this work are given in the text.

690. Paul Tillich, *Systematic Theology* 2, 1957, 159.

691. Kurt Hübner, *Die Wahrheit des Mythos*, 1985, 339: The resurrection of Christ consists 'only in the fact that it is a bloody and miraculous reality'. Like Hübner, I am certain that at that time people believed 'literally in the resurrection. That cannot and must not be relativized by kerygmatic ploys. But there is no foundation – from a philosophical point of view – for

Hübner's hidden conclusion that in that case today, too, we must believe in the bloody reality of the resurrection. That is the typical genetic fallacy that he commits everywhere. *Where the body of Christ has not been revived, no revival of myths will help us.* If Jesus did not rise in that way, this has serious consequences for our religion, though I do not believe that it would be its end. But one certainly cannot conclude unconditionally, i.e. without an evaluative intermediate assumption, that, e.g., the original historical state of a religion in all its elements is always the best one and the only one possible (religiously speaking) from the fact that the earliest Christian religion was once associated with belief in the revival of the corpse of Jesus that if we want to be proper Christians today we too must believe in this revival of the corpse. We do not need to, but in that case we must honestly concede the fact. For more recent discussion about the significance of myth for theology cf. Ulrich H. J. Körtner, 'Arbeit am Mythos? Zum Verhältnis von Christentum und mythischen Denken bei Rudolf Bultmann', *NZST* 34, 1992, 163-81 (with bibliography).

692. Cf. only Berthold Klappert, in id. (ed.), *Diskussion um Kreuz und Auferstehung*, ³1968, 10: 'The resurrection of Jesus Christ . . . is a real event in history and as this event which took place at a particular time and among particular people has a definite "historical periphery". On 18 n.29 and 18-23 of the same book Klappert makes further remarks on the 'historical periphery'.

693. Cf. Hans von Campenhausen, 'Tod und Auferstehung Jesu als "historische Fakten"', in J. M. Hollenbach and Hugo Staudinger (eds.), *Moderne Exegese und historische Wissenschaft*, 1972, 94-103: 103.

694. Cf. C. G. Jung, 'On the Resurrection', Collected Works, Vol. 18, *The Symbolic Life*, 1977, 692–6:696: 'It is funny that Christians are still so pagan that they understand spiritual existence only as a body and as a physical event. I am afraid our Christian churches cannot maintain this shocking anachronism any longer.'

695. Emanuel Hirsch, *Hauptfragen christlichen Religionsphilosophie*, 1963, 326f.

696. Strauss, *Glaube* (n.672), 13-94.

697. Thus e.g. even Georg Strecker, who in his Göttingen inaugural lecture of 1969 had still disputed any possibility of certain knowledge of the historical Jesus ('Die historische und theologische Problematik der Jesusfrage' [1970], in id., *Eschaton und Historie. Aufsätze*, 1979, 159-82), says that he has 'got a step further in the question of the authentic Jesus tradition' (id., *Die Bergpredigt. Ein Exegetischer Kommentar*, 1984, 6).

698. To exaggerate: it was not Jesus or his message that needed the 'Easter event' but Peter and the disciples (cf. Walter, 'Jesus' [n.676], 330f.). That is the historical truth of the messianic secret in the Gospel of Mark, however one may connect its literary formation with Mark himself and/or his tradition. Cf. the classic study by Wrede, *Messianic Secret* (n.36), whose idea of an unmessianic life of Jesus in my view goes back to an unconscious

wish to play down the Jewish side of Jesus. Here he is a pupil of Paul de Lagarde.

699. Therefore in many impressive works Ernst Fuchs has attempted to show that there were no differences between Jesus of Nazareth and the 'Risen Lord'. Cf. e.g. his view in Ernst Fuchs and Walter Künneth, *Die Auferstehung Jesu von den Toten. Dokumentation eines Streitgesprächs* (edited from a tape recording by Christian Möller), 1973, 33: 'One must not only, as is traditional, assert the identity of the Risen Christ with the crucified Jesus): 'But I think that one should make *use* of the identity. And so at any rate I come back to the historical Jesus. I can see no difference between the Risen Lord and Jesus of Nazareth . . . That is Jesus himself!' See also the penetrating remarks by Peter Carnley, *The Structure of Resurrection Belief*, 1987, 266-96 ('The Raised Christ as the Remembered Jesus') and especially 327-68 ('Easter Faith and the Self-Giving of Jesus').

700. To this degree he makes the historical presupposition that Jesus of Nazareth accepted death as life.

701. However, historically it is clear that 'the figure of the historical Jesus had to be raised to that of the mythical Christ, to the dominance of the eschatological Lord of the Worlds and cosmocrator' (Theissen, *Miracle Stories* [n.685], 37), in order to have the well-known great effect. But Theissen, ibid., may be underestimating the power that emanated from the historical Jesus. Similarly, I would want to examine in connection with the historical Jesus Paul Althaus's statement directed against Emanuel Hirsch's christology ('In truth even the one who thinks he can get by in his faith without Easter secretly lives by Easter, namely by the Easter image of Jesus of Nazareth', in P. Althaus, 'Christologisches. Fragen an Emanuel Hirsch', in Hayo Gerdes [ed.], *Wahrheit und Glaube, Festschrift für Emanuel Hirsch zu sein 75. Geburstag*, 1963, 22-30: 30). I have no doubt what the result would be.

702. Cf. Ulrich Luz, 'Einheit und Vielfalt neutestamentlicher Theologien', in id. and Hans Weder (eds.), *Die Mitte des Neuen Testaments (FS Eduard Schweizer)*, 1983, 142-61, about the proclamation and activity of Jesus as the basis for the possibility of the multiplicity of New Testament witnesses to Christ and also as a criterion for limiting them.

703. Wilhelm Herrmann, *The Communion of the Christian with God. Described on the Basis of Luther's Statements* ([4]1903), 1972. Further references to this work are given in the text. Relatively late in writing the present work I came to treasure Wilhelm Herrmann as someone who thought through the question of the relationship between history and faith in all its radicality, and am all the more delighted to follow this significant Marburg theologian of the Ritschl school here.

704. Cf. also Hans Grass, 'Glaubensgrund und Glaubensgedanken' (1954), in id., *Theologie und Kritik, Gesammelte Aufsätze und Vorträge*, 1969, 28-37.

705. Emanuel Hirsch, *Christliche Rechenschaft* I, 1989 (= 1978), 32f.

706. Cf. Herrmann (n.703), 235: 'Indeed, I can conceive a man getting a most vivid impression of Jesus' power, just when he thinks he sees that his historical appearance has been swathed in a thick mist of legends, and that, nevertheless, the glory of his inner life breaks through all these veils. a man who thinks he sees this has, at any rate, a firmer ground for his faith than another who *determines* to believe in the resurrection of Jesus in order that he may have his feet planted on a fact that overcomes the world.'

707. Cf. Jung, 'Resurrection' (n.694), 744f.

708. Cf. Herrmann, *Communion* (n.103), 293.

709. Cf. for the above Herrmann, ibid.

710. Cf. Hans Küng, *Eternal Life?*, 1984; Andreas Resch (ed.), *Fortleben nach dem Tode*, 1981; Raymond A. Moody, *Leben nach dem Tode*, 1977; Eckart Wiesenhütter, *Blick nach drüben. Selbsterfahrungen im Sterben*, 1974; Hans Bender (ed.), *Parapsychologie. Entwicklung, Ergebnisse, Probleme*, WdF IV, ⁴1976, See also the *Journal of Near Death Experiences*.

711. The interesting work by Volney P.Gay, *Understanding the Occult. Fragmentation and Repair of the Self*, 1989, does not even attempt to judge the truth of occult faith but demonstrates when it arises and what is contributes (xiii).

712. Cf. the impressive example of a sermon on I Cor.15 from 1532/33 (*WA* 36, 595-7) in Traugott Koch, '"Auferstehung der Toten", Überlegungen zur Gewissheit des Glaubens angesichts des Todes', *ZTK* 89, 1992, 426-83: 463.

713. Cf. Bernhard Lang and Colleen McDannell, *Eine Kulturgeschichte des ewigen Lebens*, 1990, 248-78.

714. The references to Hirsch, *Osterglaube* (n.61), will be put in the text in what follows.

715. Koch, *Auferstehung* (n.712), 481.

# Index of Authors

# Select Index of Subjects